Verse

Verse

An Introduction to Prosody

Charles O. Hartman

WILEY Blackwell

This edition first published 2015
© 2015 John Wiley & Sons, Ltd

Registered Office
John Wiley & Sons, Ltd, The Atrium, Southern Gate, Chichester, West Sussex, PO19 8SQ, UK

Editorial Offices
350 Main Street, Malden, MA 02148-5020, USA
9600 Garsington Road, Oxford, OX4 2DQ, UK
The Atrium, Southern Gate, Chichester, West Sussex, PO19 8SQ, UK

For details of our global editorial offices, for customer services, and for information about how
to apply for permission to reuse the copyright material in this book please see our website at
www.wiley.com/wiley-blackwell.

The right of Charles O. Hartman to be identified as the author of this work has been asserted in accordance
with the UK Copyright, Designs and Patents Act 1988.

Library of Congress Cataloging-in-Publication Data

Hartman, Charles O., 1949– author.
  Verse : an introduction to prosody / Charles O. Hartman.
    pages   cm
  Includes index.
  ISBN 978-0-470-65600-6 (cloth) – ISBN 978-0-470-65601-3 (pbk.)   1. Versification.
2. Poetics. I. Title.
  P311.H28 2015
  808.1–dc23

                                        2014017660

A catalogue record for this book is available from the British Library.

Cover image: Serge Gladky, design from Nouvelles Compositions Decoratives, pochoir print, late 1920s.
Private Collection/The Stapleton Collection/The Bridgeman Art Library.

Set in 11/14pt Garamond by SPi Publisher Services, Pondicherry, India

Printed in Singapore by C.O.S. Printers Pte Ltd

1   2015

Contents

Sidebars

Sidebars

Introduction

This book explores what seems like a simple question: why are poems usually written in lines? This small puzzle turns out to be connected to larger mysteries. When we read a poem, more of our being is engaged than when we read an instruction manual or an editorial. We feel that poems are a use of language distinct from other uses of it – that in poems words *work on us* in uncanny ways. How might the power of poems' language be linked to the custom of printing them in lines, that is, as *verse*?

Suppose for a moment that you had never learned to read silently. (Nobody did until the Middle Ages, thousands of years after writing was invented.) Every word on the page would pass not only before your eyes but through your mouth and ears. Poetry remembers the time when reading always meant reading aloud. Most of the writing that deluges us every day – newspapers, business letters, emails, tweets – can be read silently with no great loss and with a gain in speed. But in ways we'll examine throughout this book, the meaning of a poem depends on its sound at least as much as on ideas that it may convey. A poem needs the time to be heard.

If you're reading aloud, what happens when the text is divided into units that are (usually) larger than a word and smaller than a sentence – that is, into lines? Isolated this way, a short stretch of language is easier to *hear*. The visual fact of lines paradoxically encourages us to listen to the sounds of the words. Whether or not we can specify exactly what you do at the boundary between lines, and whether or not we can be sure that every reader will do the same thing, you're

Verse: An Introduction to Prosody, First Edition. Charles O. Hartman.
© 2015 John Wiley & Sons, Ltd. Published 2015 by John Wiley & Sons, Ltd.

bound to take the line breaks as signals for *some* kind of shift in your almost-internal performance of reading. They're cues in a script.

One name for all the aspects of language that silent reading jettisons for the sake of speed, a name that emphasizes how the complex auditory action of words distributes itself through time, is *rhythm*. All language performances – conversation, singing, recitation – have some kind of rhythmic character, but in poems there is a tendency for rhythm to be noticeably *organized* in various ways. (Lines are most often the basic units of organization.) Some of these rhythmic arrangements are based on counting, and we call them *meters*. Others are not. A term that covers all these kinds of rhythmic organizations and focuses on the ways they're shared by poet and reader and therefore become available for the making of meaning is *prosody*. (Linguists use "prosody" in a different though related way. See the Glossary at the end of this book.) All poetry makes use of some kind of prosody, some means by which the poet controls the reader's experience of rhythm. These chapters examine the kinds that poets in English have used.

Formal arrangements of language such as meter and rhyme aren't merely devices or decorative patterns. Like all prosodic controls, they help us hear the poem as a speaking voice. Considered from one odd angle, a poem is a miracle of *bandwidth*. The poet imagines a whole speaking, gesticulating person, complete with a tone of voice and a situation, and compresses that living being into a stream of data only a few bits wide: a few dozen letters and punctuation marks. This stream (after traveling for a day or for hundreds of years, a mile or thousands of miles) reaches a reader who, perhaps without being aware of the process, from this impoverished text imaginatively *reconstitutes* the voice and the speaker, as alive again as at creation. What we call poetic techniques are methods of supporting this marvel of recovery. They often work subliminally on us while we think we're paying attention to what's merely being *said* by the poem.

If the reader doesn't need to be aware of the details behind the work of reading, what use is a book like this? Even as children, after all (or especially as children), we respond to language arranged for the sake of its sounds. Yet the image of transmission I just gave – a poem-channel with a writer and reader at the two ends – is incomplete. There is not one reader but many, perhaps widely distributed in space and time, who read not one but many poems. These expansions change the process. We read as communities and these communities evolve elaborately over time. Just as native speakers of English don't confine themselves to the few hundred words required for a barter language, so readers and writers of poetry in English have built up rich and varied frameworks of assumption and reference. This book introduces and explains the core elements of those traditions of reading that have to do with rhythm. Rather than cataloguing formal devices as an encyclopedia would, it aims to connect the forms with the meaning and movement of the poetry at as many points as possible.

For a long time – at least from the seventeenth century to the middle of the twentieth – poets, critics, and teachers assumed that readers shared knowledge of the traditional poetic norms and terms. Now, for a variety of reasons, people who want to discuss how poems work can no longer count on that widespread, more or less unified understanding. Though this doesn't render all poetry alien, it makes a great deal of English poetry from the past millennium only half-audible to many readers. At the same time, the many school and college courses that introduce students to poetry have too much material to cover – history, biography, cultural background, interpretive techniques, and so on – to give the study of verse *as verse* the class hours it requires. This book tries to fill that gap in as self-contained a way as possible. I've tried to make the book readable for advanced secondary-school students but accurate and detailed enough for a graduate student brushing up on the fundamentals. There's no reason why combining these goals should be especially difficult. After all, my premise is that meter and other formal properties of poems operate as *common ground* among poets and readers. They aren't in the poem so much as in the context we bring to the reading of the poem. It should be possible to explain them in terms available to everyone. There's nothing in this territory so abstruse as to prevent a motivated person from learning it even without classroom help.

I also mean the book both for people who want to learn more about reading poems and for those learning to write them. Again, I can't think of this as a difficult combination. Poetry is a reciprocal act. As poets we read other people's poems as well as our own – otherwise the communities of reading would disintegrate. As readers we're continually recapitulating the poet's act of speaking and hearing the poem as its sound unfurls in time. Reading poems and writing them are, on the most fundamental level, impossible to distinguish.

Though the six chapters in this book sometimes refer to each other, to some extent you can pick and choose. Everyone will want to read the first chapter, "The Iambic Pentameter Line," because it introduces the process of *scanning* a metrical line and the terminology necessary to talk about this process. We start with the iambic pentameter not because it's the simplest metrical line, but rather because it's the most dominant historically and the most fully elaborated over time. Even if you've already learned about scansion, you'll want to skim this chapter to see how its approach may differ from those you've encountered before. While introducing metrical reading, the chapter fills in some theoretical and historical background as needed.

The next chapter, "Other Meters," extends the methods of Chapter 1 to lines of different lengths and with different metrical bases. These first two chapters concentrate almost exclusively on what happens within a line of verse, the basic unit that poems are usually made of. Chapter 3, "Beyond the Line," examines the ways in which lines are combined – by rhyme, by the groups of lines called stanzas, and by sentences – into larger structures and ultimately into poems.

Chapter 4 deals with what has become a dominant mode in poetry in the past hundred years, nonmetrical or "Free Verse." It asks how this modern mode resembles the metrical verse that predates it and continues alongside it, as well as how the two modes differ. Chapter 5 is devoted to a topic not as commonly included in discussions of poetic form: "Songs." In our experience of poetically formed language, songs may be even more prevalent than free verse, and their prominence goes back much farther.

Chapter 6, "Advanced Topics," will interest a different group of readers. The approach to poetic meter that this book takes as its foundation and develops is not the only one available. The first two sections of this chapter compare it to a couple of the systems developed by linguists and by other literary critics. Different approaches to meter embody different assumptions about how poetic language works rhythmically, and those assumptions suggest different ways of reading. The chapter ends by describing a computer program that can perform a certain kind of metrical scansion and asking what its limitations say about the nature of meter.

Technical terms are printed in **bold face** at a principal point of explanation; this may occur more than once for some terms. These terms are all collected in the Glossary at the end, which lists the page on which the term is introduced as well as page numbers for any extended discussion of the term. In this way the Glossary serves also as the most useful kind of subject index for this book. There is also an index of poets and poem titles.

A website to accompany this book is at charlesohartman.com/verse. At least two programs can be found there: a downloadable version of the Scandroid, described in Chapter 6, and a web-based tutorial on scansion.

* * * * *

Though this book distills my own experience as a teacher, critic, and poet, I could not have written it without a world of help. We write in communities too. I thank Natalie Gerber for her generosity and informed intelligence as correspondent and foil, and for enlisting her own classes to locate soft patches in the ice. Tom Cable and other members of the West Chester University Poetry Conference provided useful responses and pushed me in unexpected directions. Wendy Battin, Martha Collins, Mary Kinzie, and other poet friends have given me the benefit of their compatible but distinct views on the intricacies of the art. Davis Oldham and Geoffrey Babbitt not only gave close scrutiny to particular chapters, but tried them out on their own students; many tactics adopted in Chapters 1 and 4 have changed as a result. Julia Proft and Jim O'Connor have provided the expertise I lacked to make the Scandroid (see Chapter 6) into a program someone besides its author might be willing to use.

I'm grateful to Janet Gezari for lending me her faultless editorial eye, her astute sense of what an actual reader might see and want to see, and her encyclopedic delight in English poetry. Alan Bradford provided some crucial historical details. My own students, not only during the several years when I tested parts of this book's method on them, but for the several decades when they helped goad me into formulating it, deserve my cumulative thanks. Looking farther back, I see how indebted I am to my teachers, especially Howard Nemerov, Donald Finkel, Naomi Lebowitz, and Barbara Herrnstein Smith, who gave me help I can no longer extricate from my own thought. The same is true of my father, Carl Frederick Hartman, who (I think I remember) paid me twenty-five cents an hour in junior high school to read Robert Frost's "The Most of It" and write down what I thought it meant; told me to type out some poems by Yeats as prose to see how they changed; and suggested by his example that music and poetry might live together in one person.

1

The Iambic Pentameter Line

This book is about **verse**: the form of written language most often used for poems.

"Verse" refers to a channel, a medium, not to the content or value of the writing it carries. "Poetry" is a different kind of term, more fluid and value-laden – "sheer poetry," "poetry in motion." "Poetry" has no opposite. But **verse** is so clearly opposed to **prose** that you can see the difference from across the room:

some verse   some prose

For centuries there has been a close association between verse and poetry. Though prose-poems exist and though some print forms like advertisements show the kind of attention to line breaks that poets pay to them, generally when we see a page like the one on the left we're sure that a poem waits to be read.

Verse: An Introduction to Prosody, First Edition. Charles O. Hartman.
© 2015 John Wiley & Sons, Ltd. Published 2015 by John Wiley & Sons, Ltd.

The polarity between verse and prose looks so simple as to be bald and bland. But it turns out to be freighted with meaning for poems. Poems use verse because verse is language in **lines**. Prose is in lines too, of course (unless it's printed sideways on a very long tape), but the breaks between lines don't mean anything. They're just the places where the text is cut up to fit into the page-box. Verse is verse because every line and line break represents a *decision* by the writer. Poems use verse because poetry, whatever else it may be, does its work by being a tissue of decisions about language. When we read a poem we retrace the poet's path (often without thinking about it) and mimic those decisions within ourselves. Grouping words into lines and dividing the lines carefully turn out to be powerful ways to focus the reader's attention. They contribute to the reader's understanding whether the understanding happens consciously or not.

Verse can be made up of either **metrical** or **nonmetrical** lines. In English, for most of the past thousand years until about World War I, poems almost always used some type of **meter** to organize their lines, and we'll begin with metrical verse. (This will help us make sense of "free verse" in Chapter 4.) The dominant kind of metrical line in English poetry has long been what is called the **iambic pentameter**. We'll work out formal definitions soon, but it's more important to *hear* the tune or movement of the line. Here are two iambic pentameters, both from sonnets by William Shakespeare (1564–1616). Read them *out loud* – this will be an important step throughout this book:

> If thou survive my well-contented day …
> So long as men can breathe or eyes can see …

Let's consider some differences between these two lines before we get to what they have in common. The first line begins by focusing on the charged verb "survive." Then it pauses momentarily, then gathers itself even more tightly around the **polysyllabic** compound "well-contented." (Shakespeare made up this word, which adds to the line's intensity: if we imagine him speaking the line, we see him having to reach for new language, like a singer reaching for a note almost out of range.) The second line consists entirely of **monosyllables** and spreads emphasis fairly evenly among the five main words, "long," "men," "breathe," "eyes," and "see." Again there's a small pause (it sets up a balance between the verbs "breathe" and "see," with their shared vowel sound), but this time it comes just after the midpoint of the line rather than just before it. These are a few of the ways in which the two lines move or unfold differently. (You can find more.) Within the small, concentrated space of a single line words can speed up and slow down and group themselves in a wide variety of ways. To sum all this up in a single word, the two lines differ in **rhythm**.

Syllables

The terms "monosyllable" and "polysyllable" assume that we're always sure how many syllables a word has. That's not quite true. People from different parts of the English-speaking world may hear words like "fire" and "hour" as having either one syllable or two. How many syllables does "comfortable" have? Or "towards"? In practice, as we'll see, it's unusual for these uncertainties to make any important difference in the *metrical* workings of a line. Notice and enjoy the variety English offers, but don't be anxious about it. When in doubt trust your dictionary, which always gives the syllabification of a word.

Here are two more lines in iambic pentameter, one by Sir Philip Sidney (1554–1586), the other by Theodore Roethke (1908–1963). Again begin by reading them aloud:

> Desiring nought but how to kill desire …
> I hear my being dance from ear to ear. …

Listen, as before, for how rhythmic variations in the speed and groupings of words and in the position and strength of the pauses combine to give each line its own "tune." Both lines are organized around repetitions, but the repetitions have different effects on the movement of the line. Sidney begins and ends with forms of the word "desire." (This is the final line of a poem about being trapped by one's own desire.) Roethke, in contrast, repeats "ear," which echoes "hear" at the beginning. In the ballroom in his head all those long *e* sounds (including "being") gambol around the different resonance of "dance." Though we might think of the rhythm in both lines as somehow symmetrical, the symmetry feels like imprisonment in Sidney's line but celebration in Roethke's.

All of these variations may be subtler than any we're routinely conscious of hearing in speech – though we hear a lot more than we're conscious of. Part of a poem's business is to make us more aware of the sound and movement of what we speak.

Rhythm and Meter

We've been listening to differences, but what do these four lines of verse have in common? They're all ten syllables long and the even-numbered syllables are all stronger or louder or more intense than the odd-numbered ones. You may have been aware of these similarities in the lines when you spoke them aloud. (If not, listen to them again.) This common ground is the **meter**. Here's a way to make it visible, using '/' for the stronger syllables, 'x' for the weaker syllables, and a plain vertical bar to demarcate the repeated units:

> x / | x / | x / | x / | x /
> If thou survive my well-contented day ...   (Shakespeare)
> x / | x / | x   / | x / | x /
> So long as men can breathe or eyes can see ...   (Shakespeare)
> x /| x   / | x / | x / | x /
> Desiring nought but how to kill desire ...   (Sidney)
> x / | x / | x / | x / | x /
> I hear my being dance from ear to ear. ...   (Roethke)

The row of marks above each line is a **scansion** of the line.

Learning how to **scan** iambic pentameter is the goal for this chapter, and the skills this involves underlie everything later in the book as well. In fact the scansion itself is much less the point than the kind of detailed listening that scansion requires. Scansion is just a system of notation, but using it encourages us to apply a close awareness that helps connect the details of the words' sounds with the larger gestures of meaning that the sequence of words performs.

Though later in this section we'll discuss several kinds of variations used in iambic pentameters, in a nutshell this similarity among the lines *is* the meter. All of the many lines we call "iambic pentameters" have the same meter, but each one of those millions of iambic pentameter lines has its own characterizing rhythm. An iambic pentameter is a set of words that fits the pattern

> x / | x / | x / | x / | x /

This is obviously not a line of verse, just a skeleton. Marks aren't syllables, of course, but the distinction goes farther than that. We began by noticing differences in rhythm among several lines of verse, and then we noticed the meter which is common to all of them. An unvarying meter underlies the varying rhythms. The poetic meter of a line and the line's rhythm are closely related – after all they're both embodied in the same row of syllables – but while meter is an abstract pattern, rhythm is the far more detailed, textured experience that's available to us as we read each particular line of verse.

There's an analogy with faces. Meter is like *the human face*: a pattern of two eyes either side of a nose, mouth below, ears outboard, and so on. Rhythm is individual like *a human's face*: crow's-feet, the left eyebrow a millimeter higher than the right, the mouth narrower than average, ears sticking out especially far, and so on. Humpty Dumpty complains to Alice that "if you had the two eyes on the same side of the nose, for instance – or the mouth at the top – that would be *some* help." We recognize a face in a way and with an ease that Humpty Dumpty just doesn't get. "The human face": our brains are so good at picking out human faces from a visual field that we do it even when they aren't there – in the random knots in a pine wall or leaves in a row of bushes. "A human's face": we can recognize a friend's face in profile thirty yards away in the dusk. As we gain experience in reading metrical verse we soon learn to identify a line as iambic pentameter without stopping to scan it. At the same moment we may well notice its rhythm: the new and individual way in which *this* iambic pentameter embodies the familiar design.

While rhythm can include any and all aspects of language sound, a meter abstracts just a few features from the line's language and organizes them into a pattern. In scansions, which make metrical structure visible, the main marks correspond to the main features that the meter organizes. This mark:

/

indicates a **stressed syllable** or **stress**. This one:

x

indicates an unstressed syllable or **slack**. (In the scansions given earlier, a third mark, |, indicates the division between "feet." We'll return to it later.)

Marks

If you've worked with scansions before, you may remember using different marks. It doesn't matter deeply; we could use * and $ if we wanted, though it would be helpful if we all agreed so we could talk about the scansion (which in a sense is what scansions are *for*). A mark often used in the past for a slack syllable was this: ˘. But historically that mark, the **breve**, really complements the **macron**: ¯ Macrons and breves were used by scholars of Greek and Latin poetry to indicate long and short syllables. In English, while some syllables are inevitably longer than others, what *counts* about a syllable – what we count when we're paying attention to the meter – is not long versus short but stressed versus slack. Much of our vocabulary for talking about meter is inherited from Greek and Latin, but the English language is different from the Classical languages and our meters are based on a different selection of features. It seems unnecessarily confusing to employ the old marks. The stress, /, has long been a common mark, and x for a slack has become fairly common also.

A scansion diagrams just the essential aspects of the *interaction* between meter and rhythm. If we know that a poem is in iambic pentameter, there's no point in diagramming its *meter* alone. That would just be a long list of lines that are all the same: x / | x / | x / | x / | x /. On the other hand, diagramming the *rhythm* in any complete way would be enormously complicated. We would have to have marks to indicate all the degrees of stress (in "Desiring nought but how to kill desire," is "how" more or less strongly stressed than "kill"?); the grouping of words into phrases (in reading the line we might pause after "Desiring" or "nought" but we're unlikely to pause after "to"); the boundaries between words (we would never pause after the first syllable of "desire"); echoes of sound that link separate parts of the line (the hard 't' at the end of "nought" and the hard 'k' at the start of "kill" help give the line its tone of bitter distaste); and many other characteristics of the line's language that distinguish it from other lines but don't participate directly in its meter. If rhythm is like a face and meter is like the human face, scansion is like a police artist's sketch. We know the person is likely to have eyes and a nose, but the sketch can guide our attention to the details and patterns that let us recognize that particular person.

Stress

What is a stressed syllable? Explaining what stress is is easier in person than in print – sound and gestures help – but your own imagination can come to the rescue. Suppose you go to the multiplex with a friend but without much of a plan. You look over the movies being offered and your friend says, "What do you want to see?" Polite companion that you are, you say, "What do *you* want to see?" Your friend starts reading down the list and rejecting one movie after another. Finally you get a little exasperated and say, "Well, what *do* you want to see?"

What you have done with your voice to emphasize one word rather than another, in that sentence whose words never change, is called stress. You stress a word by speaking it a little louder, or lengthening it, or raising (or lowering) the pitch of your voice, or some combination. For our purposes here the physiological and acoustical components of stress don't matter much. But whatever produces it, the psychological phenomenon of stress is a crucial part of our speech. (This is true in English, though not in all languages.)

Stress plays a number of different roles in English speech. The sentences at the multiplex illustrate **contrastive stress**, which is the most conscious kind, a device we use all the time to emphasize how one word is opposed to another. ("I said *dis*courage them, not *en*courage them!") Stress also marks the difference between a **phrase** ("a *French* teacher": someone who teaches French) and a **compound** ("a French *teacher*": a teacher who is from France). At an even finer level of detail, words with the same spelling sometimes function either as verbs or as nouns (or adjectives), and in English speech we distinguish these by stressing different syllables: "If the members of the jury convict him, he'll be a convict." "Did some colonies rebel? Which were the rebel colonies?"

Hearing Stresses

Again it's important to say these sentences out loud. It's not exactly that you're training your ear to hear stress. If you didn't already hear stress very accurately, you wouldn't understand what people say or be able to make yourself understood. Stress is that important in English speech. Rather, you're helping yourself to make your hearing conscious. In many kinds of reading (newspapers, legal briefs, textbooks) you don't need to be aware of stress, though along with other elements of linguistic rhythm it subliminally influences how you read a text and how much pleasure you take in reading it. When you're reading poetry, though, hearing is essential. Read it aloud whenever you can. Stress is just one kind of detail you'll come to feel in play and at play. To put it another way, read the lines aloud until you can hear the stresses *without* having to make sound to do it.

All these kinds of stress make one syllable feel more prominent than the others around it. This is the basis of the most common kinds of poetic meter in English.

In any English word with more than one syllable, one of them gets primary stress: the first syllable of "butter," the middle syllable of "decision," the last syllable of "insist." These stresses are built into the language, and this has the handy result that if we're not sure which syllable gets the stress we can look it up in a dictionary. (Make sure you know how your dictionary marks stress; there are various systems.) You can practice – again not to train your ear as much as your awareness – by noticing what you stress when you say words like these:

delight	diesel	ridiculous	werewolf
employ	fortification	appreciative	handle

Similarly, in simple phrases made up of monosyllables one is often clearly stressed more than the others: "the *house*," "in *front* of," "on a *dare*." Unfortunately, while the dictionary will tell you which syllable of a longer word gets the stress, it can't tell you whether a monosyllable is stressed or not in all the different contexts where it might appear. But there are fairly reliable rules of thumb that depend on the part of speech of the word. (The terms used here for parts of speech aren't quite the ones linguists would use these days, but they should be familiar.) Some monosyllables are almost always stressed:

nouns	*hand, force, time, itch*
adjectives and adverbs	*blank, first, wild, soon*
verbs	*sit, close, dream, tell*

(An exception: words like "can" and "do," when used as *auxiliary* verbs, aren't usually stressed. Neither are forms of "be" when they're linking other words together: "Sharon is president.") Some additional words are *automatically* stressed because of what they mean or how they're used, especially interjections – *Ha! Wow! Nuts!* – though they're not very frequent in poems. Other monosyllables are typically *not* stressed:

articles	*the, a, an*
conjunctions	*and, but, or*
prepositions	*in, of, for*

Rather than memorizing lists, you might find it useful to notice what distinguishes these two groups of categories of words. Linguists call them **open class** and **closed class** words. A class of words is "open" if we can easily add new items to it. Nouns and verbs are open classes: the nickname of the Nike logo, "swoosh," is a verb that someone at Nike turned into a noun, and the verb itself was invented in the nineteenth century by someone imitating a certain kind of sound. Since it's easy to create new nouns and verbs, it follows that there are a very large number of both. "Closed" classes, on the other hand, contain far fewer words and almost no new ones. It's extremely difficult to make up a new preposition and get English speakers to agree to use it. When we speak or write, the words we think about choosing in order to convey our meaning are mostly open-class words, so they're sometimes called "content words." The closed-class words that glue the sentence together ("grammar words") mostly get chosen as if automatically, behind our backs. This difference in purposefulness correlates with the fact that open-class monosyllables are stressed and closed-class monosyllables generally aren't. If you're trying to say "The bridge is closed" over a bad phone line, you don't bother to articulate "The" or "is" carefully. You stress "bridge" and "closed" because those carry the key pieces of information.

These lists of parts of speech omit one important category, the pronouns. Again there's a reliable rule of thumb, just one step more complex: pronouns are almost never stressed except through *contrast*. In those sentences at the multiplex, it's contrastive stress that makes one word or another stand out, always in comparison to something else: "What do *you* want to see?" implies, "Never mind for a moment what *I* might want to see." In the same way, in poems we generally hear words like *I, you, her, theirs*, and *us* as unstressed unless something in the context suggests a contrast. (In "Leda and the Swan" by W. B. Yeats (1865–1939), the blow-by-blow account of the mortal woman's rape by the self-transformed Zeus includes the line, "He holds her helpless breast upon his breast." The opposition between her female human "breast" and the hard, white, alien "breast" of the bird may show up as a stress on "*his* breast" at the end of the line when we read it aloud.) As we scan more lines, we'll watch for examples of how pronouns behave. One pattern is already predictable: *demonstrative* pronouns are frequently stressed because they often imply contrasts (*this* book, not *that* one).

Here we need to take a short detour – it will turn out to be important later – first to complicate this idea of stress and then to simplify it again. Though examples like *improve* and *fragile* suggest that stress is clear and simple, something you can look up in a dictionary, stress can become quite complicated in English speech and even in particular English words. There are actually at least four *levels* or *degrees* of speech stress. Even in a single word like "volunteer" we can hear some of the intricacy that technical phonetic analysis would reveal in more detail. The last syllable clearly gets the primary stress. But the first syllable, while weaker than the third, is still stronger than the second. If we represent degrees of stress with numbers (with 1 for the strongest) the word might look like this:

2   3   1

vol – un – teer

Similarly, the first syllable of "caveman" is stronger than the second (we could diagram it as 1–2), but not as *much* stronger as it is in "chairman" (1–3). We hear "chairman" as a single word, while "caveman" still feels like a compound of two words, so that the second syllable retains some of its original stress.

Scoring the changing degrees of stress throughout a word like *incendiary*, let alone an entire iambic pentameter line, could be a daunting task if we needed to achieve this kind of precision. When we're discussing the rhythm of a particular line, it's occasionally useful to seek this high degree of auditory resolution. Yet when we're discussing meter rather than rhythm, we don't need such elaboration. In almost all English metrical contexts, stress basically operates in a *binary* way: a syllable is stressed or not. Though the rhythm of a line like this one by William Wordsworth (1770–1850),

A sight so touching in its majesty

is quite complicated, as you can hear when you say the line aloud, nevertheless for metrical purposes we can begin by marking the syllables this way:

x / / / x x x / x x
A sight so touching in its majesty

This isn't yet a complete scansion, but it does capture the facts about stressed and slack syllables in the line that are basic to how it realizes the meter.

Feet

The one mark of scansion that we saw earlier but haven't yet discussed is the vertical line that divides **feet**. A **foot** is simply a small pattern of stresses and slacks. The abstract iambic pentameter we saw earlier –

x / | x / | x / | x / | x /

– is clearly made up of five units that are the same, and it's useful to have a name for this repeated unit. The traditional names have been around for so long that they're in Greek. In iambic pentameter the unit repeated is the **iamb** – a slack followed by a stress.

The Names of Meters

The names of meters combine an adjective denoting the dominant kind of foot – such as "iambic" – with a noun that signifies a number (also in Greek!) with "-meter" added to it (because what we call a foot the Greeks sometimes called a "metron"). Here are all the nouns in use:

monometer	mon-o-me-ter	a line 1 foot long
dimeter	di-me-ter	2 feet
trimeter	tri-me-ter	3 feet
tetrameter	te-tra-me-ter	4 feet

pentameter	pen-*ta*-me-ter	5 feet
hexameter	hex-*a*-me-ter	6 feet
heptameter	hep-*ta*-me-ter	7 feet
octameter	oc-*ta*-me-ter	8 feet
nonameter	non-*a*-me-ter	9 feet

So "iambic pentameter" means a line of five iambs. In practice the extremes of length (1, 2, 8, 9) are rare.

Now that we've plunged into foreign vocabulary, a word about why we use it might be appropriate. This traditional terminology of feet isn't the only way to analyze meter or metrical lines; it may not even be the most precise. (In Chapter 6 we'll look at a couple of alternatives.) Its greatest advantage is that it *is* traditional: poets and readers have been using these terms for centuries, frequently thinking of and hearing lines as composed of these conventional units, and using these names when they want to discuss what goes on in a metrical line. Presumably an iambic pentameter that falls in the forest makes the same sound as one that has all its parts labeled, and it's possible to feel the movement of the line like a dancer or hear it like a musician without knowing the terminology. But to discuss how we feel and hear the lines we read and write, some analytical tools like names are useful. These are the names that lie to hand.

If all iambic pentameter lines were composed of five iambs, scanning them would be easy but there would be little point to it. In fact only a minority of iambic pentameters are exactly regular. There are two main kinds of variation. We'll investigate "promoted stress" a little later. First we'll discuss **metrical substitution**: replacing one or more of the iambs in the line with a different kind of foot. There are many possible candidates – over two dozen Classical feet with lovely names like "molossus" and "antispast" – but in practice, to scan the vast majority of iambic pentameters in English we need almost nothing besides these four feet:

iamb (*i*-am)	x/	(adj.) iambic (i-*am*-bic)	"improve"
trochee (*tro*-key)	/x	trochaic (tro-*kay*-ic)	"badger"

spondee (*spon*-dee)	//	spondaic (spon-*day*-ic)	"Duck Soup"
anapest (*an*-a-pest)	xx/	anapestic (an-a-*pest*-ic)	"in a bind"

Almost, but not quite. We need to add two special items. One is the **bare stress**, sometimes called a **defective foot**:

/

The other is a tricky beast that replaces *two* iambs. Reasonably enough, it's often called a **double iamb**:

x x / /

The traditional name for this double iamb is **rising ionic**.

A Twist on the Double Iamb

An alternative is to break the double iamb into two feet. The second is a spondee (//), but we don't yet have a name for what precedes it. A name does exist: the **pyrrhic** (xx). But including pyrrhics among the feet that can replace the iamb creates problems. We would need to attach a special rule to it – not just a rule of thumb, but an absolute decree that the pyrrhic can *never* occur *except* before a spondee. (Spondees could still occur without pyrrhics before them, which adds to the confusion.) Forgetting this rule and sprinkling pyrrhics arbitrarily throughout a scansion creates several kinds of confusion. The most important is that it compromises our hearing of many lines by undermining the important concept of promoted stress, which we'll explore shortly. Keeping a special rule in mind that is attached to just one foot is an extra burden. I've excluded pyrrhics in this book's scansions. If you'd rather use the pyrrhic and remember the rule you can, but most people find it easier to remember that the double iamb replaces two iambs.

Incidentally, excluding pyrrhics also lets us declare that every foot contains at least one stress. It's tempting to make this part of a dynamic definition of feet, but this would require a lavish theoretical digression.

At first this looks like a pretty random collection of syllable patterns (x/, /x, //, xx/, /, xx//). It becomes less arbitrary when we think of each of these potential substitutes for the iamb as performing a particular kind of *operation* on one small segment of a line:

- put more weight on the iamb by adding a stress: spondee (x / → / /)
- stretch the iamb out with an extra slack: anapest (x / → x x /)
- truncate the iamb by removing the slack: defective foot (x / → /)
- swap a slack and the adjacent stress:
  - within the foot: trochee (x / → / x)
  - between feet: double iamb (x / | x / → x x / /)

Each of these variations alters the tune of the iambic pentameter in a characteristic way. Some of them, and some combinations, disrupt the basic meter more violently than others. Any substitution that confuses the meter enough to make it unrecognizable tends to be shunned by poets. For the same reason, notice that our list excludes some theoretically possible feet that would combine *two* operations. The poet could reverse *and* stretch the iamb (making a **dactyl**, /xx), or both stretch *and* load it (making either a **cretic**, /x/, or a **bacchius**, x//). But these double operations distort the iambic pentameter too much, and poets usually avoid them.

Let's look at how these metrical substitutions work in real lines. Here are some rules of thumb for the use of metrical substitutions in iambic pentameter. Though you may find or create lines that violate these rules and yet work recognizably as iambic pentameters, poets follow them most of the time:

1. A spondee can replace an iamb anywhere. An extreme example from John Milton (1608–1674):

   /___/ | /___/ | /___/ | x / | x /
   Rocks, caves, lakes, fens, bogs, dens, and shades of death

2. A double iamb can replace two iambs anywhere. A start-of-line example from Theodore Roethke:

   x x / / | x / | x / | x /
   In a dark time, the eye begins to see

3. A trochee often replaces an iamb at the beginning of a line. A typical example from Alexander Pope (1688–1744):

    /___x | x / | x   / | x   / | x   /
    Vexed to be still in town, I knit my brow

4. A trochee can also replace an iamb after a major pause in the line, a break between sentences or a strong break within the sentence, as in this line by Robert Browning (1812–1889):

    x / | x / | /___x | x   / | x   /
    Ye mark me not! What do they whisper there

Trochaic substitution is much less common at other points in the line. Substituting a trochee for the last iamb in the line is so confusing to the meter that it's virtually never done. Two or more trochees in a row are fairly rare, since this tends to turn the iambic meter around.

5. A slack can be omitted – so that the iamb becomes a bare stress – at the beginning of a line. Then it becomes a **headless line** (or **acephalous line**, to use the Greek term), like this one by Gerard Manley Hopkins (1844–1889):

    /| x / | x   / | x   / | x   /
    Glory be to God for dappled things

Like trochaic substitution, this truncation of the iamb to a bare stress – which normally reduces the pentameter to nine syllables – can also occasionally happen after a major pause within the line. This variation tends to disrupt the meter, though, so poets handle it with care.

These are rules of thumb, not traffic laws. If you come up with a scansion that breaks one of these rules, the point is not that you must be wrong or that the poet must have written an unmetrical line. Rather, it's a good idea to go back and look for an alternative way to hear the line. If no alternative that is more regular turns out to be possible, so be it: you've found an exceptional line and its effect in the verse will be especially worth listening for.

This list of five guidelines by themselves will let you scan a huge proportion of the iambic pentameters you'll run across. In the example lines we'll scan in the rest of this chapter, we'll rarely need more than these five rules of thumb. There are two other variations in the iambic norm, though, which arise with some frequency and require a little more explanation: extrametrical final syllables and the anapest (xx/).

An iambic line generally ends with a stress, because an iamb does. But the line can end with an extra slack syllable. Here's an example from Samuel Taylor Coleridge (1772–1834):

$$x \;\; / \;| x \quad / \;| x \quad (/) \;| x \quad / \;| x \quad / \;\; x$$
By woman wailing for her demon-lover!

(We'll discuss that third stress in parentheses in a moment.) The sound of urgent yearning in this line seems to come partly from its extension by yet one more slack syllable. We call this final slack "extrametrical" to declare that we're leaving it outside the metrical system. Only a slack gets this treatment, and only at the end of a line.

Traditionally this extra slack at the end of a line has been fitted into the system of metrical scansion in a different way. We might speak of the iamb being replaced by an **amphibrach** (x/x). There are two problems with this. First, it might suggest that the amphibrach is on the list of generally suitable substitutes for the iamb, like the trochee or the spondee. But in fact amphibrachs would badly confuse the iambic meter if they occurred anywhere except at the end of the line. To be included in the system, therefore, this foot would have to come with a special rule attached saying that it could *only* be used at the end of the line. An extra rule is yet another apparently arbitrary item to remember.

Lines that End with x

The special rule that the amphibrach would require, like the rule that would have to accompany the pyrrhic if we didn't use the double iamb, is absolute: *never* an amphibrach *except* at the end of a line (and *always* an amphibrach at the end of a line that ends with x / x). In this case, however, you don't quite have the same liberty as with pyrrhics – to use the foot and remember the rule – because of the *second* problem that arises when the line's last foot isn't an iamb.

Second, if the iamb has been replaced by another foot at the end of the line, we would need yet *more* special terms with special rules. A spondee plus an extra-metrical slack would be a **palimbacchius** (/ / x); an anapest plus slack would be a third **paeon** (x x / x); those too would have to be restricted to the ends of lines. The terminology seems too cumbersome for what's really a straightforward phenomenon: some iambic lines end with an extra syllable, and it doesn't desta-bilize the meter, perhaps because the meter's "contract" has already been fulfilled. If the verse **rhymes**, these extra syllables will participate in the rhyme: ". . . a winner / . . . his dinner." Rhyming contexts can even occasionally entail *two* extra-metrical slacks. We'll look further at rhyme and its metrical effects in Chapter 3.

The possibility of an extrametrical final slack reinforces a rule of thumb mentioned earlier, that the last iamb in the line is virtually never replaced by a trochee. If a line ends with an unstressed syllable, the scansion will end with an extrametrical slack added to the last foot, not with a trochee.

The final kind of metrical substitution, replacement of the iamb by an anapest (x x /), has a knotty history. In some periods poets hardly ever used it; in others it has been more common. Especially in the late nineteenth century, theorists debated fiercely whether "trisyllabic substitution" (the anapest's three syllables versus the iamb's two) was legitimate or not. The anapest, because it loosens the iambic meter, carries special risks and creates special effects. It can make the metrical line seem more conversational, and this is why Shakespeare uses anapests with moderate (and increasing) frequency in his plays:

$$ /\quad /\,|\,\mathrm{x}\qquad /\,|\,\mathrm{x}\qquad /\,|\,\mathrm{x}\ \mathrm{x}\ /\,|\,/\quad / $$
Good morrow, neighbor, whither away so fast?

Elision

For the sake of completeness we should note one more twist in this question of trisyllabic substitution. Sometimes an anapest barely differs from an iamb because the unstressed syllables are "elided." **Elision** generally means leaving something out (like the vowel we omit when we say "I'm"). In meter what's omitted is a boundary: two syllables merge into one – perhaps in pronunciation, or per-haps only notionally. It can happen only to unstressed syllables. It may happen when the meeting points of the two syllables are both vowels: "to a cloud" may act like an anapest or an iamb. Even some consonants don't interrupt this merging of syllables: 'l' and 'r', 'm' and 'n', and 'h'. So in Shakespeare's line, the "-er a-" in "whither away" may be elided.

Elision as a factor in meter varies historically. Periods of greater metrical strictness tend to resort to it more often by way of compensation. For our purposes it's not vital to introduce an extra mark of scansion to indicate elisions. Instead we'll treat lines like this one by Shakespeare as containing anapests. It's worth keeping in mind, though, that this approach makes anapests seem more common than is accurate for some periods. Also, anyone *writing* iambic verse should be aware that anapests which *can't* be elided disrupt the line more than ones that can.

But if the lines become *too* conversational we lose sight of their belonging to a poem. To put it as a rule, the anapest can be substituted for the iamb anywhere, but not too often – though what "too" means is always debatable. Here's an example from Yeats:

> ... she would of late
> x / | x / | x x / | / / | xx /
> Have taught to ignorant men most violent ways

He uses the *pair* of anapestic substitutions to make us hear a relation between the men's violence and their ignorance.

As always, the point isn't an arbitrary rule but how the sound of language actually works. Though it's hard to determine the average number of slacks between stresses in ordinary, intense English speech, we can guess that it's around two-and-a-half. Iambic meter, which guarantees at least one stress in every two syllables, condenses those speech rhythms, and it tends to make the language more packed and strong even before the poet does anything else to heighten it. Anapests, with just one stress in three syllables, go the other way, toward relaxation. Furthermore, a series of anapests in a row produce a "runaway horse" effect – *sentences galloping recklessly over whatever they try to communicate* – that tends to drown out any subtler music. Poets are wary of these "triple threats to duple rhythm," as the critic Edward Weismiller has called them. (A duple rhythm is one based on a two-syllable foot like the iamb.) If a line has a string of especially light stresses – "I do not at this point in time agree" – it can be all too easy to hear and scan as an anapestic tetrameter:

x x / | x   x   / | x   / | x /   (?)
I do not at this point in time agree

(This is a made-up bad example; poets avoid this kind of uncertainty in meter.) The solution, when scanning a line, is to remember to hold the *number of feet* in the line constant.

The Persistence of Line Length

If the poem begins in iambic pentameter, expect every line to have five feet. (Remember that the double iamb counts as two.) What the five feet are can vary, but not their number. It's useful to think of this rule as absolute: when you're scanning a poem in iambic pentameter, always check to make sure every line has five feet, not four or six. These are easy mistakes to make.

You'll encounter two kinds of exceptions to this rule. First, when lines are collected into **stanza** forms (which we'll discuss in Chapter 3), those repeated stanzas may *systematically* vary the number of feet in particular lines. The Spenserian stanza, for example, is eight iambic pentameters followed by one iambic hexameter. Keats's "Ode to a Nightingale" is mostly in iambic pentameter, but he shortens the eighth line of each stanza to an iambic trimeter. Second, in the period when iambic pentameter dominated English poetry most thoroughly – roughly, the "long Eighteenth Century" – an accepted source of variety was to introduce an occasional hexameter. These exceptions are specialized, somewhat rare, and fairly easily identified when you run across them.

So far we've mostly seen isolated examples of metrical substitutions, but many combinations are possible. Just one example: in this line by Pope,

/   x| /   / | x   / | x / |x   /
Count the slow clock, and dine exact at noon

the combined trochee and spondee, by foregrounding the heavy stresses at the start of the line, help us hear the tedium of the clock-ticks and feel the tiresome crawl of time. This effect depends partly on the presence of the word "slow." A century later, John Keats (1795–1821) begins a number of lines in his "Ode to a Nightingale" with the same pair of substitutions, but the pattern produces quite a different sound in his line about wine:

/   x| / / |x x /   /| x /

Cool'd a long age in the deep-delvèd earth

If time is stretched out here too, in this case it feels luxurious. The double iamb later in the line may be one reason for the difference. Comparing Pope's line to Keats's shows that though a particular pattern of metrical substitutions may well have a meaning, its meaning depends on context, as the meaning of a word or a musical chord does. When Keats uses the same metrical pattern later in the same poem, it seems to have an oppressive weight not so different from the ennui expressed by Pope:

/   x| / / |x / | x / | x /

Here, where men sit and hear each other groan;

Then again, near the end of the poem Keats repeats the trochee-and-spondee opening in two successive lines:

/ x| /   / | x /|x x /   /

Past the near meadows, over the still stream,

/   x|/ / | x / | x /|x /

Up the hill-side; and now 'tis buried deep

Here the pattern acts out the urgency of imagined perception – his mind's eye is following the bird that has flown away – rather than the more passive misery of "Here, where men sit and hear each other groan." Although this is quite a wide range of effects, none of these lines could be characterized as light, carefree, sedate, or complacent. Apparently metrical patterns (and patterns of metrical substitution) can express broad kinds of movement within the kinetics of feeling – "weightiness," perhaps – though they signify particular feelings only when the sense of the words themselves also conveys those feelings.

Promoted Stresses

Besides substituted feet, the other sort of variation in the metrical structure of a line is called **promoted stress**. Let's look into the process that produces it.

When we call a syllable "stressed" in a metrical context we don't claim that it's *strong* in some absolute sense – only that it's a little stronger than what immediately precedes and follows it. One factor that can help make a syllable feel stressed, besides contrast or the habit recorded in a dictionary entry, is the syllable's position within the metrical line. As we've already noticed, when we listen to an iambic pentameter line we're hearing two things at once: the rhythm of the line itself and the underlying meter. Sometimes the meter makes us expect a stress where the rhythm of the line's actual words wouldn't otherwise enforce one. Speak this line (by Wordsworth) aloud:

> The ghostly language of the ancient earth

When we mark the clear stresses, we get only four –

> x / x / x x x / x /
> The ghostly language of the ancient earth

– but the definition of iambic pentameter requires the line to have at least five ("at least," because one or more spondees might add to the normal five). No combination of the feet listed earlier will divide this line into the five we need for an iambic pentameter because each of the "legal" feet on the list contains at least one stress.

This looks like a problem. Yet as you say the line aloud you may hear yourself naturally giving a little extra emphasis to "of" in the middle of the line, a preposition that would ordinarily be heard as unstressed in speech. A combination of factors works to *promote* this syllable from unstressed to stressed. There's the immediate phonetic context: though "of" may be weak, it's not as shy and retiring as "the" after it, which is phonetically swallowed up in the following word

27

"ancient." Also, between "language" and the prepositional phrase that modifies it, there's probably a tiny pause that also gives "of" a slight boost. Most important, we're simultaneously hearing a regular metrical pattern that *wants* a stress at this position. And yet to scan the line as perfectly regular,

x   / | x / | x / | x / | x   /

The ghostly language of the ancient earth

crudely overrides the line's audible rhythm. Instead, we can mark that middle stress in a way that shows it has been *promoted* to stress by the metrical context:

x   / | x / | x (/) | x / | x   /

The ghostly language of the ancient earth

Though readers may or may not hear promoted stresses clearly as stresses, the scansion registers them as part of its job, which is to diagram the interacting forces of meter and rhythm. Once we're hearing that interaction, debating whether a particular stress is promoted or is a full stress in the speech rhythm is not much to the point metrically, though it may be part of a discussion about rhythm and about possible performances of the line.

    Wordsworth's line shows the most common situation for promoted stress. If your preliminary scansion of a line is one stress short of a pentameter's five and somewhere in the line you see this pattern:

... / x x x / ...

it's a good bet that the middle slack will get promoted. (Of course this hypothesis must be tested by ear. Try out any alternatives you can find.) Another common situation occurs at the end of a line. If you have only four clear stresses and the line ends with

... / x x

then the last syllable is likely to be promoted to stress. Here's another line by Wordsworth, one that we've seen before, which contains (besides a spondee) *both* of the common situations for promotion:

x / | / / | x (/) |x   /|x (/)
A sight so touching in its majesty

As you read and listen to more pentameters you'll come to recognize these common patterns easily. A less usual and more difficult situation occurs when not three but four slack syllables intervene between stresses:

... / x x x x / ....

Then you have to decide whether to promote the second or the third slack. You'll end up with either an iamb and an anapest or an anapest and an iamb, and the choice may not make much difference to the overall metrical feel of the line. A good guess: if just one of those two middle slacks is a monosyllabic word, promote it.

The mechanism that underlies promoted stresses relies in part on our sense that a syllable is often stressed not absolutely but relative to what surrounds it. This works against the possibility of a promoted stress being immediately adjacent to a full or "real" stress. If you find

... / (/) ... or ... (/) / ...

in your scansion, be very suspicious. It *can* happen, but when it does you'll almost always find that the line contains, right at the gap between the full and the promoted stress, a strong pause, probably signaled by a major mark of punctuation like a period or semicolon. What allows the slack to be promoted in this case is that it's adjacent not to a weaker syllable but to a silence.

Caesura

Several times we've seen rules that depend on the presence of a "strong pause" in the line. It's called a **caesura** (plural **caesurae**). It occurs where a major juncture in the syntax of the words, such as between phrases or clauses, comes in the midst of a line rather than at its end. It's an encouragement to some metrical substitutions: a trochee or defective foot most easily replaces an iamb after a caesura.

In some cases caesura plays a role worth noticing and commenting on. When we need to we can mark it ". Notice that it can occur either within a foot –

x   / | x / | x "(/) | x / |x   /
The ghostly language of the ancient earth

– or between feet:

x /|x   / " | x / | x / | x /
Desiring nought but how to kill desire.

Because caesura is not part of the meter itself and because it adds to the clutter of marks, we'll leave caesurae out of scansions except when we want to call particular attention to them.

The two major kinds of metrical variation that we've examined stand in a close logical relation to each other. Both of them arise from the interplay between the metrical skeleton and the particular rhythmic flesh that clothes it:

- *Metrical substitutions show the influence of rhythm on meter.* If a line begins with "Greater than time ...," then instead of asking us to drastically distort the rhythm of the words ("great-*ER* than *TIME*") the meter flexes slightly, and we hear a trochee substituted for the first iamb.
- *Promoted stresses show the influence of meter on rhythm.* Instead of steamrolling the regular alternations of slack and stress in the metrical base, the words' rhythm adjusts itself by lifting slightly where the meter pushes up at it.

This symmetry is a fundamental principle of the system of scansion used here.

Neither kind of variation can run completely wild without derailing the whole enterprise. If the poet tries to substitute too many feet too often, the reader loses the ability to hear the meter at all. Our reading ceases to be guided by a metrical context. If the poem has been metrical up to this point, then the reader feels that the poem has somehow run off the road. At best the rules of the game have been changed without warning. (Meter as a game between poet and reader is almost as common a metaphor as meter as a contract.) At worst, the poem's coherence disintegrates. It turns out that our confidence that a poem is *making sense* depends partly on its rhythmic continuity. (When the band is cooking along, if the bass player suddenly goes off into a rhythmic wilderness there's no *song* any more.) If the poem is metrical, then this continuity centers on meter.

Scansion

All the terms and phenomena we've examined so far come together in the process of scanning a line. In 1903 W. B. Yeats, who has already given us several examples, wrote "Adam's Curse" in rhymed iambic pentameter **couplets**. (The "curse" in the title is the necessity of labor, as forecast in Genesis 3:19, which the poem extends to the labor of creating beauty.) Here's the first couplet, in which Yeats sets a scene of conversation:

> We sat together at one summer's end,
> That beautiful mild woman, your close friend …

As you read these lines aloud you can hear that they are not very regular. Does the irregularity make them feel casual? excited? troubled? The speaker's tone of voice (we're almost as good at reading tones of voice as we are at recognizing faces) becomes actual when you give voice to the lines. How would you speak them? The adjectives listed here may all be reasonable guesses about the state of mind of the speaker with his two companions, a "you" to whom the poet is in some intimate relation and her "beautiful" friend. Only reading the rest of the poem would clarify the question of tone – if not definitively answer it – but these jittery opening lines alert our ears to listen for some disturbance.

To get a more concrete sense of *how* the lines are irregular, which could ultimately help us decide *why*, we scan them.

Steps in Scanning a Line

Here's a compressed account of the algorithm for scanning a line of verse:

0   Read it aloud. (This could be repeated as step 6, step 4.5, etc.)
1   Pick out and mark one stress in each polysyllable.
2   Decide which monosyllables are stressed: nouns, verbs, adjectives and adverbs yes; conjunctions, prepositions, articles no; pronouns only through contrast.
3   Mark the slacks.
4   Consider ways to divide the preliminary line of marks into feet, checking that the substitutions are plausible and that the line has the right number of feet.
5   Decide whether any stresses are promoted (though this question arises as early as step 2 and interacts with step 4).

We begin by marking the polysyllables and their stresses, checking with a dictionary if necessary:

>   /   /
> We sat together at one summer's end,
>   /   /
> That beautiful mild woman, your close friend, ...

Next we mark the stressed monosyllables:

>   / /   / /   /
> We sat together at one summer's end,
>   /   / /   /   /
> That beautiful mild woman, your close friend,...

The verb "sat" and the nouns "end" and "friend" are all pretty clearly stressed: these are the words that tell us what Yeats is talking about. The adjectives "mild" and "close" and the number "one" aren't far behind in prominence. (It also feels interesting that both adjectives apply to the "woman," the "friend," who seems to get more of the speaker's attention at the beginning of the poem than the "you" the poem is addressed to.)

The third step is relatively mechanical – just fill in the slacks:

<pre>
 x / x / x x   /   /   x   /
We sat together at one summer's end,
 x   / x x   /   / x   x   /   /
That beautiful mild woman, your close friend, ...
</pre>

Yet we could wonder about some of these. "That" at the beginning of the second line is a demonstrative pronoun, and those are often stressed ("Not *that* prisoner, Igor, *this* prisoner!"). "Your" is another pronoun, and we can imagine its being stressed ("Not *my* friend, *your* friend!"). Yet these lines don't seem to be interested in either of those possible contrasts. In the absence of contrastive stress, let's leave "That" and "your" as slacks.

We've finished marking the lines to indicate the basic binary distinction between stresses and slacks. To get from this preliminary set of marks to a complete scansion, we need to figure out where to divide the syllables into feet.

Substitutions for the Iamb

As a reminder, the "legal" substitutions for the iamb (x/) are:

> trochee (/x)
> spondee (//)
> anapest (xx/)
> double iamb (xx//) for *two* iambs
> bare stress (/) more rarely

It's often best to start from the end of the line. The first line of this pair certainly looks as if it ends with an iamb:

<pre>
 x / x / x x   /   / | x   /
We sat together at one summer's end,
</pre>

And before that? Perhaps it could be a bare stress (as at the beginning of a headless line, like the one by Hopkins that we saw earlier: "Glory be to God for dappled

33

things"), but this would have to be preceded in turn by an anapest. That's a bizarre combination. A good rule is always to prefer *the most regular scansion that will fit the rhythmic facts*. In this case, the more regular alternative is the double iamb:

$$\text{x} \ / \ \ \text{x} \ / \ \underline{|\text{x x} \ \ / \ \ / \ |} \ \ \text{x} \ \ \ /$$
We sat together at one summer's end,

Since the double iamb counts as two feet, we need only two more at the beginning of the line, and it's fairly obvious that they have to be iambs:

$$\underline{\text{x} \ /|} \ \ \underline{\text{x} \ /} \ \ |\text{x x} \ \ / \ \ / \ | \ \ \text{x} \ \ \ /$$
We sat together at one summer's end,

That's it – except for reading the line aloud again, now with a more detailed awareness of its movement, including the way it circles (nostalgically? yearningly?) around that double iamb.

In this case, if we had started at the beginning of the line we would have met the same choices in a different order. We'd begin with the two clear iambs and then we'd have to choose between the double iamb and an anapest that would have to be followed by either a bare stress and an iamb or a trochee and a bare stress, both of which yield unnecessarily peculiar scansions. But it's not always true that starting at either end of the line provides equally well-paved paths to metrical understanding. More lines begin in some tempestuous way, resolving into metrical clarity at the end, than the other way around. (Why? Robert Frost (1874–1963) called poetry "a momentary stay against confusion," and the poem may tend, in each line as well as over all, to work toward order rather than away from it. More directly: a line as a *unit* of verse seeks formal closure.) This is why starting at the end of the line often makes scansion easier.

Starting at the End of the Line

Starting your scansion at the end of the line is not completely foolproof. If the line (*excluding* any final extrametrical slack) contains more than ten syllables, it must include at least one anapest. You can't predict where the anapest will occur, and in some cases it's easier to locate when you start from the beginning of the line.

Another approach to the foot-division task may occur to you: just divide the ten marks into pairs. In this case, that works fine – though we have to remember to erase the foot division in the middle of the line since "x x" isn't a foot on our list. (As we saw earlier, it's called a pyrrhic, but it never occurs *except* before a spondee – that is, as the start of a double iamb – and our approach is not to consider feet that need special rules.) In fact this simplified approach will work for a large number of iambic pentameters. It fails, though, with any line that has nine syllables (usually a headless line), or eleven or more (including anapests). More treacherously, it fails with a *ten*-syllable line that contains both an anapest and a bare stress:

$$/ \mid x \quad / \mid x \quad / \quad \mid x / \mid x \quad x \quad /$$
Why did Gretel shove her into the stove?

Remember that the rules of thumb for metrical substitutions frown on multiple consecutive trochees. While this line could be scanned as four trochees followed by an iamb, in an iambic pentameter context the ear very much wants to hear the second through seventh syllables ("did Gretel shove her in-") as a series of iambs. If this marking-off-pairs approach appeals to you as a shortcut, try it, but remember to check the result carefully. One more caveat: for someone learning to *write* metrical verse this method is useless.

> You can always construct a line of ten
> syllables without thinking about stress,
> but the pairs of them aren't likely to make
> a really coherent series of feet.

A reader can sometimes get away with beginning from the assumption of two-syllable feet, but the poet has to begin from the rhythm of the words and particularly the positions of stressed syllables. Notice that much of what goes wrong with these lines as iambic pentameters falls under the heading we saw earlier, "triple threats to duple meter":

$$x \quad x \quad / \mid x \quad x \quad / \mid x \quad / \mid x \quad /$$
You can always construct a line of ten ...
$$x \quad / \mid x \quad x \quad / \mid x \quad / \mid x \quad x \quad /$$
a really coherent series of feet.

Yeats's second line seems a little more complicated than the first. Here are the preliminary marks:

x   / x x   /   / x   x   /   /

That beautiful mild woman, your close friend,

To be thorough, let's double-check alternative ways to divide this sequence into feet. Again we'll start at the end of the line. While the last stress *could* be a foot by itself, that would just get us into trouble: it could be preceded by an iamb, but what could come before that? Our list of usual feet contains only one that would fit, a trochee, and before that we would have to use an anapest preceded by an iamb:

x   / | x x / | / x | x   / | /

That beautiful mild woman, your close friend, ...

This is a theoretically possible scansion, but it's a highly unlikely iambic pentameter. Besides offering just two iambs, it contains a peculiar jumble of three different other kinds of feet. A better alternative isn't hard to find:

x   / | x x / / | x   x   /   /

That beautiful mild woman, your close friend, ...

This is still out of the ordinary, made up of only one iamb and two double iambs. Yet partly because it preserves the two-syllables-per-foot norm (four for a double iamb) rather than a mix of one- and three-syllable feet – always more disruptive – this scansion seems easier and more natural. In this case we might want to mark the caesura, which delicately moderates the massiveness of the double iambs:

x   / | x x / / | x ″ x   /   /

That beautiful mild woman, your close friend, ...

It matters which scansion we choose, though this isn't the same as saying that there is a single *correct* scansion of this complicated line. Within the system we're using here, different scansions embody different ideas about how the line moves and therefore what it means. The first version – an anapest, a trochee, a couple of lonely iambs, and a final bare stress – feels arbitrary. Neither the trochee nor the bare stress follows a caesura (as urged by our rules of thumb). The scansion sketches an unstable line in which the basic iambic movement is confirmed only at two apparently random points (the first and fourth feet). Does the line actually *sound* as strange as that? If the poem were about the contingent nature of constraints, metrical or social, or if it were more about chaos than about mortality, then a line scanned that way might conceivably fit. The second scansion, on the other hand, diagrams a line that, while irregular and even edgy, remains committed to the fundamental iambic movement – a movement that the doubled doubling of the iamb could even be heard as emphasizing. To put it another way, this scansion treats the "rules" of meter as encompassing a set of unexpected possibilities like the rules of chess or tennis, while the other scansion treats them as obstacles to be gotten around like ordinances against jaywalking. If we hear the line that other way, we hear the poet squirming uncomfortably among rules; but Yeats is after deeper discomforts than that.

After these two irregular opening lines Yeats gives us a third whose metricality is much easier to hear:

> And you and I, and talked of poetry.

Except for the promoted stress at its end this line is entirely regular. (Scan it for yourself to check.) Yeats wrote this poem more than a decade before World War I, at a time when he knew readers would assume that he was writing metrical lines. ("Free verse" didn't begin to be popular until a few years later.) Even so, he's careful to reaffirm our hearing of the basic metrical pattern after those two more tumultuous opening lines. More broadly, the rest of his poem develops a larger rhythm, one spanning multiple lines, similarly characterized by departing from regularity and returning to it.

To see how the poet can build on the sense of meter that he has established, let's look at one more couplet from the same poem. Thirty lines after the opening pair we've been reading, near the end of the poem, while thinking about all that he would like to but can't quite say to "you," he mentions almost as an aside,

> A moon, worn as if it had been a shell
> Washed by time's waters as they rose and fell

Almost as an aside: yet it's clearly also a description of himself and her, or his feeling about her, or what they have become, or what he imagines them becoming as time carries them onward.

The preliminary marks for these lines look messy:

```
x    /    /   x x x x   x x   /
A moon, worn as if it had been a shell
 /     x /      / x x   x / x   /
Washed by time's waters as they rose and fell
```

In the first line only three syllables are clearly stressed out of the five we'll ultimately need for a pentameter. (Already this tells us something: the line isolates these three reverberant words, "moon" and "worn" and "shell," to bring them into the center of the poem's contemplation here at its end.) There must be two promoted stresses in the last seven syllables of the line, but which? If a promoted stress can't normally fall next to a full stress (or, for the same reasons, next to another promoted stress), then the only possible combinations would be "if" and "had"; "it" and "been"; or "if" and "been." But what reason is there to stress "it"? And what would "had" be contrasted with? The most likely candidates, then, are "if" (which is exceptionally substantial for a conjunction and is the stronger element in the phrase "as if") and "been" (which may be just a linking verb, but carries the burden of connecting the line's three main words not only in the sentence but also as a simile):

```
x    /    /    x(/) | x x   (/) | x   /
A moon, worn as if it had been a shell
```

This seems the best choice for the second half of the line. But at the same time it's worth noticing – as Yeats, like any poet accustomed to working in meter, would have been aware – that the choice among these alternatives doesn't make a drastic difference. They shuffle one anapest and two iambs into various orders, none with much emphasis until the very last syllable. However we scan it, everything about the line's realization of the metrical pattern minimizes *all* the syllables after "A moon, worn ...," so that "shell" arrives with the sound of discovery.

Earlier in the line we have one more decision to make. We can either mark "worn" as a bare stress followed by an iamb, or take it as the beginning of a trochee. If we do the latter, it would have to be followed by another trochee whose stress is promoted:

x   / | / x|(/) x |x (/) | x   /

A moon, worn as if it had been a shell

There are reasons to think this scansion is unlikely. As mentioned earlier, two or more trochaic substitutions in a row destabilize the iambic movement by reversing it. On the other hand, the word "worn" is so emphatic and so isolated between an early caesura and a long run of slack syllables that hearing it as a bare stress doesn't add much further turbulence to the line. This is probably the best scansion:

x   /″ | / | x (/) |x x (/) | x   /

A moon, worn as if it had been a shell

Near the end of the poem, Yeats is giving us an unusually irregular line. It's difficult to scan, and the difficulty is useful because it calls our attention to the deliberate irregularity. (If you've followed the arguments for scanning it this way you have a good grasp of the principles.) The remainder of the poem works toward a solid, regular close ("As weary-hearted as that hollow moon" is the last line). Even the second line of this couplet is considerably easier to scan than the first:

/   x | /   /| x (/) | x   / |x /

Washed by time's waters as they rose and fell

This line's ending has a clear iambic movement, and the beginning doesn't throw us off either: the initial trochee is very common, and the following spondee makes a pattern that we've seen previously in lines by Pope and Keats. The promoted stress on "as" is easy to locate. What makes the scansion worth doing in this case is not that it's difficult, but that it helps point out the developing motion of the line: the dense cluster of stresses at the beginning, the middle syllables' receding wave, and the regular tide of the ending, "they rose and fell." We hear something of the speaker's erotic yearning in this line.

An Example

This chapter has given you the information you need to scan most iambic pentameter lines, some methods for applying that information, and hints about why it's worth doing. Later chapters will build on these fundamentals, examining metrical and nonmetrical alternatives to the iambic pentameter and exploring more of the territory that surrounds this core topic in English metrics.

To bring all this together in one more extended exercise, let's examine a well-known **sonnet** (we'll explore sonnets more generally in Chapter 3), Wordsworth's "Composed upon Westminster Bridge, September 3, 1802."

> Earth has not anything to show more fair:
> Dull would he be of soul who could pass by
> A sight so touching in its majesty:
> This City now doth, like a garment, wear
> The beauty of the morning; silent, bare,
> Ships, towers, domes, theatres, and temples lie
> Open unto the fields, and to the sky;
> All bright and glittering in the smokeless air.
> Never did sun more beautifully steep
> In his first splendor, valley, rock, or hill;
> Ne'er saw I, never felt, a calm so deep!
> The river glideth at his own sweet will:
> Dear God! the very houses seem asleep;
> And all that mighty heart is lying still!

You might want to scan this poem yourself before reading on. The best way to do this is to type it out – having the poem flow through your own fingers (as well as through your own mouth and ear) helps in hearing its details – with double spacing between lines and then sketch the scansion first in pencil. In any case be sure to read the whole poem aloud before going on.

The first line is both irregular and insistent:

/   x | x /|x (/) | x   / | /   / .
Earth has not anything to show more fair:

Metrically, the least certain part of this line is its beginning, not because of the standard initial trochaic inversion but because it's hard to be sure whether "not" is stressed. (Even "has" might ordinarily be stressed, since it's a verb, but any emphasis seems to get lost between "Earth" and "not anything.") But as we've seen before with such ambiguities, the line is arranged so that the decision doesn't affect anything else: the line begins with either a trochee and a spondee (fairly common) or a trochee and an iamb (extremely common) and everything after that is settled. (The final spondee does more to clinch the meter than to unsettle it.) This neat compensation for metrical uncertainty doesn't signify *exceptional* cleverness on Wordsworth's part: it is the usual practice of poets to keep rhythmic ambiguities confined in their metrical impact so that they complicate and enrich the reader's rhythmic sense without dislocating it. If the second half of the line were less definitely iambic, the uncertainty about "not" would be more destabilizing. As it is the poem begins with an enthusiastic exclamation that's still recognizably grounded in firm metrical soil.

$$/ \quad x \mid x \ / \mid x \ / \mid x \quad x \mid / \ /$$
Dull would he be of soul who could pass by

Though its syntax is a little unfamiliar, this line is not difficult to scan – until the end. What's stressed? Our guidelines say that monosyllabic verbs are and prepositions aren't. Why not "could," which is a verb, and why "by," which looks like a preposition?

The line provides two important footnotes to our rules of thumb. First, the stress on verbs doesn't automatically extend to *auxiliary* verbs, such as "could" and "would" in this line. Unlike main verbs, auxiliary verbs are a "closed class" of words: there are only a couple of dozen of them and none have been added to English for a long time. Like pronouns, they're stressed when they participate in a contrast – "I *could* have told you, but I didn't want to" – but often that doesn't apply. Here, though the auxiliaries collaborate in creating the line's contrary-to-fact condition, "could" near the end is no more stressed than "would" near the beginning. (An unusual performance of the line that stressed "would" would almost certainly have to stress "could" as well. Try it out.)

Second, some verbs are spelled as two words. These **phrasal verbs** are important and common in English. They consist of a main verb plus a particle which resembles an adverb or a preposition. Many common verbs form multiple phrasal variants whose meanings can't be predicted from the meaning of the main verb: *catch on* ("comprehend" or "become fashionable"), *catch up* ("overtake"), *catch* [someone] *out* ("detect in a fraud or error"), and so on. In another context "pass by" might be an ordinary verb and a preposition ("He could only pass by cheating"). Here, though, "pass by" is a phrasal verb. Ending a line with a preposition would be awkward, but the end of this line yields a more natural suspense: we wait to hear the object of the (two-word) verb, what it is that only a dullard could "pass by." Because the meanings of phrasal verbs reside in the contrast between possible particles – between *running up a bill* and *running down a lead* – the particle gets at least as much stress as the main verb. Here "by" is perhaps even more strongly stressed than "pass." Since stress is binary, we don't need to decide; we just mark the pair as a spondee.

<pre>
 x   / | /   / | x (/) | x   / | x (/)
</pre>
A sight so touching in its majesty:

We've seen this line before. One additional point is that except for "anything" in the first line "touching" and "majesty" are the first polysyllables in the poem. Wordsworth has chosen them partly for their odd relation to each other: what's *majestic* might inspire awe or fear, but what *touches* us is more intimate and personal. The line's rhythm focuses on this odd couple of words, and the meter uses promoted stresses to clear a little auditory space after each of them.

Wordsworth's fourth line tells us what we're actually looking at, the panoramic view from the bridge:

<pre>
 /   / | x   / | /   x | x   / | x   /
</pre>
This City now doth, like a garment, wear

Whether to stress "This" or not is a question like several we have seen before: it's worth thinking about, but the answer won't change anything else in the scansion. Here it's marked as stressed because it calls attention to the sense of *presentness* in the scene that Wordsworth seems to want to emphasize. The middle of the line is slightly more puzzling: should we stress "doth" (an obsolete form of "does") or hear a promoted stress on the preposition "like"? "Do" is an auxiliary verb, but in contexts where it's not required, including it often makes it emphatic.

Separating it from the main verb it supports tends to strengthen the emphasis: "I *did*, despite everything they told me, read that book."

Even though the line's only punctuation is the commas marking off "like a garment," in reading we're more likely to pause not after "doth" but after "now," which augments the sentence's subject. Caesura always has to do with syntax, but it doesn't always correspond to punctuation marks, which sometimes conform more to logical than to rhythmic aspects of syntax. We might want to mark the caesura to show how it helps make the mid-line trochee feel natural:

/   /|x / "|/   x| x / | x   /
This City now doth, like a garment, wear

What does the city "wear"?

x   /| x(/) | x   / | x   /| x   /
The beauty of the morning; silent, bare,

This line, the most metrically regular in the poem so far, is also the beginning of its second **quatrain** (a unit of four lines linked by rhyme). At the same time it continues the poem's second sentence, which began in line 4 before the first quatrain was finished. In other words, the sentences and the quatrains are out of synchronization. This isn't particularly puzzling or disturbing, but it does help us (since the two quatrains use the same rhyme sounds) hear this fifth line as forming a rhyming couplet with the line before it:

This City now doth, like a garment, wear
The beauty of the morning; silent, bare, ...

Though all this may sound convoluted, the resulting pattern has a direct effect: it strikingly rhymes "wear" with its near-antonym "bare." We don't actually know what the adjectives at the end of this line ("silent, bare") will turn out to modify, but for the moment it seems to be the "City," so we have the apparent paradox that the city is made naked by wearing something. Of course, since what it wears is not "a garment" but "beauty," the paradox dissolves: "beauty" is *all* it wears. Behind the simile ("like a garment") lies a metaphor: the city as a kind of nymph perhaps. Wordsworth is a poet better known for celebrating flowers and fields than industrial capitals. Yet London at this early hour, "smokeless," not yet cloaked or shrouded, is for once able to compete with "Nature" for the poet's enthusiasm.

The next line does give us new nouns for the adjectives "silent, bare" to modify:

/   / | x   / | / x | x   x   / | x   /
Ships, towers, domes, theatres, and temples lie

These things are not the object we expected (the city) but they do constitute it. This line enacts a shift of focus from wide view toward sharper detail. The opening spondee and iamb, as a density of stresses, emphasize the catalog this line presents to us. The list of nouns is the equivalent, for us as readers, of the panorama that the speaker is seeing. (What the poet sees, he tells us; what he tells us, we see. This is a magic of language, basic but not simple.) Besides the list, the line contains only a final verb. At least until we go on to the next line, "lie" doesn't seem to detract or to add much (it appears to be a mere synonym for "are situated"), though as a verb it's certainly stressed.

In the middle of this line, if "theatres" has three syllables it creates a momentary puzzle about how to divide the line into feet. By trying out the alternatives, you can confirm that only the trochee and anapest shown here will ultimately work. (The trochee upholds our rules of thumb: it follows a strong pause in the middle of the line.) If "theatres" is reduced to two syllables, as in colloquial American speech, the scansion becomes even simpler: a trochee and an iamb. Even putting a stress on the middle syllable, as in some regional American dialects ("the-*ay*-ters") doesn't disturb the pentameter too badly (an iamb and an anapest). The metrical line can be surprisingly flexible.

The seventh line amplifies what seemed so minor in the sixth, the verb "lie":

/   x | /   x | x   / | x (/) | x   /
Open unto the fields, and to the sky;

Unlike "lie" by itself (as in the bland expression "the town lies on the coast"), "lie / Open" furthers the idea, established earlier by "bare," that before the city wakes up to business it's exposed and available to affectionate perception: it's a "touching" sight. The initial trochee on "Open" may emphasize this.

44

The scansion shown here begins with two trochees in a row, and this should set off a warning bell. The rules of thumb are only that, and when we find an exception the point is not to reject it as illegal but to ask why it happens where it does. In this case, the exception might be smaller than it seems. Though "unto" has two syllables, it's just a preposition (a more familiar one in 1803 than now). Its first syllable is stressed more than the second, but the whole word, as a member of a closed class, is de-emphasized. (In some systems of metrics "grammar words" like this are excluded from the scansion's rules entirely.) So in a broader view the line has just three main stresses, the nouns "fields" and "sky" and the beginning of "Open." These words that mainly carry the meaning of the line have a lot of room to resonate among all the unstressed syllables.

An alternative explanation, if we want to stick with this scansion of the line, might emphasize the exception instead of minimizing it: Wordsworth deliberately diverts the meter, not far enough for us to lose track but far enough to startle us, just as he is startled and drawn in by the city's unwonted aspect. Different readers may prefer one or the other of these explanations. They follow from and contribute to different ways of hearing the voice of the poem as a whole: is our speaker feeling primarily expansiveness and relief or energetic wonder? A scansion can't answer such a question, but it can help frame it, as we've just seen.

A different scansion might occur to you:

> / | x / |x   x   / | x (/) | x /
> Open unto the fields, and to the sky;

This avoids the troublesome double trochee, though at the cost of an unusual headless line with a later anapest. There are interesting arguments to be made on both sides. It may not be worth arguing about: as always, if the process of scansion has made us hear the line's bargain between meter and rhythm, its job is done.

> /   / | x   / | x x (/) | x   / |x   /
> All bright and glittering in the smokeless air.

In a slightly earlier period than Wordsworth's, a poet might well have written the word in the midst of this line as "glitt'ring." The middle syllable disappears easily in pronunciation, and this would yield a thoroughly iambic line. Yet the text does give us "glittering," which may even enhance the word's contribution: something in the coruscation of the line's middle syllables suggests the visual sparkle of the scene. (It's a spooky word. Wordsworth's friend Coleridge uses it to describe the eyes of his Ancient Mariner. Yeats speaks of the "ancient, glittering eyes" of his mysterious sages in "Lapis Lazuli.")

The resulting four slacks in a row, when we make our preliminary marks, present the problem mentioned earlier, whether we should promote the second or third:

/   x   x   x   x   /

All bright and glittering in the smokeless air.

As usual, the best judge here is the ear: when you speak the line aloud you'll probably find *"glittering in* the *smoke*less air" easier to say in a natural way than *"glittering* in the *smoke*less *air*." As a general rule, if only one of the two candidate syllables is a separate word, that one will be promoted.

We've finished the first eight lines of this sonnet (the **octave**) with six to go (the **sestet**), and this is the point where most poems written in this form make some kind of turn. Here, for one thing, the rhymes change: the previous eight lines used just two rhyme sounds and the next six lines will shift to two different ones. Even though the poem is printed without any stanza break, we're beginning a new part, and Wordsworth uses its first line to make a subtle but striking point about the poem's own language and meter:

/ x | x   / | /   /|x (/)|x   /

Never did sun more beautifully steep

In conversation we hardly ever enunciate "beautifully" this way. We shorten it to "beautif'ly." Generally poems don't make it their business to quarrel with our habits of speech. But this line can't very well be scanned as the iambic pentameter we know it must be unless we give that word its full complement of four syllables. Similarly, when we say "beautifully" in conversation we often don't mean it. We mean something like "quite well enough" or just "OK." Here Wordsworth means it, and he uses our metrical hearing to guide us too into giving this word its full potential wingspread.

"Steep" is a puzzling word at the end of this line; if it's an adjective ("a steep hill") it seems odd as a modifier for "sun," the only noun in the vicinity. (So early in the day, the sun may appear to be rising "steeply," but we apply the adjective to paths, not to things following those paths.) The next line begins with the surprise that "steep" was in fact a verb — it refers to bathing or soaking, like what we do with tea. In this context the sun "steeps"

$$x \ \ x \ | \ / \quad \ / \ | \ x \quad / \ | \ x \quad / \quad | \ x \quad /$$
In his first splendor, valley, rock, or hill;

The line ends with a second list of nouns. As in line 6, the catalog is a celebration, though the things listed contrast with the earlier ones. He isn't presently looking at valleys and hills but at theaters and domes, which in this moment of "splendor" compare well with his more usually beloved landscapes. The strictly iambic list is preceded by a double iamb, and the fact that it's the only one in the poem (though there are a number of spondees) makes it sound all the more forcefully solemn.

The first word of the next line is a contraction, possibly still familiar from the compound "ne'er-do-well":

$$/ \quad / \ | x \quad / | x \quad / \quad | x \quad / \ | \ / \quad /$$
Ne'er saw I, never felt, a calm so deep!

Though "ne'er" and "e'er" were common enough in poetry at the time, Wordsworth takes the unusual step of immediately pairing the contracted word with its full form, "never." This increases the insistence of the repetition. The two verbs "saw" and "felt," governed by the repeated negative adverb, are placed in a strong contrast which paradoxically links them: the scene's "calm" is one that joins seeing with feeling, or that only seeing and feeling conjoined can appreciate. The unspooling of the iambs from the initial spondee on "Ne'er saw" emphasizes the expansiveness of his feeling.

$$x \ / \ | \ x \quad / | x \quad (/) \ | \ x \quad / \quad | \quad / \quad /$$
The river glideth at his own sweet will:

It was a convenience to poets of the early nineteenth century that some conventional linguistic options made metrical composition a little easier. In the previous line the contraction of "ne'er" is an example – though it's also an example of how a poet like Wordsworth could turn a mere option into a pointed opportunity by adding the full "never." Another example is the availability of both "glides" and "glideth" (one syllable or two) as present-tense third-person-singular forms of the verb. Again, though, Wordsworth doesn't simply take advantage of "glideth" to fill up the required number of syllable slots in the pentameter. Rather he uses its extended length within this sinuous line as part of a soundscape that we, listening readers, readily associate with the scene that he, the speaking witness, sees. The name he selects for the river's movement, "glideth," becomes the truth of what our mind's eye creates. Sound and sight, hearing and seeing, interact this way frequently in poems, and meter is among other things a framework for this symbiosis.

/　　/ | x　/|x　/| x　/ | x　/
Dear God! the very houses seem asleep;

It would be hard to find a more definite spondee than "Dear God!" The rest of the line is perfectly regular. We're near the end of the poem, and just as iambic pentameters tend to resolve toward regularity at their ends, so poems tend to reassert their metrical foundation at or near the close.

x　/ | /　/ | x　/ | x /|x　/
And all that mighty heart is lying still!

This final line is shocking, of course: the city is beautiful because it's dead. (What about the people?) Yet the death is temporary, momentary, a kind of miraculous interval. Metrically the line maintains the regularity of the one preceding it, again with one spondaic substitution that doesn't much counter the iambic regularity and might even reinforce it. Comparisons of the iambic meter to a heartbeat are common, though impossible to substantiate. (So are comparisons between the length of the iambic pentameter and the typical duration of the breath.) In any case, this line does the pair of apparently contradictory, climactic things that many poems' last lines do: it reaffirms the life-giving pulse of the poem, and brings it to a close. Through its sound the poem says of itself what Wordsworth says of London.

2

Other Meters

In Chapter 1 you learned how to hear complex lines of five iambic feet and scan them to make your hearing clear to yourself and others. Though the pentameter has been the dominant English line for centuries, lengths other than five feet are common too. Also, though a majority of poems in English are iambic, different feet can be used as the basis for metrical lines. In this chapter we'll begin by exploring variations in length and then turn to lines based on other feet such as anapests and trochees. Finally we'll explore some metrical systems that aren't based on feet.

Other Iambics

Almost everything you learned about the pentameter applies when you're reading iambic lines of other lengths. The possible foot substitutions stay the same: the spondee, the double iamb, the trochee, and so on. Stresses get promoted by metrical context as in the pentameter. So there isn't much to learn in the way of new terminology or methods of scansion. But there are subtler differences.

When the line has fewer than five feet, the effect of each variation tends to increase and fewer combinations of variations are possible. At an extreme, lines

Verse: An Introduction to Prosody, First Edition. Charles O. Hartman.
© 2015 John Wiley & Sons, Ltd. Published 2015 by John Wiley & Sons, Ltd.

of one foot, iambic **monometer**, show up occasionally. Here's a poem by Robert
Herrick (1591–1674), "On His Departure Hence":

```
        /   /
    Thus I
        /   /
    Pass by
    x       /
    And die:
    x     /
    As one
    x       /
    Unknown
    x     /
    And gone:
    x     /
    I'm made
    x   /
    A shade
    x       /
    And laid
    x       /
    I'th grave,    ["in the"]
        /   /
    There have
    x     /
    My cave.
      /   /
    Where tell
    x     /
    I dwell.
      x   /
    Farewell.
```

This is a famous example mostly because it's so rare. The rigidly curtailed lines
certainly help to act out the extreme concentration of mind which a meditation
on one's own death can call for, though they break up any complicated train of
thought. The only substitutions Herrick uses are spondees. (Even those aren't

very definite: is "Thus" really stressed in the first line?) Obviously a trochee would seriously disrupt this meter. The contraction in line 10 ("I'th") suggests that even a single anapest felt like too much for the fragile monometer structure to contain.

The iambic **dimeter** offers a little more flexibility, and poets have used it for a number of effects. In *A Midsummer Night's Dream* Shakespeare gives his comic character Bottom a song whose buffoonish crudity owes a lot to the fast clash of feet in the cramped line:

            x   / | x /
        The raging rocks
        x   / |x x   /
        And shivering shocks
          x   / | x   /
        Shall break the locks
         x / | x   /
        Of prison gates;
          x   / | x   /
        And Phibbus' car   [Phoebus Apollo's chariot, the sun]
          x   / | x   /
        Shall shine from far
          x   / | x   /
        And make and mar
         x   / |x /
        The foolish Fates

This is meant to be loud nonsense. Notice that scanning it is a fairly trivial exercise, mostly because the dimeter invites little more variation than the monometer. Thomas Hardy (1840–1928) begins "The Robin" almost as lightly, though it's less boisterous:

             x / | x /
          When up aloft
         x / | x   /
          I see in pools
            x   / | x   /
          The shining sky,

<pre>
        x   x / | x   /
        And a happy bird
        x   / | x /
        Am I, am I!
</pre>

But he gives his short lines more weight as the poem goes on, as the last of the poem's four stanzas shows.

The "it" here is winter:

<pre>
        x   (/) | x   /
        But when it lasts,
        x   / | /   /
        And snows still fall,
        x / | x /
        I get to feel
          /   / | x /
        No grief at all,
         x x / | x x /   /
        For I turn to a cold stiff
         /   x|x   /
        Feathery ball!
</pre>

Stanzas

This chapter can't entirely avoid mentioning stanzas or the rhymes which often define them, though it's Chapter 3 that will go into detail about these aspects of verse that organize it beyond the level of the line. For now it's enough to think of a stanza simply as a group of lines, usually linked by similar-sounding words at their ends.

The second-to-last line isn't easy to account for metrically. If we treat it as ending with a double iamb then the line has the equivalent of three feet, which breaks the dimeter rule the poem has set for itself. Instead, just as dubiously, we might try to hear the final word "stiff" as a kind of extra metrical syllable, like ones we've seen at the ends of some pentameters, but here stressed instead. A third alternative – perhaps the most likely though the most complex – is that Hardy hears "stiff" as really belonging to the following line, which we then read as:

$$/ \quad / \mid x \, x \quad /$$
stiff Feathery ball!

(The more allied to music the verse is – and an exceptionally short line is one factor that might produce this effect – the more fluid the boundaries of *lines* become. We'll see more of this in Chapter 5.) One way or another, the extra weight of this line combines with the preceding spondees to create the increased gravity we feel at the poem's end, despite "Feathery."

Iambic dimeter poems are almost as scarce as iambic monometer ones. The iambic **trimeter** line is more common, though as we'll see in Chapter 3 it is most often used in combination with lines of other lengths. Still, some well-known poems are entirely in iambic trimeter. Theodore Roethke's "My Papa's Waltz" varies the meter in different ways in its four stanzas. Here's the last of them:

$$x \quad / \mid \; / \quad x \mid x \quad /$$
You beat time on my head
$$x \; x \; / \mid \; / \quad / \mid x \quad /$$
With a palm caked hard by dirt,
$$x \quad / \quad \mid \; x \; / \mid x \quad /$$
Then waltzed me off to bed
$$/ \quad / \mid x \; (/) \mid x \quad /$$
Still clinging to your shirt.

The trochee in the middle of the first line is a bit of metrical play: it unsteadies the line so as to imitate the father's half-drunk dancing with his son – the "time" goes awry. (The poem begins, "The whisky on your breath/ Could make a small boy dizzy.") Though the spondee in the second line may emphasize the hardness of the palm and through that the hard work the father does, the one in the final line emphasizes the fondness of the recollection. The poet, through memory, continues to cling. As we've seen before, a certain metrical substitution doesn't have a fixed, uniform effect. We interpret the spondee's added force under the influence of context – in particular the words "hard" in the second line and "still" in the fourth.

W. B. Yeats gives the trimeter line a more reflective movement in his short poem "Memory," though the nostalgic surface is troubled by a current of bitter yearning. Here is the whole poem:

```
 /   x | x /  | x /
One had a lovely face,
   x  / | x   / | x    /
And two or three had charm,
   x   /  | x  / |  x  x   /
But charm and face were in vain
   x /   | x  /  | x   /
Because the mountain grass
 /  x | x   /  | x  /
Cannot but keep the form
   x   x   /  | x  /  | x  /
Where the mountain hare has lain.
```

He begins by recollecting various women, but then says their allure had no power (it was "in vain") to stick vividly in his memory – as the offhand "two or three" also suggests. The second half of the poem shifts to metaphor: "Because" doesn't make literal sense as a logical connection between several women and one hare. "Form" has a technical meaning here: the nest a hare presses out in tall grass. The one woman, the "mountain hare," who has left an ardent trace in his memory, is gone from her place in the "mountain grass." (If the "grass" is his *faculty* of memory, the "form" is the memory *impression* she's left there.)

Within the poem's single sentence, Yeats arranges the movement of his trimeter lines to underscore the structure of his metaphorical thinking. The lines in the dismissive first half are relatively self-contained in syntax; they're complete clauses. This emphasizes the shortness of the lines and makes the trimeter feel like a light and casual meter. The second half, where the metaphor gets under way and the feeling turns more urgent, is more continuous in syntax: it's all one subordinate clause. Yeats distributes one anapest and one trochee in each half of the poem. ("Cannot" is a word that can be stressed in various ways. In this old-fashioned phrase which means "can't help but keep," and in Yeats's Irish English, the first syllable gets the stress.) Even the poem's two regular lines move differently and contribute different effects. The second line has the sound of casual brushing off. The fourth line initiates the metaphor, and the line's end is emphatically suspended on the first strong image in the poem, in contrast to the second line's brusque closing-off of the topic of those other women.

If a similar combination of speed and gravity arises from the trimeter in these lines from "Maud" (section XI) by Alfred, Lord Tennyson (1809–1892), it's projected into the future rather than the past:

> / / | x /|x /
> O let the solid ground
>   / / |x / | x /
>   Not fail beneath my feet
> x / | x / |x /
> Before my life has found
>   x / | x / | / /
>   What some have found so sweet;
>   /| / / / | x /
>   Then let come what may,
>   / /| x x(/)|x /
>   What matter if I go mad,
> x / | x / | x /
> I shall have had my day.

Spondees underscore the tone of petition in these lines. Tennyson seems to balance the loss of a syllable in the headless line 5 with the anapest in the following line. The compressed scope of the three-foot line tends to foreground symmetries of this kind. More importantly, the strong variations in this pair of lines underscore their role as the center of intense feeling in the poem. On the whole the iambic trimeter is a wonderfully versatile line with space for one or two vivid metrical gestures, and it's a little surprising that poets haven't relied on it more often.

We'll come back to the large topic of four-foot lines, iambic tetrameters, in a' moment, after we've glanced briefly at lines *longer* than the pentameter.

Some poems in English are written in iambic **hexameters** and longer lines, though not a great many. One set form, the stanza invented by Edmund Spenser (1552–1599) and known as the **Spenserian stanza**, always ends with a hexameter. Also, writers of unrhymed iambic pentameter verse in the seventeenth and eighteenth centuries sometimes inserted a hexameter for the sake of variety. Other poets, imitating the Greek and Latin epics which were written in a different kind of hexameter, tried to adapt iambic hexameters to large-scale purposes in

English. *Poly-Olbion*, by Michael Drayton (1563–1631), which was published in 1612, comprises over 15,000 lines rhymed in couplets describing the beauties of England (Albion). The large majority of these hexameter lines have a caesura, a strong pause at a syntactical juncture, right in the middle:

```
 x /   |x     / |  x  / " |  x  /  |  x    /  |x   /
Of Albion's glorious Isle the wonders whilst I write,
  x  /  |  x / |x     / " |  x  /  |  x / | x (/)
The sundry varying soils, the pleasures infinite ...
```

Each line falls easily into two equal pieces. This holds true until line 31, where the caesura shifts back by one foot:

```
  x / |x    /  " |  x (/) | x   /   |   x / |   x   /
Ye sacred Bards, that to your harps' melodious strings ...
```

Within the first 500 lines of the poem, no polysyllabic word ever crosses the midpoint, the boundary between the sixth and seventh syllables, so at least *some* pause is possible in the middle of every line.

This may be why, as a continuous meter, iambic hexameter hasn't taken root to the same degree as lines one or two feet shorter. It's difficult to keep a line of six feet from breaking so consistently at a midpoint caesura that it merely feels like an oddly printed pair of trimeters. Six syllables is a reasonable length for a syntactical unit, while twelve (the length of the whole hexameter) is too long to hold together syntactically, and phrases of four syllables or fewer seem unusually short. In a pentameter the caesura generally produces an asymmetry which is easy to modify pleasingly from line to line, but the hexameter's caesura is most often stuck in the middle. It's too bad: six is a good number, dividing into two threes or three twos for attractive variety. In some styles of music – African, Medieval European, flamenco, and so on – frequent shifts between treating six beats as two groups of three and as three groups of two is a constant source of rhythmic interest. (The musical term is "hemiola.") Maybe someone will find a way to realize the same lively possibilities in lines of six iambic feet.

Lines longer than the hexameter are even more breakable. In particular, the iambic **heptameter** – also known as the **fourteener** for the number of its syllables – usually has a caesura after the eighth or ninth syllable. When it does it feels exactly like the first half of what's called "common measure" or "ballad stanza" or "hymnal stanza," an extremely popular form that we'll examine later. The great Christmas vision of the Jesuit priest and poet Robert Southwell (1561–1595), "The Burning Babe," written late in the sixteenth century, shows this regular break at work:

```
x / |x  / |x /  | x   /  " |  /   / | x x (/) |x   /
As I in hoary winter's night stood shivering in the snow,
   x   /  |x (/) | x   / | x   / " | x    /  |  x  / |x   /
Surprised I was with sudden heat which made my heart to glow ...
```

You may sometimes see this poem printed as ballad stanzas, with a line break at each caesura. In these cases the iambic heptameter comes to seem like an arbitrary choice of typography rather than an integral meter.

One of the few notable English poems in heptameters that vary enough to sound like heptameters rather than spliced-together tetrameters and trimeters is the translation by George Chapman (1559/60–1634) of Homer's *Iliad*. (He chose pentameter instead for his *Odyssey*, so much admired by John Keats in his poem "On First Looking into Chapman's Homer.") It was published at the beginning of the seventeenth century, around the time of Shakespeare's death:

```
   x   /  | /   /  | x /  | x / " | /   x |  x   / | x   /
The stern fight freed of all the Gods, conquest with doubtful wings
 / x  | x   /  | x"/ | x  / | x   / | x  / | x   /
Flew on their lances; every way the restless field she flings
 x  /  |x   /  | x  /| x (/) | x  / |x  " (/) | x /
Betwixt the floods of Simois and Xanthus, that confined
 /   x | x  / | x / |x(/)" |x   /  |x  / | x    /
All their affairs at Ilion, and round about them shined.
```

(Notice how the meter tells us how to pronounce the unfamiliar river name Simois.) It's true that all these lines have at least a slight break after the eighth syllable, but there are more conspicuous pauses at less predictable spots: after the fifth syllable in the second line and after the eleventh in the third line. There are pauses on all scales in almost any line, and they can't all be prominent enough to interact noticeably with the meter. If we need to pick one pause in the line to call the caesura, then these lines have caesurae that dance around the dead center of the line. Along with variously distributed trochees and promotions, this syncopation of the parts of the line makes Chapman's verse a supple instrument that keeps our ears entertained throughout his very long poem.

Our review of lines of different lengths has skipped over the iambic **tetra-meter**. After iambic pentameter, it's by far the most common meter in English. So many poems have used it over so many centuries that it's worth examining several examples of how poets have handled it.

Andrew Marvell (1621–1678), writing at the same time that his friend John Milton was solidifying the dominance of iambic pentameter in poems like *Paradise Lost*, himself preferred the tetrameter, usually rhymed in couplets. Partly because of the rhyme and partly because it's simply 20% shorter, Marvell makes the tetrameter feel tighter than the pentameter, more witty and less grandiloquent. Here is the first stanza of his "A Dialogue Between the Soul and Body." The soul is complaining about its imprisonment:

```
  /   /  |  x   (/)  |  x   /  |  x     /
O, who shall from this dungeon raise
x    /  | x  /  |  /   /  | x   /
A soul enslaved so many ways ?
   x    /  | x   /  |   x   /  | x     /
With bolts of bones, that fettered stands
x    /   | x    /| x (/) |x     /
In feet, and manacled in hands ;
   /    /  |x  (/)  | x /  |  x      /
Here blinded with an eye, and there
   /   x  | x     /   |  x   (/) |x  /
Deaf with the drumming of an ear ;
x    /  |  /    /  | x  (/)  | x     /
A soul hung up, as 'twere, in chains
x    /   | x    /| x (/)  |x    /
Of nerves, and arteries, and veins ;
 /   x   | x  /  |  /    /  | x  /
Tortured, besides each other part,
x x   /   /  | x   /  | x /
In a vain head, and double heart?
```

The foot substitutions and promotions in these lines all operate exactly as in iambic pentameter. Marvell mostly uses the tetrameter as if it were a condensed pentameter, exploiting the same kinds of rhythmic adaptability. The shorter line can help bring out witty details like the play on "manacled": the word comes from the Latin for "hand" because that's where manacles are usually fastened; here the soul complains that *having* hands is a burdensome restraint. Similarly "fettered" comes from a root meaning "foot" – though here the etymology is more distant, so that "fettered ... / In feet" feels like a pun.

Some of Marvell's lines (such as the last one) use the four stresses that anchor the four feet to emphasize symmetry and balance in a way that might be less clear in pentameter lines. Other poets take even more advantage of the stable, four-square nature of the line to shape a whole poem's structure. A striking example is Yeats's "An Irish Airman Foresees His Death," which you can easily find online. Almost from the beginning the doomed pilot is posing oppositions:

<pre>
x   / | x (/) |x   / | x   /
I know that I shall meet my fate
  /   x | x / | x   / | x /
Somewhere among the clouds above;
  /   x | x / | x / |x   /
Those that I fight I do not hate,
  /   x | x   / | x / | x   /
Those that I guard I do not love ...
</pre>

(He is flying for Great Britain at a time (1918) when Ireland is about to go to war with Britain for its own independence.) In most of the poem, *pairs* of lines present opposed terms. At the end of the poem (lines 13–16) the "on the one hand, on the other hand" gesture becomes explicit:

<pre>
x / | x   / | /   / | x   /
I balanced all, brought all to mind,
  x / | x / | /   / | x   /
The years to come seemed waste of breath,
x   / | x   / | x   / | x /
A waste of breath the years behind
x   /| x   x   / / | /   /
In balance with this life, this death.
</pre>

In a wonderful twist, Yeats moves the paired lines up into the *middle* of this last four-line group. (Elsewhere the pairs usually divide the four into halves.) This leaves his emphatic final line to summarize the whole poem's stance of fascination with oncoming death.

The Kinesthetics of Poems

When this book or literary criticism in general talks about "balance," "movement," and so on, you should feel welcome to think in terms of bodily motion. In fact, otherwise such talk is empty abstraction. Poems appeal not only to your senses of sight and sound, but also to your *kinesthetic* sense, the one that tells you whether you're standing on one foot or not. Reading poems is unlike reading newspapers partly because the poem wants to be *felt* as dance, as movement through space organized in some interesting way. The French poet Paul Valéry said that "Poetry is to prose as dancing is to walking": a more exciting way to cross a room.

The elegy for his wife, "The Exequy," written by Henry King (1592–1669) around 1624, opens with lines that measure actualities against possibilities:

<pre>
x / | x   / |x x /   /
Accept, thou shrine of my dead saint,
x   / | x / |x   / | x   /
Instead of dirges this complaint;
  x x   /   / | x / | x /
And for sweet flowers to crown thy hearse,
  x / |x   / | x /|x   /
Receive a strew of weeping verse
  x   x   /   / | x   / | x   /
From thy grieved friend, whom thou might'st see
  /   / |x (/)|x / | x   /
Quite melted into tears for thee.
</pre>

The second line announces the poem's theme: before he can resignedly commit her to God's hands ("dirge" comes from a Latin verb meaning "direct" or "lead") King has grieving to do, and the poem's 120 lines will work through the welter of his feelings. In the third line "for" means "instead of," so this line and the following one balance the sweetness of funeral flowers with the stubborn "weeping" of this verse. (If this unusually strong use of the preposition "for" makes you want to stress it, go ahead. The choice of double iamb versus iamb and spondee won't alter anything else in the line's foot structure.) The word "strew," especially as a verb, is often connected with flowers, which emphasizes the balance of the substitution.

The fifth and sixth lines connect himself and his dead wife in a complicated mutual pose: he imagines how she *might* see him if she were here, as he weeps because she is not. The "thou" who sees is also the object ("thee") of the grief. Throughout this opening passage the balance enacted within lines and pairs of lines is reinforced on a smaller scale by the doubled stresses of spondees, some standing alone and some within double iambs. Late in the poem King includes this couplet:

<pre>
 x / | x / | x x /   /
But hark! My pulse like a soft drum
 /   x|x   / | /   x |x /
Beats my approach, tells thee I come;
</pre>

Here the abstract sense of balance is overcome by direct sound painting. We're certainly meant to hear the "soft drum."

The iambic tetrameter runs like a thread throughout English poetic history, never disappearing even in ages when the pentameter dominates most strongly. At the end of the nineteenth century, A. E. Housman (1859–1936) favored the same meter as Marvell and King two centuries before, as in his famous elegy "To an Athlete Dying Young."

<pre>
 x / | x / | x   / | x   /
The time you won your town the race
 x / | x (/) | x / | x   /
We chaired you through the market-place;
 / |x   / | /   /|x   /
Man and boy stood cheering by,
 x / | x / | x   / | x /
And home we brought you shoulder-high.
</pre>

<pre>
 x / | x   / | / / | x /
To-day, the road all runners come,
 /| x / | x / | x /
Shoulder-high we bring you home,
 x / | x (/)| x   / | x   /
And set you at your threshold down,
 / | x (/)|x / |x /
Townsman of a stiller town.
</pre>

These are the first two of seven stanzas. Housman uses headless lines frequently (here the third, sixth, and eighth). Otherwise his lines include somewhat fewer substitutions than Marvell's. These differences reflect the difference in tone between Housman's brave requiem and Marvell's exuberant dialogue.

In his three-part elegy "In Memory of W. B. Yeats," W. H. Auden (1907–1973) begins with rather florid **free verse** ("The peasant river was untempted by the fashionable quays"), moves through tighter but still orotund hexameters ("Now Ireland has her madness and her weather still"), and settles at last on a special meter that can be seen as a version of the iambic tetrameter. Though Auden is writing well into the twentieth century, here he makes the four-foot line sound more primitive than Marvell's or Housman's, as if the lines were chiseled into stone:

> / | x / |x / | x /
> Earth, receive an honoured guest;
> / |x / | x / |x /
> William Yeats is laid to rest:
> / | x / | x / | x /
> Let the Irish vessel lie
> / | x (/) | x / |x(/)
> Emptied of its poetry.

The forceful opening with its very well marked stresses helps set up the sorrowful falling-away of the fourth line, whose two promoted stresses make the line sound as if it were reduced to just two beats. (Auden's choice of meter is also part of his tribute: the final poem in Yeats's final book, "Under Ben Bulben," makes use of the same hard, epitaphic measure.) In this stanza the headless tetrameters which Housman occasionally intersperses have come to dominate the verse. Headless lines are more common in tetrameter than in pentameter, but this case is extreme. The effect is one of strength combined with emotional restraint.

You might notice that the lines as scanned are perfectly symmetrical. Logically we could call them either headless iambic tetrameters or "tailless" (**catalectic** is the technical term) trochaic tetrameters:

> / x| / x | / x | /
> Earth, receive an honoured guest;

This ambiguity occurs whenever the tetrameter is used consistently with neither an opening nor a trailing slack syllable. There is some debate among critics about how such lines should be classified. Perhaps it doesn't matter much – not in the way that *hearing* how these lines proceed matters – but the question may be an entry point for deeper matters. In Chapter 6 we'll examine some other approaches to meter that treat lines like these as crucial evidence.

Here's the first half of an older example, an elegy by William Browne (1590–1645), "On the Countess Dowager of Pembroke," which along with "Under Ben Bulben" probably served Auden as a model:

```
  /  x  /    x  / x  /
Underneath this sable hearse
  /  x / x  x /  /
Lies the subject of all verse:
  /  x  / x  /  x    / x
Sidney's sister, Pembroke's mother;
  /  x   (/) x  /  x / x
Death, ere thou hast slain another,
  /  x  /  x  /  x  /
Fair, and learn'd, and good as she,
  /  x  / x / x  /
Time shall throw a dart at thee.
```

Here I have omitted foot divisions so as to acknowledge the ambiguity of the meter. In the third line the consistent use and placement of two-syllable words might suggest a trochaic scansion. (Notice that this argument would shift the boundary we've been maintaining between meter and rhythm. Word boundaries have an effect on rhythm, but we have not treated them as part of meter.) The second line with its final double iamb would be difficult to scan any way but iambically. We'll return to this puzzle of categorization when we examine trochaic meters.

It happens that four of these five examples show the tetrameter at work in poems of mourning. There's certainly no necessary connection: many well-known elegies are in iambic pentameter and tetrameters are often used for chatty or comic verse. But one thing the tetrameter lends itself to, especially when it's slowed down and agitated by spondees, promotions, and varying pauses, and particularly when lines paired by rhyme can intensify balanced and conflicting thoughts and feelings, is stately and reserved meditation in circumstances of grieving.

Other Feet as the Basis of Meter

Meters can be divided into **falling** and **rising**: the stress either initiates the metrical unit or anchors its end. Meters are also usually classified as **triple** or **duple** depending on whether the number of syllables in the basic unit is three or two (so that stresses are separated by either two slacks or one). Logically there are four possibilities, each a meter built on one of the feet we have already seen:

	RISING	FALLING
DUPLE	iamb (x /)	trochee (/ x)
TRIPLE	anapest (x x /)	dactyl (/ x x)

The iambic pentameter and tetrameter are rising duple meters. The fact that iambic lines can contain trochees and anapests as substitutions doesn't change the basic, normative movement of the meter. In English duple meters are more often used than triple meters, and rising meters are far more common than falling ones. Trochaics, which we'll look at briefly a little later, are quite uncommon, and dactylic meters are scarce as hens' teeth. This is worth noting because the Greek and Latin poems that have been so influential in English poetry, especially epics like the *Iliad* and the *Aeneid*, are in dactylic meters. In his North American epic *Evangeline*, Henry Wadsworth Longfellow (1807–1882) tries to capitalize on this historical connection:

> / x x | / x x | / x   x | / x x | /   x   x | /   x
> This is the forest primeval. The murmuring pines and the hemlocks,
> /   x   x | /   x   x | / x | /   x x | / x x | / x
> Bearded with moss, and in garments green, indistinct in the twilight,
> /   x | / x   x | /   x | / x | / x   x| / x
> Stand like Druids of eld, with voices sad and prophetic,
> /   x | / x | /   x | /   x | / x   x | / x
> Stand like harpers hoar, with beards that rest on their bosoms.

After he establishes his unusual dactylic hexameter very clearly in the first line, Longfellow can afford to begin interspersing more variations, specifically the shortening of the dactyl to a trochee. The dactyl can't be lengthened, and reversing it (to an iamb or anapest) would destroy the meter. Whether its weight could be increased (like the shift from iamb to spondee) by making one of the slacks a stress is an interesting question — but examples are tellingly hard to find.

Anapestics

A more significant minority of English poems are in anapestic meters. This is especially true of light and comic verse, and those modes of poetry are perennially popular. As we'll see, though, anapestics can be used for serious purposes as well.

From the poet's point of view, both the strength and the risks of anapestics lie in the extreme *catchiness* of a regular triple rhythm. The usual rhythms of English speech, at least when we're speaking vigorously or listening very closely, put one or two unstressed syllables between stresses on average.

Stress-Timing and Syllable-Timing

English is a **stress-timed language**. This means that as we speak we tend to keep the stressed syllables coming at roughly equal intervals of time no matter how many unstressed syllables intervene. Obviously this is only a tendency. If we say, "Why don't you go down to the corner and pick up a cooked chicken," we don't hesitate before "chicken" long enough to equal the interval with the one set up by "*Why* don't you go *down* to the …"

The tendency is strong enough, though, to be one of the clues our brains use as we decode the speech we hear. By contrast, in a **syllable-timed language** like French the stresses come at irregular intervals while the syllables move at a quick, steady pace. These are obstacles that English speakers listening to French or French speakers listening to English have to overcome. Understanding speech is an amazingly difficult feat – decades of research have not yet made computers humanly good at it – and unconsciously we use countless tricks and hints to do it. Since poets, even though working in print, are more interested than journalists or writers of legal briefs in reproducing our sense of language as *spoken*, they use (consciously or unconsciously) an array of techniques corresponding to these habits that we rely on as speakers and hearers.

Principles like these presumably underlie the dominance of iambic meters in English verse. In our speech, stresses tend to alternate with slacks and the intervals of time between stresses tend toward being equal. Iambic meter is a close fit to this pattern.

Iambics (and trochaics) compress these speech rhythms, making the poems that use them feel more weighty than speech, more intense and incisive. Continuous anapestics, on the other hand, expand the speech rhythms and make us more aware of the regular recurrence of the stresses. A little more than in iambic meter, the stresses take on the character of a *beat*, a "meter" in the musical sense of that word. As a result the lines can seem typically light or quick or, at an extreme, unstoppable. Robert Browning isn't the only poet to have associated the movement of anapests with that of horses, as in his anapestic tetrameter poem "How They Brought the Good News from Ghent to Aix":

```
x  /  | x x  / |x  x  /|x  x  /
I sprang to the stirrup, and Joris, and he;
x /| x    /    /| x   x  /| x  /  /
I galloped, Dirck galloped, we galloped all three;
 /    / |  / x   /  | x x / | /   x  /
"Good speed!" cried the watch, as the gate-bolts undrew;
 /   /| x   x   /| x x  /|x  x     /
"Speed!" echoed the wall to us galloping through;
 x /  |  /  x  /| x   x   / | /  x  /
Behind shut the postern, the lights sank to rest,
 x  / |x  x  /|  x  x   / | x x  /
And into the midnight we galloped abreast.
```

(In a moment we'll look at details of the substitutions used here.) This kind of relentless motion can be exhilarating, but it can also seem crude, and it can wear us out. The pitfall that regular anapestics have to avoid is blithe shallowness. They are "rhythmic," but too obviously so for many contexts. If the poet wants to use an anapestic meter for serious, delicate, or meditative tones, then substitutions become even more important than they are in iambics. In iambic pentameter strict regularity can at its best lend a kind of stateliness to the verse. In anapestics it can be the kiss of swift death. Substituted feet add rich resilience to iambics, and the same is more urgently true of anapestics.

The substitutions used in anapestic meters, however, differ from the standard variations in iambics. Let's go back to some categories we examined in Chapter 1. Abstractly, we can think of all foot substitutions as ways for the poet to do one (or more) of four things to the foot:

- stretch it
- trim it
- load it
- reverse it.

In iambics, stretching produces the anapest, trimming produces the "defective foot" or bare stress, loading produces the spondee, and reversing produces the trochee. Reversing the stress and slack across the boundary between two feet generates the double iamb or rising ionic.

In anapestic meters the same four actions produce a different range of possibilities. Stretching the anapest can mean adding an extra metrical slack syllable to the end. (Technically this produces the third **paeon**, xx/x.) Just as in iambic verse, this happens at the ends of lines, where it's often part of a rhyme pattern. The reason it doesn't happen elsewhere in the line is the same as the reason why the other possible stretching action – adding an extra slack before the stress (producing a fourth paeon, xxx/) – won't work. In either case, three unstressed syllables would intervene between stresses, and the verse would become too loose to feel rhythmically controlled. We would lose our sense of a meter at work. To put it another way, hearing such a long row of slack syllables we'd feel a strong urge to promote one to stress; but that would produce another foot, breaking the basic constant of line length.

Trimming, on the other hand, is far more common in anapestics than in iambics, whether at the beginnings of lines or even in the middle. Of the six lines by Browning quoted earlier four begin with an iamb, which in this context counts as a trimmed version of the anapest. The frequency of iambic substitutions in anapestic lines is probably a gesture toward the average of one or two slacks between stresses in speech. When anapests are used as substitutions in iambic pentameter a comparable compromise with speech occurs, but the effect is the opposite: anapests loosen the iambic line but iambs tighten the anapestic line. In anapestic meters, even doubly trimming the anapest to a single bare stress is not unheard of at the beginnings of lines.

The most interesting variations come from loading the anapest. There are two candidates: the bacchius (x//) and the cretic (/x/, also called **amphimacer**). Browning's second line uses the bacchius twice and his third and fifth lines contain two cretics each. Technically it's possible to "double-load" the anapest and make a **molossus** (///), though one of the three always seems to fade away from stress. (The previous foot will have ended with yet another stress. It's difficult to compose a sequence of four equal stresses: "…on a bet. Hey! Wait! Where are you going?") These "loading" substitutions, the cretic and the bacchius, slow the line down and complicate it even more subtly than the spondee does in iambics. This feeling of rhythmic complexity is due to the same principle that makes the fourth possible alteration, reversing the anapest to a dactyl (/xx), more or less impossible: the need to preserve the "beat" so characteristic of anapestics even while taming it. To stay rhythmically oriented, the reader needs to know when to expect the main stress of the foot; this is the other side of the "stress-timing" coin. As accustomed readers we come to know the variations of iambic pentameter so thoroughly that the poet can hardly throw us, but anapestics – when not galloping regularly along – require more care on both our parts. A dactyl substituted for an anapest would put the beat too early for a reader to be prepared to hear it and would also create a bewildering run of four slack syllables, one of which the reader would try to promote to stress. The bacchius and the cretic, on the other hand, make the game interesting while keeping it fair. The final stress is where we expect it; the earlier stress is a bonus, an unexpected emphasis. Especially by using these two substitutions the poet can keep the reader just slightly off balance and therefore intrigued. The reader slows down to pay attention yet continues to feel the forward momentum of the anapestic norm.

It's also possible to combine loading with trimming by using the spondee, though it can be tricky to keep the meter clear. Browning uses spondaic substitution at the beginnings of his third and fourth lines; the beginning of a line is the most common, least disruptive place for it.

As an example of how much more delicate the movement of anapestic verse can be in a different context, here is "Ah! Sun-flower" (1794) by William Blake (1757–1827):

```
 /   /  | /  x   / | x x  /
Ah, Sun-flower! weary of time,
   x   / | x   x   / | x   x   /
Who countest the steps of the Sun,
 /  x  / | x   x    /  | /  x    /
Seeking after that sweet golden clime
   x   x  /  | x x   /  | x  x  /
Where the traveller's journey is done:
```

```
x   x   /  | /   x / | x   x/
```
Where the youth pined away with desire,
```
x    x   / | / x   / |x x   /
```
And the pale Virgin shrouded in snow
```
x / | x   x   / | x  x /
```
Arise from their graves and aspire
```
x   x   / | / x  / |x  x  /
```
Where my Sun-flower wishes to go.

If we leave aside initial iambs, which create hardly any disturbance in our hearing of the meter, three of these lines are regular anapestic trimeters. They occupy strategic positions in the poem. The second line clearly establishes the meter after an opening line that – if only because of our default assumption of iambics – may have left us in doubt. The fourth line rounds out its stanza, resolving and anchoring it. The seventh line does the same for its stanza but ingeniously just *before* the end, so that the last line can repeat the celebratory emphasis on the Sun-flower.

This poem probably doesn't use the bacchius (x//), though a bacchius does come in if we stress the demonstrative pronoun "that" in the third line. Cretics (/x/) occur six times, and they come in pairs. Each time Blake mentions the "Sun-flower," framing the poem at its beginning and end, the second stress in the compound word is the first syllable of a cretic:

```
/  | / x   /
```
… Sun-flower …

Two more cretics combine to make the third line the most labored in the poem, mirroring the image of arduous quest that the line presents. Finally, at the beginning of the second stanza the identical placement of cretics in the middles of lines 5 and 6 underscores the parallel between the "youth" and the "Virgin." At the same time, Blake lays his syntax across the same array of feet at different angles: "pined away" (it's a participial adjective meaning "affected by pining away" rather than a past-tense verb) matches "shrouded," but the second participle is delayed by the adjective "pale" and the two-syllable noun "Virgin"; to compensate Blake shortens the final prepositional phrase from "with desire" to "in snow." This subtle shift keeps the parallelism from feeling rigid:

```
x   x   /  |  /   x  /  | x   x /
```
Where the youth <u>pined away</u> with desire,
```
x    x  /  | / x   / | x x   /
```
And the pale Virgin <u>shrouded</u> in snow

Only fifteen out of twenty-four feet in this anapestic trimeter poem are anapests, though all but three feet are three syllables long. The two-syllable feet, a spondee and two iambs, all occur at the beginnings of lines. All but one of the poem's lines have a regular anapest at the end. These characteristics are typical of anapestic poems and reflect the needs that anapestic verse must satisfy to keep the meter clear but also supple.

The nineteenth century saw a heyday for anapestics. Here are some examples you can find online or in many anthologies. Percy Shelley's "The Cloud" (1820), over eighty lines of anapestic tetrameter and trimeter (with some dimeters), displays the full catalogue of substitutions, especially spondees. In "Annabel Lee" (1849), Edgar Allen Poe exploits the anapestic beat for an hypnotic effect by combining the tetrameters and trimeters with pervasive repetition of words. In Algernon Charles Swinburne's "Before the Beginning of Years" (from *Atlanta in Calydon*, 1865) the form has become more mechanical, as if from anxiety that we might not recognize it, perhaps a sign that the meter was losing ground among poets and readers. By the early twentieth century anapestics had been relegated almost entirely to comic or ironic use, as in Hardy's "The Ruined Maid."

We have already noticed the ballad form, which we'll examine in more detail in Chapter 3. Though most ballads are not anapestic, many are; anapestics and ballads converge in their strong associations with traditional popular genres of song.

Two more nineteenth-century examples, both of them deft and various in their handling of substitutions, show the range of tone that poets could discover within anapestic imitations of the ballad. Lewis Carroll (1832–1898) brought the faux ballad to one kind of comic perfection in *The Hunting of the Snark* (1876). Here is Fit the Seventh, the shortest of the poem's eight parts, called "The Banker's Tale":

```
x   /  | x  x   /  | x  x   / | x x   /
```
They sought it with thimbles, they sought it with care;
```
x  x  /  | x  x   /  | x   /
```
They pursued it with forks and hope;
```
x    / | x   x  / | x  x / | x   /
```
They threatened its life with a railway-share;

```
    x    /   |  x   x    /   |  x    /
```
They charmed it with smiles and soap.


```
  x     x    /  |x  x   /   |   x   x    / |x   /   /
```
And the Banker, inspired with a courage so new
```
  x   x    /  |x  x   /  |x    x   /
```
It was matter for general remark,
```
    /        / |  x x   /   |   x    x   /  |  x   x    /
```
Rushed madly ahead and was lost to their view
```
  x   x   /   |  x   x   / |x   x      /
```
In his zeal to discover the Snark.


```
    x     /  |  x   x    / |x    x      /  |  x   x     /
```
But while he was seeking with thimbles and care,
```
  x   /  |x   /        /  |  x   /       /
```
A Bandersnatch swiftly drew nigh
```
    x    /   |  x    x   /  |  x   x     /   |  x    x  /
```
And grabbed at the Banker, who shrieked in despair,
```
    x   x    /  |x   x    / |x   x   /
```
For he knew it was useless to fly.


```
  x  /  |  x    /      /  |   x    x  /  |x   x    /
```
He offered large discount – he offered a cheque
```
      /      x  /  |x    x   / |x      /        /
```
(Drawn "to bearer") for seven-pounds-ten:
```
    x   x    /   |  x   /       /  |x   x   / |x    x   /
```
But the Bandersnatch merely extended its neck
```
  x       /    |   x    x   /  |x  x    /
```
And grabbed at the Banker again.


```
    x  /   |   /  x    /   |    x      x     /  |x  x      /
```
Without rest or pause – while those frumious jaws
```
    x    /|x   x    /  |  x    x  /
```
Went savagely snapping around –
```
    x     /   |   x    x   /   |   x  x    /  |  x      x     /
```
He skipped and he hopped, and he floundered and flopped,
```
    x   /  |x    x   / |  x    x      /
```
Till fainting he fell on the ground.
```
```

```
      x   /  |x     /     /  |x  x  /  |x  x  /
```
The Bandersnatch fled as the others appeared
```
       /  /  |  x    x  /  |  /    x   /
```
Led on by that fear-stricken yell:
```
   x     x   /  |  x  x  /  |  x x  /  |x  x  /
```
And the Bellman remarked "It is just as I feared!"
```
   x    /  |x   x    /  |  x    x   /
```
And solemnly tolled on his bell.

```
   x    x    /  |  x   x  /  |  x    x   /|  x   x   /
```
He was black in the face, and they scarcely could trace
```
   x    /    /  |x    x    /  |  x  x    /
```
The least likeness to what he had been:
```
    x   x   /  |  x  x  /  |  x  x   /|  x    /       /
```
While so great was his fright that his waistcoat turned white –
```
   x   /  |  x  x  /  |  x  x  /
```
A wonderful thing to be seen!

```
    x  x    /  |x   x  /  |  x    x      /|  x    x   /
```
To the horror of all who were present that day,
```
   x  x   /  |x   /    /  |x  x       /
```
He uprose in full evening dress,
```
   x     x     /  |  x     x  /  |x  x  /  |x     x   /
```
And with senseless grimaces endeavoured to say
```
    x     x   /       |   x   x   /  |x  x   /
```
What his tongue could no longer express.

```
    /      x  /  |x  x    /  |  /   x   /  |    x     x     /
```
Down he sank in a chair – ran his hands through his hair –
```
   x      /  |x   x   /  |  x x  /
```
And chanted in mimsiest tones
```
      /     x    /|  x x /|x x    /   |    x x  /  x x
```
Words whose utter inanity proved his insanity,
```
     x   x  /  |x   x    /  |x  x  /
```
While he rattled a couple of bones.

```
      /    x     /  |  x x  /   |  x x   /  |x   x   /
```
"Leave him here to his fate – it is getting so late!"
```
    x    /|   x   x       /  |x  x   /
```
The Bellman exclaimed in a fright.
```
```

```
    x  x     /  |  /  x   / |/ x  /  |x  x /
```
"We have lost half the day. Any further delay,
```
    x      x /  |    /   x  / |x  /    /
```
And we sha'n't catch a Snark before night!"

(The meter tells us that "gri*mac*es" was a common pronunciation in Carroll's time.) Though he uses metrical substitutions to keep the lines lively and expressive, in this mock-heroic mode Carroll is happy to rollick most of the time: "He skipped and he hopped, and he floundered and flopped." Yet dramatically ponderous lines like "Led on by that fear-stricken yell" (an anapest flanked by a spondee and a cretic) and "A Bandersnatch swiftly drew nigh" (which uses the bacchius twice) remind us that the mockery would have no point if we didn't also hear the gothic-heroic tone that shows through in these heavier lines. Echoing within this double space of tone, Carroll's anapestics are funny but never fatuous.

In contrast to Carroll's comedy, a poem by Emily Brontë (1818–1848) demonstrates the surprising darkness that a triple meter is capable of. "M.A. Written on the Dungeon Wall – N.C." was composed in 1845:

```
  x  /  | x  x  /  |x   /  |x  / x
```
I know that tonight, the wind is sighing,
```
   x  /  | / x    /   |/ x  / |x  x    /
```
The soft August wind, over forest and moor
```
   x   / |xx   /  |   /    /  |x   / x
```
While I in a grave-like chill am lying
```
   x   x  /  |   /    /  | x x   /  | x    /
```
On the damp black flags of my dungeon-floor –

```
  x   /  |  x  x   / | x   /  | x   / x
```
I know that the Harvest Moon is shining;
```
   x   / |x  x   /  | x   /  | x  /
```
She neither will wax nor wane for me,
```
   x x / | x   / |x   x   /  | x / x
```
Yet I weary, weary, with vain repining,
```
    /   /  | x  x  /  |x    /    /  | x  /
```
One gleam of her heaven-bright face to see!

```
   x   x  /  |x   /  |  x  x  / |x   x   / x
```
For this constant darkness is wasting the gladness

73

/　/　| x　　x　/　| x　x　/　| x　/
Fast wasting the gladness of life away;
x　/　| x　/　　/　　| x /　| x　/　x
It gathers up thoughts akin to madness
　x　/　| x　　x　　/　| x　　/　| x　/
That never would cloud the world of day

x　/　| x　x　/　　| x /　| x　/　x
I chide with my soul – I bid it cherish
　x　/| x　　x　/　| x　　x /| x　/
The feelings it lived on when I was free,
　x　　/　| x　x　　/ | x　　/　/| x　x /　x
But, shrinking it murmurs, 'Let Memory perish
x　/　| x　x　　/　| x　　x /| x　/
Forget for thy Friends have forgotten thee!'

x /　| x　/　　/　| x　　　/　| x　　/　x
Alas, I did think that they were weeping
/　　/　| x /　/　|　x (/)　| x　/
Such tears as I weep – it is not so!
　x　　/　| x　/　　/　| x　/　| x　/　x
Their careless young eyes are closed in sleeping;
　x　　/　| x　x　/ | x　　x　/　|　x　/
Their brows are unshadowed, undimmed by woe –

　x　　x /| x　x　/　| x　/| x　/　x
Might I go to their beds, I'd rouse that slumber,
x　/　| x　x　/ | x　x /　| x　/
My spirit should startle their rest, and tell
x　/　| / x　/| x　/　| x x　/　x
How hour after hour, I wakefully number
/　　/| x　x　/　| x x　/　| x /
Deep buried from light in my lonely cell!

　x /　| x　/　/　| x　　/| x　/　x
Yet let them dream on, though dreary dreaming
　x　　/ |　x /| x　x /| x　/
Would haunt my pillow if *they* were here
x /| x　/　/　| x /| x x　/　x
And *I* were laid warmly under the gleaming

```
x   x   /  | x x  /  | x   x  /  | x    /
```
Of that guardian moon and her comrade star –

```
/ |x   x / | x  /  |  /    /  x
```
Better that I my own fate mourning
```
 x    /  | x /  | x  x   / | x   /
```
Should pine alone in the prison-gloom
```
 x   /| x  /  | x x  /  | x   /   x
```
Than waken free on the summer morning
```
x   /  | x   x  / | x   x / | x    /
```
And feel they were suffering this awful doom

It's not just a question of subject matter or of words like "darkness." Brontë signals the seriousness of her mode by reining in the meter with a firm hand. She uses a high proportion of two-syllable substitutions, iambs and spondees. Lines like "That never would cloud the world of day" or the difficult "Such tears as I weep – it is not so!" would hardly stand out in an iambic tetrameter poem. The second one, especially, would be a heavy line in any context. She also uses the whole range of standard substitutions both to signal the shifts in the speaker's tone between complaint and wistfulness and to foreground the scene-painting of lines like "The soft August wind, over forest and moor," with its expansive pair of cretics.

In all the meters we've examined so far, the line can end with one or even two unstressed syllables that don't count metrically. (Often these line endings participate in some pattern of rhyme.) In anapestic meters, this can produce some odd-looking combinations, such as this from Brontë:

```
/ |x   x / | x /  |  /    /  x
```
Better that I my own fate mourning

or this from Carroll:

```
/    x   /| x x /|x x   /  | x  x / x  x
```
Words whose utter inanity proved his insanity,

We don't try to incorporate these extra slacks into the lines' meter as parts of feet. Though we could label the end of Brontë's line as a palimbacchius (//x), even the

75

Greeks never gave a name to Carroll's last "foot": xx/xx. We're better off simply recognizing how the odd sequence comes about: the anapest can be replaced by a spondee (as in Brontë's line) and either one or two slack syllables can be added to the end of a line (in Carroll's, two).

Substitution is so pervasive in anapestic poems that it's worth asking how we recognize them. Despite the neat chart presented earlier, some poems mix anapests and iambs – triple and duple rising meters – in nearly equal numbers. These poems present a challenge to classification. From one perspective, because the iambic regime is so dominant within our experience and habits of hearing, these poems are merely iambic verse with excessive anapestic substitutions. From another point of view, the hard-to-bridle insistence of the anapestic beat gives it a perceptual edge, so that if all of a poem's lines contain at least one trisyllabic foot and the lines are short, we readily hear it as anapestic. No poem is ever simply "in" a meter. Meter is something that happens between a poem and its reader (as well as between the poem and its writer). Recognizing the meter of a poem is an experience of synchronizing with the poem so that we and it click into place at once. Here is a short lyric by John Dryden (1631–1700) from the end of *The Secular Masque*:

```
 /    /  |x x  /  |    x     /
All, all, of a piece throughout:
   x   / |  x  x  / |x   /
Thy chase had a beast in view;
    x   / |   /     /  | x  x  /
Thy wars brought nothing about;
   x / |x   x   / |x    /
Thy lovers were all untrue.
   x   /  | x  /   /| x  /
'Tis well an old age is out,
   x   /  |x x / |x  /
And time to begin a new.
```

Heard within an anapestic framework, this passage, one of the last that Dryden wrote, is very satisfying. If we tried to read the lines as basically iambic they would feel metrically unstable. The bacchius in line 5 would be bizarre in iambic verse but feels natural in anapestics.

Trochaics

Though trochees are used all the time as substitutes for iambs, as a basis for meter the trochee is unusual in English. This is interesting because a large majority of two-syllable English words (including people's names) follow the trochee's /x stress pattern. Apparently poets have generally found it more useful to keep the falling rhythms of words syncopated or counterpointed against the rising rhythms that underlie English meters. It's also true that while trochaic disyllables are very common in English, stressed mono-syllables preceded by an unstressed particle are even more so: "the chair," "in time," and so on.

Longfellow, whose *Evangeline* demonstrated dactylic hexameter for us, also gave us *Hiawatha* as one of the best-known examples of trochaic tetrameter:

>   /   x | / x | /   x | / x
> Down the rivers, o'er the prairies,
>   /   x | /   x | (/) x | /   x
> Came the warriors of the nations,
>   /   x | / x | /   x | /   x
> Came the Delawares and Mohawks,
>   /   x | /   x | (/) x | /   x
> Came the Choctaws and Camanches,
>   /   x | /   x | (/) x | /   x
> Came the Shoshonies and Blackfeet,
>   /   x | /   x | (/) x | / x
> Came the Pawnees and Omahas ...

In order to keep the meter clear to our ears, which aren't used to hearing it, Longfellow avoids metrical substitution. Though dactyls and spondees are possible in trochaic meters, even a single iamb – even at the beginning of a line, usually a forgiving place – would throw the whole thing into disarray. (In contrast, a trochaic opening in an iambic line is almost normal.) We can be sure, for example, that Longfellow heard the last word of this passage, the name of the Native American tribe, not as we pronounce the name of the city that took its name from the tribe ("Omaha"), but as "*Oma*has." He's willing to promote a stress on "and" (as he does also two lines earlier), but he can't use the dactyl that would be required if "Omahas" were stressed on its first syllable. In fact trochaic verse generally can make only limited use of the foot substitutions that are a major expressive resource of the familiar iambic and anapestic meters. The success of iambics breeds success. We easily hear them even where some other kind of meter is possible, and trochaic and dactylic regimes have to keep up strong defenses against the iambic.

Trochaics occur most frequently as short songs. If they are set to music (either at the time when they're written or later) the musical rhythms can help underline the trochaic rhythm. The witches' song from Shakespeare's *Macbeth* is a clear example:

/ x | / x | / x | / x
Double, double toil and trouble;
/ | / x | / x | / x
Fire burn, and caldron bubble.

The witches' song (and their speech as well) stands against the iambic norm created by the pentameters in which most of the play's characters speak. This heightens our sense of them as uncanny visitors from a different world.

Here is a lighter lyric that seems clearly trochaic. It's by Sir John Suckling (1609–1642), a Cavalier poet and dramatist (and the inventor of the game of cribbage). The repeated lines and phrases underscore the poem's association with songs, where we're more used to such repetitions than in printed poems:

/ x | / x | / / | / x
Why so pale and wan, fond lover?
/ x | / x | /
Prithee, why so pale? –
/ x | / x | / x | / x
Will, when looking well can't move her,
/ x | / x | /
Looking ill prevail?
/ x | / x | /
Prithee, why so pale?

/ x | / x | / / | / x
Why so dull and mute, young sinner?

```
 /  x  |  /  x  |  /
```
Prithee, why so mute? –
```
  /   x   |  /  x  |  /  x  |  /   x
```
Will, when speaking well can't win her,
```
 / x  | /   x  |  /
```
Saying nothing do't?
```
 /  x  |  /   x  | /
```
Prithee, why so mute?


```
  /    /  |  x  /  |  x  /  |  x   /
```
Quit, quit, for shame! this will not move,
```
  x  /  |  x  /   x
```
This cannot take her –
```
 / x |x  /  |  x  /  | x   /
```
If of herself she will not love,
```
 /  x  |  x   /    x
```
Nothing can make her:
```
 x   / |x  /   x
```
The Devil take her!

For two stanzas Suckling maintains the trochaic movement even though many
lines end with a stress. Omitting the final slack in trochaics is as common as
omitting the opening one in anapestics. But if you try to scan the last stanza's
first line as trochaic tetrameter, you run into trouble from which only an anoma-
lous palimbacchius can rescue you:

```
  /   /  x |  /    x  |  /  x |  /   (??)
```
Quit, quit, for shame! this will not move

The ease of scanning these lines as iambic is telling:

```
  /   /  |x  /   |  x  /  |x   /
```
Quit, quit, for shame! this will not move

It's better to acknowledge the shift to a new meter, even though such shifts are
unusual. In Blake's "The Tyger," too, though it's easy to hear the beginning as
trochaic because all the lines start with stresses –

/ x | / x | / x | /
Tyger, tyger, burning bright
(/) x |/ x | (/) x| /
In the forests of the night

– by the time we reach the last line the iamb has again reasserted itself:

x / | x   / | x / | /   /
Did he who made the lamb make thee?

As with the ambiguous meter we saw earlier in Auden and Browne –

/ x/ x/ x/

– these odd cases point toward alternative ways to understand meter which we'll look at briefly in Chapter 6.

Trochaic meter, then, is inherently somewhat unstable. Longfellow maintains it throughout his book-length epic by means of rigid regularity. As suggested before, reasons for the difficulty of trochaic verse may be its too-neat correspondence to the rhythms of innumerable two-syllable words and its exclusion of common stress patterns ("the chair") at the beginnings of lines. A broader reason, though, is the hearing expectations of countless readers in favor of rising meters and especially iambic meters. A few critics have gone so far as to declare that *all* English meters are iambic. If we adopt Charles Darwin's distinction between "lumpers" and "splitters" (Darwin was referring to scientists who tended to see very few or very many species within a continuum of individuals) these critics are on the lumping side. They have a point: whatever poets try to do, ultimately the question is what readers can be made to hear and get used to.

The *Meter in English* Debate

Readers interested in how and to what extent scholars find consensus on questions of this kind might turn to *Meter in English* (Arkansas, 1997), a collection of essays edited by David Baker, in which over a dozen scholars of prosody all address a list of ten questions. The essays outline some of the range of modern opinion.

But it seems unnecessary to abandon all classification. Some species of verse are written and recognized frequently enough to stand apart from the dominant iambic reign, and dragging them all into iambic scansions falsifies the way they sound to us. The job of readers is to hear the life of individual poems, and the job of careful readers is to understand their rhythmic workings. If categories like trochaic meter can help us do that they're worth keeping in mind, even if we ultimately reject the categorization in a particular case. Whether we classify Auden's "Earth, receive an honored guest; / William Yeats is laid to rest" as iambic or trochaic, what's more important is to hear the terseness of his line and its effect on the funeral tone of the poem. But noticing the ambiguity, which depends on contradictory classifications, can help focus our awareness.

Similar cases arise in the rare poems that use longer trochaic lines. The most famous is Edgar Allen Poe's "The Raven" (1845), which is usually scanned as trochaic **octameter**. Emphasizing how the long line staples together two tetrameters, Poe frequently rhymes the first half of a line with the second:

```
  /   x| /  x|  /   x   |  /  x |  /  x| /  x   |   /   x  |  /  x
Once upon a midnight dreary, while I pondered weak and weary
 / x |   / x x |   /    x|   / x x | / x  |(/) x | / x  |  /
Over many a quaint and curious volume of forgotten lore,
   /   x | /  x|   /  x | /  x  |  /  x |(/)  x  | ˙ /  x | / x
While I nodded, nearly napping, suddenly there came a tapping
 / x  |  / x  |   / x |/  x   |  /  x |(/)x  |  /    x | /
As of someone gently rapping, rapping at my chamber door.
```

These lines call our attention to two technical points about the scansion of trochaic meter. First, the logical place for promoted stresses is the beginning of the foot, not its end. Second, the triple-meter substitution for the trochee isn't the anapest but its reverse, the dactyl, as in the second and fourth feet of the second line.

Tennyson's "Locksley Hall" (1842) is also presumably in trochaic octameter, though all the lines reenact a familiar ambiguity by both starting and ending with stresses. Unlike Poe, Tennyson deliberately shifts the division of the line into variously syncopated parts and also adjusts the placement of promoted stresses. One pair of lines from early in the poem (about 200 lines altogether) shows some of his means of variation:

/ x x | /   x | / x | / x | /   x | (/) x| /   x | /
Many a night from yonder ivied casement, ere I went to rest,
(/) x | / x | /   x |/ x| / x | /   x|(/) x | /
Did I look on great Orion sloping slowly to the West.

The balance tips toward calling this trochaic for several reasons. The simplest is that iambic lines without the initial slack (headless lines) are rarer than trochaic ones that drop the final slack.

Accentual Meter

The meters we've explored so far are all **accentual-syllabic**: they organize a line by counting and patterning both the stresses and the syllables (though we've also seen how the metrical context modifies those dictionary properties of the words). It's because these meters are founded on two separate elements – the number of syllables and the number and position of stresses – that it's convenient to analyze them in terms of feet, defined as certain combinations of the two elements. More important, because there are two kinds of rules at work each of them can be more relaxed than if the whole meter depended on one alone. Because the stresses are approximately fixed in position, the number of unstressed syllables can vary around them. Because the syllable counts are roughly constant, the stresses can vary within them. As we've seen, all this variation happens within limits, but it's central to the rhythmic expressiveness that the meter encourages.

English verse didn't begin with accentual-syllabic meters. Instead our earliest poems were written in lines measured only by the number of stresses or (equivalently) accents without any counting of unstressed syllables. This **accentual meter** was typically used in lines of four stresses, though the half-line of two stresses was an important unit which could sometimes stand alone. We know these poems only from old manuscripts in which line breaks weren't indicated, but the accentual meter tends to be very clear to the ear and it hasn't been very difficult for scholars to locate line ends for modern printing.

These poems were written in an early form of our language called Old English or Anglo-Saxon, which English readers must learn almost as if it were a foreign language. Anglo-Saxon is even more easily identified than modern English as belonging to the family of languages called Germanic or Teutonic. Stress is extremely prominent in all these languages, which makes accentual meter seem like a natural fit. Then as now, a large majority of two- and three-syllable words are stressed on the first syllable. This encourages a kind of reversal of what we normally think of as rhyme: certain words are linked not by their ending sounds but by the sounds they begin with (or rather the sound that begins the *stressed* syllable). This sound patterning is called **alliteration**: "park" and "peaceful" alliterate, and we say that "appear" alliterates with both since it's the stressed syllable that counts. Every consonant alliterates with itself ("clout" and "accord") and all vowels alliterate with each other, so there's alliteration between "earth-ling" and "applesauce." Roughly speaking, the Anglo-Saxon metrical line was two half-lines of two stresses each in which the third stress alliterates with either or both of the first two. Here's a brief example:

/　　　　/　　　　　/　　　　/
Ærest min hlaford gewat,　heonan of leodum
First my lord went away from his people
/　　　　/　　　/　　　/
ofer yþa gelac;　hæfde ic uhtceare
over the wild waves; I felt dawn-care
/　　　/　　　　/　　　/
hwær min leodfruma　londes wære.
where my lord in the lands might be.

This is from a poem called "The Wife's Lament." We don't know whether it was written by a woman or not. Virtually all Anglo-Saxon poetry is by now entirely anonymous.

A different example, however, may be easier for us to hear. William Langland (c.1325–c.1390) wrote his great allegorical narrative poem *Piers Plowman* between 1360 and 1387. This is just when Geoffrey Chaucer (1343–1400) was writing *The Canterbury Tales*, whose popularity helped established iambic pentameter as the dominant English meter. Langland instead maintains the old accentual, alliterative meter. Chaucer represents the beginning of the metrical world we still inhabit, Langland one that was coming to an end, and this is a major reason why people remember Chaucer better than Langland. But reading *Piers Plowman* suggests that if the following centuries had taken a different turn they would have produced a differently lovely body of poetry. Here are Langland's opening lines with an interlinear translation of his Middle English, though we don't need one to the same degree as with Anglo-Saxon:

> In a somer sesun, whon softe was the sonne,
> *In a summer season, when soft was the sun,*
> I schop me into a shroud, as I a scheep were;
> *I put on a cloak, as if I were a shepherd;*
> In habite as an hermite unholy of werkes
> *In a habit like a hermit's unholy in works*
> Wente I wyde in this world wondres to here;
> *I went wide in this world, wonders to hear;*
> Bote in a Mayes morwnynge on Malverne hulles
> *But on a May morning in the Malvern hills*
> Me bifel a ferly, of fairie, me-thoughte.
> *A marvel befell me, of enchantment, methought.*
> I was wery, forwandred, and wente me to reste
> *I was weary, wandering-worn, and went to rest*
> Undur a brod banke bi a bourne side;
> *Under a broad bank by a brook's side;*
> And as I lay and leonede and lokede on the watres,
> *And as I lay a leaned over and looked in the waters,*
> I slumbrede in a slepynge, hit swyed so murie.
> *I fell into sleep, since it sounded so merry.*

It's still not hard for us to follow both the paired accents in each half-line and the alliteration that links them.

The Anglo-Saxon meter is still easier to hear in a modern imitation by Richard Wilbur (1921-) called "Junk" (1961). These are the first of its thirty lines (or sixty half-lines):

> An axe angles
>   from my neighbor's ashcan;
> It is hell's handiwork,
>   the wood not hickory,
> The flow of the grain
>   not faithfully followed.
> The shivered shaft
>   rises from a shellheap

> Of plastic playthings,
>
>   paper plates,
>
> And the sheer shards
>
>   of shattered tumblers
>
> That were not annealed
>
>   for the time needful. ...

As the story of Langland shows, with the exception of a tour de force like Wilbur's or unusually scrupulous translations of Anglo-Saxon poems, the full metrical system including alliteration disappeared from use at more or less the same time that English was transforming itself from Old to Middle and Modern English under the influence of French and other Romance languages. Contact with the poetry of those languages strongly affected the meters that poets used in English, introducing a syllabic component. Yet the accentual roots of English poetry have never entirely disappeared. We hear them persisting in folk poetry like Mother Goose rhymes:

>   /   /
> Leg over leg,
>   /   /
> As the dog went to Dover;
>   /   /
> When he came to a stile,
>   /   /
> Jump, he went over.

These lines are clearly irregular from an accentual-syllabic point of view. At the same time they're clearly regular in having two strong stresses. That's enough to carry us past minor worries about whether "went" in the fourth line is stressed or not. In the third line, "when" might worry us a little more if we let iambic habit try to promote a stress because of the unstressed syllable on one side of it and the silence of the line's start on the other. But the context isn't accentual-syllabic, so promotion doesn't happen.

Once we're alerted to the possibility of accentual meter we can hear it in an experimental poem by Samuel Taylor Coleridge called "Christabel," which opens this way:

>   /   /   /   /
> 'Tis the middle of night by the castle clock,

>   /   /   /   /
> And the owls have awaken'd the crowing cock;
>   /   /
> Tu – whit! – – Tu--whoo!
>   /   /   /   /
> And hark, again! the crowing cock,
>   /   /
> How drowsily it crew.

Tellingly, Coleridge felt that he had to put readers on the right track: in his Preface he says that the meter "is not, properly speaking, irregular, though it may seem so from its being founded on a new principle: namely, that of counting in each line the accents, not the syllables." As we've seen, the principle was not new but very old, although Coleridge was probably the first to revive it in over 300 years. Readers occasionally stumble over Coleridge's third and fifth lines, but we can recognize them as half-lines like those in Anglo-Saxon verse.

Yet if Coleridge hadn't called attention to the "new principle" of his poem's meter, we might just as easily have heard it as anapestic tetrameter with a moderate amount of iambic trimming. This is the problem with accentual meters in a modern English context. We're so used to accentual-syllabic meters, and iambic and even anapestic meters are so flexible, that it's difficult for accentual lines to maintain their separate identity. It can be done: the stresses have to be unusually clear, their number must be exactly constant because the single-element foundation of the meter doesn't permit flexibility, and the numbers of unstressed syllables have to vary at least as widely as in accentual-syllabic lines. Here's an invented example:

>   /   / /
> Dark as the night falls
>   /   /   /
> the winter falls darker
>   / / /
> still: yields stars
>   /   /   /
> innumerable, fierce and clear …

Conversely, it's also true that the accentual pulse is so deep-rooted in the sound of the stress-timed English language that we may hear some kind of underlying more-or-less regularity even in verse that isn't metrical at all. But when the critic Helen Gardner tried to argue that T. S. Eliot (1888–1965) wrote the long poem *Four Quartets* not in free verse but in variations on the four-beat accentual line, though she made an intriguing point about the lines' *rhythmic* character she couldn't convincingly prove her case with regard to *meter*.

Accidental Species

Bird-watchers have a category, "accidental species," for individuals that show up in a territory where they aren't usually sighted. They may have been blown off course during migration or be escaped pets or be pioneers shifting their breeding or feeding range in advance of other members of the species. We could adopt this term for some kinds of meter used at least occasionally in poetry in English that are *not* based either on the accentual-syllabic foot or on the native accentual foundation.

These poems are still metrical, not the nonmetrical or "free" verse which we'll examine in Chapter 4. The question is tricky, though, because from inside the perspective of any one kind of metrical system (such as iambics or accentual-syllabic meters generally) a poem that doesn't follow the rules of that system looks "free" even if in fact it rigorously adheres to some other metrical system.

> ### Meter as Numerical Prosody
>
> What *is* a meter on this abstract level? At least informally, we can define a meter as a system of rhythmic control – a **prosody** – that depends on some kind of *numerical* rule.

So poems in English whose meter stands outside the accentual-syllabic norm have a sort of public-relations problem: to hear them as metrical the reader has to recognize the alien system, which requires being aware that it exists. Suppose a poet were to arrange for every third character in each line to be a vowel:

> The scent of dinner lingers in her mind

This might or might not be a useful discipline for the poet, but it hardly works to control any rhythm we're likely to hear. It's a numerical rule, but it wouldn't operate as a meter for us as readers unless the poet somehow advertised the system. (Notice that this example makes the recognition problem even worse because the line is *also* an iambic pentameter.) It's a premise of this book that some awareness of a poem's metrical underpinning enriches and expands our understanding of the poem – if only because we can, if we like, share the poet's concentration on how the system is working itself out. A truly secret meter would abandon this resource of engagement.

In practice, therefore, only a small number of metrical systems have established themselves as even occasional rivals to the accentual-syllabic system. The useful ones have been imported into English from other languages, particularly the languages that for historical reasons most closely adjoin the territory of English: French on the one hand, which gives us **syllabics**, and Classical Greek and Latin on the other, which offer a range of forms that were originally composed in **quantitative** meters. The prominence of these sources of importation is what gets these meters over the "public relations" threshold, though it may not be enough to naturalize the meter in its new residence.

Syllabics

French is a syllable-timed language, as discussed earlier in this chapter. It's reasonable that French meters are based on a strict count of these regularly recurring units of the language. As iambic pentameter is the classic line in English, in French poetry the classic line is the Alexandrine, a line of twelve syllables with a caesura after the sixth. The English pentameter is a little heedless of syllable counts – it can have anywhere from nine to twelve or thirteen – and conversely, in the French Alexandrine stress (which is light in French words anyway) is merely a secondary aspect of the meter. Sometimes English iambic hexameters are called Alexandrines, but this is not quite accurate: the basis of metrical perception is different. Like accentual meter, **syllabic** meters depend on a single element. Therefore they tolerate variation less resiliently than accentual-syllabic meters. It doesn't make sense to analyze them in terms of feet.

Particularly in the twentieth century and after, poets have experimented with syllabic verse in English. The difficulty of writing well in these meters is *avoiding* the normal and expected iambic movement – a problem the French poet doesn't have. By the same token, though, when handled attentively the syllabic line can be richly expressive in its unpredictable rhythms.

In the first section of *My Sad Captains* (1961), by Thom Gunn (1929–2004), as in Gunn's previous two books, the poems are all iambic, mostly pentameters. In the second section the poems are in syllabics. Except for two that are in lines of eight syllables, they're all composed of either seven- or nine-syllable lines. When poets set out to write in a syllabic meter they often choose an odd number for the line length because lines with an even number of syllables more easily slide into iambic rhythms and the poet working in syllabics wants to forestall those rhythms. Here is Gunn's poem in seven-syllable lines called "Considering the Snail":

> The snail pushes through a green
> night, for the grass is heavy
> with water and meets over
> the bright path he makes, where rain
> has darkened the earth's dark. He
> moves in a wood of desire,
>
> pale antlers barely stirring
> as he hunts. I cannot tell
> what power is at work, drenched there ["power" as 1 syllable]
> with purpose, knowing nothing.
> What is a snail's fury? All
> I think is that if later
>
> I parted the blades above
> the tunnel and saw the thin
> trail of broken white across
> litter, I would never have
> imagined the slow passion
> to that deliberate progress. ["deliberate" as 3 syllables]

It would be inappropriate to *scan* this poem as if it were accentual-syllabic, because scansion as we have defined it diagrams the relation between the poem's speech rhythms and the double-element accentual-syllabic meter. Numbering the syllables would be fitting but mostly redundant. Of course we can still mark stresses. (If necessary we could mark slack syllables too. What we can't do is insert foot-boundaries.) The number of stresses in this poem's lines varies from about two –

/   /

litter, I would never have

– to about four:

/   /   /   /

the bright path he makes, where rain

This range of stress counts would be possible in an iambic trimeter or tetrameter poem (where promotions would fill out the metrical quota), but here the unusual freedom with which the poet shifts his stresses around is foregrounded. Even more clearly, we can hear that lines like "has darkened the earth's dark. He" completely defeat iambic expectations:

x / x   x /   / x

has darkened the earth's dark. He

In the line "with water and meets over," our hearing is drawn to the chime between "water" and "over," and away from questions about whether "over" receives any stress at all. Lines like "imagined the slow passion" are organized for us by the play of vowels, not by some conceivable scansion:

x /| x   x /   / x   (??)

imagined the slow passion

As English readers we can hardly *hear* syllabic meter as a meter. Our ears are tuned to stresses. In another sense, therefore, syllabic meters free the poet, and us as readers, to hear a wider range of the rhythms that English speech makes potentially available to poetry than we might in a meter founded directly on stress – though those rhythms will inevitably organize themselves around stress, an unavoidable fact of English. It's worth noticing that the three lines last quoted (lines 3, 5, and 17 of the eighteen-line poem) all have the same basic stress rhythm: x/xx//x. Would an accentual-syllabic context invite us so warmly to notice this pattern linking the beginning and end of the poem? By avoiding any regular recurrence of stresses, the poet puts us in a state of continuous low-level suspense. In that condition we tend to pay close rhythmic attention, and that's the resource the poet in syllabics takes advantage of.

Another master of syllabic poetry, Marianne Moore (1887–1972), takes a radically different approach from Thom Gunn. Here is her poem "To a Steam Roller":

> The illustration
> is nothing to you without the application.
> You lack half wit. You crush all the particles down
> into close conformity, and then walk back and forth on them.
>
> Sparkling chips of rock
> are crushed down to the level of the parent block.
> Were not "impersonal judgment in aesthetic
> matters, a metaphysical impossibility," you
>
> might fairly achieve
> it. As for butterflies, I can hardly conceive
> of one's attending upon you, but to question
> the congruence of the complement is vain, if it exists.

With its irregular rhythms and drastically varying line lengths, this certainly doesn't look or sound like a metrical poem. Even a syllabic meter seems impossible at first since the lines don't have a set number of syllables. The lengths of lines in the first stanza – five, twelve, twelve, and fifteen syllables – seem completely arbitrary. Yet the rhyming of the first two hints that the lines aren't formed by random cuts in a continuous stream of prose. Moreover, the next stanza and the next exactly duplicate those syllable counts in their corresponding lines. Moore's method is a **stanzaic-syllabic** meter because the numerical rule can be formulated only on the level of the whole stanza, not the line – unlike every other meter we've explored in this chapter.

91

As in Gunn's poem, however, Moore's holding strictly to a syllabic pattern seems to liberate other rhythmic resources. Between corresponding lines of equal length there is hardly any resemblance in rhythm. Here are the first lines of each of the stanzas, which Moore's method invites us to isolate and compare:

<pre>
      x / x   / x
The illustration
  ...
      / x   / x   /
Sparkling chips of rock
  ...
      x   / x x   /
might fairly achieve
</pre>

Her method, operating on the scale of the whole stanza, invites us to pluck matching lines out of the poem and compare the different materials framed by the same syllable-count window. The fourth line of each stanza, for example, is devoted to the usual task of completing the business of that stanza. At the same time, though, it belongs to a more abstract community – defined only over the scope of the whole poem – of lines that share the same elaborately extended fifteen-syllable length. Especially in Moore's longer poems, this produces an odd kind of dual reading: we're aware of each line both as participating in a local continuity of sense and image and also as corresponding with other lines distributed throughout the poem. It's like being aware of historical parallels to events in our own time.

Again, these kinds of reading happen in our eyes and minds, not in our ears. As the basis for a meter syllable counts are – for English readers – more abstract than accentual-syllabic or accentual ones. Yet, paradoxically, the more or less silent net of syllabic meter can be used to capture a wide range of English rhythms and make them even more audible.

Classical Imitations

Imitations of French meters are mostly confined to the past century or so – if we leave aside the fact that very early on, the example of French and Italian helped Chaucer and others replace the old accentual meter with an accentual-syllabic system. In contrast, until perhaps the past century Greek and Latin poetry have been enormously prestigious and influential throughout English literary history. One sign of this prominence is that so much of our metrical terminology, such as the names of the feet, is Greek in origin. Another result is that poets from Thomas Campion (1567–1620) to Robert Bridges (1844–1930) have worked to adopt Classical meters into English verse.

The problem is that the languages are different. In English, as we saw in Chapter 1, stress is a distinctive feature – it distinguishes the noun and verb uses of "rebel" for example – but the *length* of syllables is not. It's not even easy to say which English syllables are "long" and which are "short," despite the old classroom labels for the long 'a' in "rate" and the short 'a' in "rat" and so on. Your dictionary will tell you which syllable in a word gets stress but it won't tell you the length of the syllables. In Greek and Latin, in contrast, syllable length, usually called **quantity**, could distinguish one word from another. "Liber" with a short 'i' is Latin for "book," but with a long 'i' it means "free." Naturally enough, then, Classical meters are quantitative. Latin also had strong stresses and Greek had accents based on pitch, but the central principle of a Classical Greek or Latin meter is the organization of long syllables (marked with a macron, ‾) and short syllables (marked with a breve, ˘) into feet. The Classical iamb, for instance, is ˘ ‾, which is exactly analogous to – but *only* analogous to – the English x/. On another level, Classical meters also differ from English ones in that they're typically based not on repetition of one kind of foot but on set patterns of combinations of feet.

It's possible, barely, to duplicate the Latin rules for syllabic quantity in English. For example, one standard Classical line is the **hendecasyllabic**. The word is Greek for "eleven syllable," and the line is scanned this way:

$$\begin{matrix} \bar{} & \bar{} & \bar{} & \breve{} & \breve{} & \bar{} & \breve{} & \bar{} & \breve{} & \bar{} & \bar{} \\ \breve{} & \breve{} & & & & & & & & \breve{} & \end{matrix}$$

(Certain positions, here marked with ‾ over ˘, could be filled by either a long or a short syllable.) Tennyson composed a self-referential poem that includes these lines:

> Loōk, Ī cōme tŏ thĕ tēst, ă tīňy pōĕm
> Āll cōmpōsĕd ĭn ă mētrĕ ōf Cătūllŭs,
> Āll ĭn quāntĭtˇy, cārefŭl ōf mˇy mōtiŏn,
> Līke thĕ skātĕr ŏn īce thăt hārdlˇy beārs hĭm …

Let's take a moment (and maybe a deep breath) to see how this works. We count as "long" all syllables with "long" vowels (assuming we're always certain what that means) *or* whose vowel is followed by more than one consonant (even if one of them comes after a space and is in the next word). It looks, then, as though Tennyson has achieved the scansion shown here. The word "come" counts as long either because a final silent 'e' customarily makes the previous vowel "long" ("note" versus "not") or because its final *sound* is the consonant 'm' and the next word begins with another consonant, 't'. It's consonant sounds that count, not spellings, so that if he'd used the word "box," the 'x' (the double consonant 'ks') would make it a long syllable.

If this all seems hopelessly complicated, at least in this case it also turns out to be needlessly so. Notice that Tennyson's lines scan perfectly well in English terms:

/ x |/ x x | / x|/ x | / x
Look, I come to the test, a tiny poem
/ x | / x x| / x | (/) x|/ x
All composed in a metre of Catullus,
/ x | / x x | / x |(/) x| / x
All in quantity, careful of my motion,
/ x| / x x |/ x | / x | / x
Like the skater on ice that hardly bears him …

What does it mean to say that this scans correctly as English? We can replace the longs and shorts of Latin with the stresses and shorts of English in the hendeca-syllabic scheme:

/ / | / x x | / x | / x | / /
x x x

Tennyson's lines still contain the same sequence of feet that defines the hendeca-syllabic meter.

This is less than what Tennyson's imitation of the hendecasyllabic so scrupu-lously accomplishes. But it is by far the most common method of adapting, not just adopting, Classical meters to English: we translate the Latin or Greek scheme into an equivalent pattern of stress-based English feet and fill them with words much as we do in the iambic tetrameter or any other accentual-syllabic meter. Even though reproducing the quantitative scansion is so tortuous a task that repeated efforts over the centuries have left it very rare, stress-based English versions of Classical metrical forms are quite common.

There's a generous catalog of available forms in Greek and Latin poetry, and by looking online or in reference books you can find the formulas for Alacaics, elegiac couplets, and various other patterns that have been used by English poets. We'll return to this topic briefly in the next chapter. For now we'll explore just one more example, the **Sapphic stanza**. It's named for its probable inventor, the early Greek poet Sappho, the most famous and influential woman poet of the Classical world, who was born sometime in the seventh century BCE and died sometime around 570 BCE. Her stanza was also used five centuries later by the Latin poets Catullus (84–54 BCE) and Horace (65–8 BCE). (As English literature has emulated Greek and Latin, Latin literature emulated Greek.) In the nineteenth century Tennyson and Swinburne and others picked up the form from Horace and Catullus and turned it into English. Ezra Pound (1885–1972) did the same early in the twentieth century, and especially in the past several decades many more poets have used it for English poems.

The scheme of the Sapphic, using stress marks rather than quantities, goes more or less like this:

```
/ x / / / x x / x / x
/ x / / / x x / x / x
/ x / / / x x / x / x
      / x x / x
```

The fourth syllable in each of the first three lines and the final syllable in all four lines can be either stressed or unstressed, though for simplicity's sake I haven't marked that choice in this diagram. We could divide this into feet – in the first three lines a trochee, a spondee or trochee, a dactyl, a trochee, and another trochee or spondee – but it may be easier to treat the whole thing simply as an extended template of stresses and syllables. Here are the last two stanzas of "Farewell Performance" by James Merrill (1926–1995). Once more it's an elegy. An imaginary performance of dancers ("they") frames the poet's "farewell" to a friend who shared his delight in dance and the other arts:

```
/    x    /   / /   x   x   /   x   / x
Back they come. How you would have loved it. We in
```

```
  /    x  /  x  /  x x  / x  /     x
turn have risen. Pity and terror done with,
  /   x      /     /  /  x   x  /  x  /  x
programs furled, lips parted, we jostle forward
  /  x  x  /    x
eager to hail them,


   /    x  /  x    /     ·x x  /  x  /  x
more, to join the troupe – will a friend enroll us
  /    x(?)  /      /      /    x  x  /   x   /  x
one fine day? Strange, though. For up close their magic
  /  x  /     /    /  x   x   /   x   /    /
self-destructs. Pale, dripping, with downcast eyes they've
  /   x   x  /   /
seen where it led you.
```

As in Marianne Moore's syllabics, we notice how the corresponding lines play out different movements while following the same pre-established pattern. The short final lines are good examples. They're a kind of signature of the Sapphic stanza. (Sometimes they let us identify a poem in Sapphics by a glance at the page.) Once we get used to the Sapphic pattern we can get pleasure from *hearing* it play out; we needn't just count it, unlike syllabics. On a smaller scale, we can hear how Merrill takes advantage of the places where stress is optional (the fourth and eleventh syllables of the longer lines) and how he uses the defining dactyl in the middle of the line (syllables five to seven) in a different syntactical context each time. Far from rigid, in Merrill's hands this exacting structure seems as pliant as the dancers' bodies. Yet his grace, like theirs, takes hard work.

Why all these English poems cast into forms imported from different languages at 2,000 years' distance? One motive has been Classics Envy and another is the sheer pleasure of technical challenge. But this doesn't entirely answer the larger question of why poets choose particular forms. A form, whether it's a metrical line like the iambic pentameter or a complex stanza-form like the Sapphic, is a kind of *tune*. Most poets work by internally playing that tune over and over and listening for what words might fit it (and fit with each other). You can get some sense of this process by speaking through the Sapphic formula given earlier, using nonsense syllables ("DUM-da-DUM-DUM-DUM-" and so on). You may well find that words begin stringing themselves together that make more sense than "da-DUM." Poets set new words to pre-existing metrical tunes just as comic and topical songwriters often put new words to a familiar melody, and just as the makers of folk ballads and blues recycle tunes from one song to another. The familiarity of the tune helps engage the listener in the words. Also, really good new singable tunes may be harder to compose than new words. Whether we can account for it or not, some tunes are more attractive than others. Similarly, some poets and readers have found particular forms productive and pleasing. The stiff movement of English dactylic hexameters hasn't appealed to many, despite Longfellow. The intricate movement of the Sapphic stanza has suggested words to many poets, and the innumerable variations of the iambic pentameter tune have been generating poems – not just constraining them – for centuries.

3

Beyond the Line

Our first two chapters have concentrated on how metrical lines are constructed and read. All this scrutiny of the line underscores the importance of verse to poetry. Lines are the most fundamental way in which poems (except prose-poems) assemble and manipulate language so as to accomplish their work of meaning. Lines are building blocks, however, not the end of the story. In this chapter we'll look at how poets combine lines into larger patterns of sense and feeling.

The most complicated of these larger patterns is the sentence, and later in this chapter we'll explore the intricate relations between sentences and lines. In a great many poems, however, the more obvious way lines are bound together is in stanzas: groups of lines, most often a constant number of lines (though irregular stanzas are certainly possible). In print stanzas are commonly set off from each other by blank lines.

Stanza: The Name

"Stanza" is Italian for "stopping place" or "room": a stanza is a little room in the palace of a poem (or the shotgun apartment). There are other terms for groups of lines. Sometimes we call them "verses": "How many verses does 'La Marseillaise' have?" But as we saw in Chapter 1 "verse" is also the general term for the form of writing that isn't "prose." Books of the Bible are made up of chapters and "verses," so the word is sometimes used to mean "line." In the courtroom scene in *Alice's*

Verse: An Introduction to Prosody, First Edition. Charles O. Hartman.
© 2015 John Wiley & Sons, Ltd. Published 2015 by John Wiley & Sons, Ltd.

Adventures in Wonderland, when the White Rabbit says that his evidence "isn't a letter, after all: it's a set of verses" we can't be sure whether he's referring to lines or stanzas. And when we're talking about popular songs, "verse" may refer to the part that comes before the "chorus." In contrast to this maze, "stanza" refers unambiguously to a regular grouping of lines.

Another term you may occasionally encounter is "strophe," but this most often refers to particular structures within the choral odes of ancient Greek drama. Just to complete the circle, "strophe" is Greek for "turning" which is also the root meaning of the Latin word from which we get "verse."

A large majority of the stanzas used in metrical poems don't just neutrally group together a set number of lines but link them by means of **rhyme**. We'll begin by looking at what we mean when we say that two lines rhyme.

Rhyme

Rhyme is an intuitively simple concept: two words rhyme when they "sound alike" and two lines rhyme when the last word of one "sounds like" the last word of the other:

/ x | x / | x / | x /
I am His Highness' dog at Kew;
/ / | x / | / / | x /
Pray tell me, sir, whose dog are you?

"On the Collar of a Dog" was written by Alexander Pope in 1738. Kew was one of the King's palaces; the dog is a royal pet. This witty little poem — it's not likely to be dogs who will read the inscription on the collar — is a couplet: a pair of lines (here iambic tetrameters) joined by rhyme. The rhyme is part of what makes the politeness so biting.

When we say that two rhyming words "sound alike" we don't mean completely alike. Otherwise "aisle" and "isle" and "I'll" would rhyme but "style" and "compile" wouldn't. Rather we mean that the last parts of the words sound the same. How much of each word? It's relevant that linguists use the word "rime" to specify just part of a syllable: the vowel and final consonants (if any) as opposed to the "onset," the initial consonant (if any). In the single syllable of "fray" the onset is "fr-" while the rime is "-ay." This fits with our instinct that "fray" can rhyme with "sleigh," since the "rime" parts of both words' final syllables are the same sound, "-ay."

Cases where rhyming words have different numbers of syllables ("fray / away") make us aware of further requirements that words must meet in order for us to hear them as fully rhyming. Why doesn't "thumb" rhyme with "kingdom"? The vowel and consonant at the end of "kingdom" are pretty much the same as those at the end of "thumb."

Rhyme as Sound

Don't be distracted by the silent 'b' in "thumb." "Thumb" rhymes perfectly well not only with "crumb" but also with "drum." Rhyme is a matter of sound. A pair like "through" and "enough" is consigned to the marginal category of *eye-rhyme*: the words *look* as though they should rhyme, but they don't.

What blocks the rhyme is that while "thumb" is a stressed monosyllable, the part of "kingdom" that is our candidate for rhyme is unstressed. The stresses need to match for us to perceive two words as fully rhyming. In fact "kingdom" doesn't rhyme with "random" either. Not only do the stress patterns have to match but the rhyming parts of both words have to be stressed. So "fray" does rhyme with "away" but not (or not fully) with "Monday."

The full definition of rhyme is a little more complicated still, because the rhyme itself can include more than one syllable. As long as the final *stressed* syllables of two words rhyme, more *unstressed* material can follow after. If that following material is identical in the two words the rhyme is sustained. So "random" does rhyme with "tandem": the stressed syllables of the two words end with the same sound ("-and-") and the unstressed syllables that follow are the same (though spelled differently).

Rhyme as Abstract Formula

A linguist would notate the formula for rhyme something like this:

$$\overset{/}{V(C)(V(C))}$$

V stands for vowel and C for consonant and anything in parentheses is optional. This allows for the rhymes "play / stray," "plate / straight," "Plato / potato," and "Platonic / laconic." The formula shown here is simplified: it doesn't distinguish a consonant from a consonant cluster ("egg" vs. "eggs"), and it doesn't allow for rhymes of more than two syllables.

When a rhyme pair includes a final, unstressed syllable it's called a **feminine rhyme**. **Two-syllable rhyme** is a fairly exact synonym. Here's a poem by Oliver Goldsmith (1730–1744), usually referred to by its first line since it has no title, in which the rhymes in lines 1 and 3 in each stanza are feminine:

x   / | x / | x   / | x / x
When lovely woman stoops to folly,
x / | / / | x   / | x /
And finds too late that men betray,
x   / | x / | x /| x / x
What charm can soothe her melancholy,
x / | x   / | x / | x /
What art can wash her guilt away?

x / |x / |x   / | x / x
The only art her guilt to cover,
x / | x   / | x / | x /
To hide her shame from every eye,
x / | x / |x   (/) | x / x
To give repentance to her lover,
x   / | x / | x (/) | x /
And wring his bosom – is to die.

Rhymes can be still longer. Three-syllable rhyme almost always has a comic effect. *Don Juan*, the long poem by Lord Byron (1788–1824), offers many examples, including the famous pair "ladies intellectual" / "hen-pecked you all" and this couplet:

<pre>
    x / | /   / | x   (/)|x   / | x   /   x x
    The wise man's sure when he no more can share it, he
    x   / | x / | /   / | x (/) | x / x x
    Will have a firm Post Obit on posterity.
</pre>

(A "post-obit" is a debt paid after one's death.) Three-syllable rhyme, incidentally, is the only context in which the rules for scanning iambic pentameter that we explored in Chapter 1 must allow for not one but two extra metrical slack syllables at the end of the line.

Two-syllable rhyme accounts for a substantial percentage of English metrical lines with one extra slack at the end, though "feminine lines" can also occur in **blank verse**: unrhymed iambic pentameter. (Don't confuse "blank verse" with the "free verse" we'll examine in Chapter 4.)

Internal Rhyme

In fact rhymes can occur not only at the ends of lines but within lines as well. This is called **internal rhyme**. Yeats uses it for emphasis in his line, "Upon the supreme theme of Art and Song." Sometimes we hear an internal rhyme across two lines. The opening of "The Conversation of Prayer" by Dylan Thomas (1914–1953) is a bravura example: "The conversation of prayers about to be said / By the child going to bed and the man on the stairs ..." where two rhyme pairs cross each other and mimic the exchange the poem is imagining.

All the pairs we have examined so far exemplify **full rhyme**. But when the rules for strict rhyming are loosened the result can still be recognizable as a rhyme. Whether the result feels more casual than full rhyme or more subtle depends on how the poet uses it.

Since rhyme is defined by multiple rules of similarity there are multiple ways it can be relaxed or modified without vanishing entirely. For example, either the vowel or the final consonant in the rhyming syllable can be held steady while the other changes. "Cause" and "loss" can be heard as almost-but-not-quite rhyming. The effect is either delicate or incompetent depending – as usual – on everything else going on in the poem. Because a pattern of repeated vowel sounds is called **assonance**, a pair like "cause" and "loss" is sometimes called an **assonantal rhyme**. On the other hand, "loss" and "mouse" half-rhyme because the final consonant is the same while the vowels differ. Since a pattern of repeated consonant sounds is called **consonance** (not to be confused with "consonants"!) this might be "consonantal rhyme," though no one seems to use that term. One factor that helps determine how clear the rhyme sounds – and, perhaps even conversely, how intentional the departure from full rhyme feels – is whether the elements that vary still feel closely related. "Lease / mouse" is more tenuous as a rhyme than "loss / mouse," because the long 'e' in "lease" is farther from the vowel in "mouse" than is the short 'o' in "loss":

lease – – – – – – mouse

loss – – mouse

These are distances in what we might call phonetic space, which is really the space inside your mouth where you shape these vowels.

There is not much agreement about how to label all the different versions of rhyme that result from various possible alterations. The terms **slant rhyme**, **off rhyme**, **near rhyme**, **half rhyme**, and others are used in various ways, sometimes with an intended technical exactness that gets lost in other contexts. New kinds of off rhyme occasionally get invented. Edmund Blunden (1896–1974) coined the term "pararhyme" for instances in which the vowels in the rhyming syllables differ but the consonants both after *and before* the vowels stay the same: "years / yours," "tigress / progress," "killed / cold." (Blunden's notion of pararhyme didn't insist on the consistency of stress position that rhyme usually demands.) These examples come from the poem "Strange Meeting" by Wilfred Owen (1893–1918; like Blunden he was in World War I, but unlike Blunden, died). An untitled poem by W. H. Auden shows how this apparent loosening of the rules of rhyme can result in a whole new kind of strictness:

```
   /    /  |   x   / | x   /
That night when joy began
 x    / |x  x    /  | x   /
Our narrowest veins to flush,
   x   /  |x  (/)| x    /
We waited for the flash
 x    /  | x    / |x       /
Of morning's levelled gun.
```

```
   x    / | x    / |x   /
But morning let us pass,
   x    / | x   / | x /
And day by day relief
 x     /  |  x   / |x      /
Outgrows his nervous laugh,
   /      / | x (/) |x    /
Grown credulous of peace,
```

```
 x     / | x    / |x   /
As mile by mile is seen
  /   /  |  x (/)  | x    /
No trespasser's reproach,
 x    /   |  /    / | x   /
And love's best glasses reach
  /    /   |   x (/)  | x   /
No fields but are his own.
```

("Glasses" are binoculars or "field-glasses.") In the first stanza "began" forms a pararhyme with "gun" because the same consonants surround different vowels in the rhyming syllables. "Flush" and "flash" do the same. In this sense the first and last lines of the stanza rhyme with each other, as do the second and third lines. At the same time, though, Auden keeps the same *vowel* in the first and third and in the second and fourth lines: "began / flash," "flush / gun." Each end word in the quatrain, therefore, participates in two different, interlocking patterns of rhyme, one a pararhyme and the other an assonantal rhyme. In case we might think this was an accident, Auden does the same thing again in the second stanza, with different sets of consonants and vowels – and then a third time.

Rhymed Stanzas: The Quatrain

It's conventional to notate rhymes by using lower-case letters. Labeling the rhymes isn't worth the trouble in the case of couplets (aa, bb, etc.). But it gives us an easy way to describe the pattern of longer stanzas. To begin with the hardest case, we can say that the poem we just saw by Auden is in quatrains (four-line stanzas) which rhyme as abba with respect to consonants but abab with respect to vowels. This double pattern is extremely rare (maybe unique) and this is as complicated a description of a rhymed form as you could ever need.

Quatrains are the most common stanzas. By far the most frequent pattern is abab. Here is one stanza from Andrew Marvell's "The Definition of Love" (published in 1681 after his death), which uses geometry to describe ill-fated love:

x / |x / |x / | x /

As lines, so loves oblique may well   a

x / | x / | x / |x /

Themselves in every angle greet;   b

x / | x /|x /|x /

But ours, so truly parallel,   a

x /|x / | x / |x /

Though infinite, can never meet.   b

Though Marvell's poem is three stanzas long we don't need to specify that it rhymes abab, cdcd, efef. Just giving the formula for the stanzaic building block, we say that the poem is "in quatrains rhymed abab." In this case the lines are all iambic tetrameters, and this is very common in quatrains, but of course quatrains can be made of pentameters and lines of other lengths.

Here is another quatrain, again in tetrameters, by Alfred, Lord Tennyson, from his long poem "In Memoriam." His rhyme scheme is not abab but abba. (In French this pattern is called *rime embrassée* or "embraced rhyme," and the reason is probably obvious.) Tennyson's poem is so famous for this stanza that the abba iambic tetrameter quatrain is often called "the 'In Memoriam' stanza":

```
x   /  |x    /  | x  /  |x  /
```
I sometimes hold it half a sin   a
```
  x  /  |x   /  | x   /  | x  /
```
To put in words the grief I feel: b
```
  x   /  |  x   /| x  /  |x  /
```
For words, like Nature, half reveal   b
```
  x   /  |x  /  |x  /  | x  /
```
And half conceal the Soul within.   a

(Internal rhyme foregrounds the opposition between "reveal" and "conceal.") The abba pattern, by joining the beginning to the end, emphasizes each stanza's closure. This one starts with a notion of "sin" and is rounded out by "the Soul within." In between is a tightly rhymed couplet ("feel / reveal"). At the same time, the syntax of the sentence is divided sharply after the second line. The rhyming structure is one of enfolding – the outer rhymes embrace the inner ones – while the structure of the sentence makes the last two lines feel like a reversal of the first two. Two different ideas about structure jostle against each other. Poets often use this kind of double patterning – in stanzas as in other aspects of the poem's language – to heighten our sense that the poem is working to organize complex thought and feeling.

Quatrains can even be made from pairs of couplets (aabb). Here is Percy Shelley's poem (1824) called "To – ":

```
    / |x    x   /   / |x  /
```
Music, when soft voices die,
```
   / |x  (/) |x   / | x (/)
```
Vibrates in the memory –
```
   / |  x    x    /  / |x  / x
```
Odours, when sweet violets sicken,
```
   / |  x /  |x  /  |  x   / x
```
Live within the sense they quicken


```
   /  |  /    x  | x  / |x  /
```
Rose leaves, when the rose is dead,
```
   x  /   | x (/) |x / |x  /
```
Are heaped for the beloved's bed;

```
x   /  | x     /      |    x    / | x   /
```
And so thy thoughts, when thou art gone,
```
 /  | x /   | x     /  | x  (/)
```
Love itself shall slumber on.

This is the least usual rhyme scheme for the quatrain. It has the oddly resonant effect of doubling each stage in the development of the rhyming structure. It might seem not to matter whether this poem is printed as quatrains or as couplets, but the four-line stanza contributes to the sense of doubling: the poem is in two parts, each made of halves, each of which is a pair of rhymed lines.

One of the most common quatrain forms, the **ballad stanza**, is originally a song form, and we'll see it again in Chapter 5, Song. As we saw in the previous chapter, in this stanza tetrameter lines alternate with trimeters. The trimeters are always rhymed and the tetrameters are sometimes rhymed. Here are two ballad stanzas (a whole poem) by Emily Dickinson (1830–1886), who strongly favored this stanza and variations on it:

```
x  /  | x / | x  /  |  x    /
```
In lands I never saw – they say
```
x  /  | x   /  |  /    /
```
Immortal Alps look down –
```
  x     / | x    /  |  x   / | x (/)
```
Whose Bonnets touch the firmament –
```
  x   /  | x   /  |  x  /
```
Whose Sandals touch the town –

```
 /  x  |  x  / | x / | x    /
```
Meek at whose everlasting feet
```
x  / | x x  / | x   /
```
A Myriad Daisy play –
```
 /    / | x   /  | x    /  | x  /
```
Which, Sir, are you and which am I
```
x  / | x   /  | x   /
```
Upon an August day?

Dickinson rhymes her second and fourth lines (the trimeters) but not her first and third (the tetrameters). Ballad stanzas are short enough not to require more internal binding than the one pair of rhymes.

The ballad stanza belongs to a small family of quatrain forms sometimes called **common measure**. There are variations in line length and rhyme. The lines can all be lengthened to tetrameters; this is called **long measure**. (In other words, "long measure" is another way of saying "iambic tetrameter quatrain.") Or the opening line can be shortened like the second and fourth, so that the stanza becomes two trimeters, a tetrameter, and another trimeter; this is **short measure**. And while the ballad stanza, as in Dickinson's poem, often rhymes only its second and fourth lines, some uses of common measure, especially for hymns, benefit from the tighter scheme of abab rhyme. Usually this regularization goes along with a tighter iambic meter as well. This **hymnal stanza**, too, can have lines of three or four feet, giving rise to **short hymnal stanza** and **long hymnal stanza**. Hymns were an important influence on Dickinson's poetry, and her lines quoted here are also an example of hymnal stanza. We'll look further into the dynamics of these stanzas in Chapter 5.

Other Stanza Types

The different kinds of metrical lines we explored in the previous chapter, together with various schemes for rhyming and various numbers of lines, combine to make a huge number of possible stanza forms. Over the centuries many of them have been tried in English, often borrowed from other literatures. Some have found widespread use or long-lasting popularity or both. Here we'll examine some of the main ones though by no means all.

An important kind of minimal stanza is the **heroic couplet**: a rhymed pair of iambic pentameters. When many of them are put together into long **verse paragraphs** the heroic couplet is hardly a stanza at all. As the term "paragraph" suggests, this is verse being used for purposes less different from those of prose than the verse of most lyric poems: arguments, epistles, extended narratives, and so on. Especially during the eighteenth century the heroic couplet dominated English poetry. A master of the form was Alexander Pope; earlier we saw his little epigram "On the Collar of a Dog" – uncharacteristically tetrameter, and just a single couplet as opposed to the thousands of lines of his Epistles and Essays, but like them in its sharp wit. (Pope summarizes the sensibility of his time in a heroic couplet: "True wit is Nature to advantage dressed: / What oft was thought, but ne'er so well expressed.")

As one among innumerable possible examples of eighteenth-century verse in heroic couplets – in this case from America just before the Revolution – here is a verse paragraph from "On Imagination" by Phillis Wheatley (1753–1784):

> *Imagination!* who can sing thy force?
> Or who describe the swiftness of thy course?
> Soaring through air to find the bright abode,
> Th' empyreal palace of the thund'ring God,
> We on thy pinions can surpass the wind,
> And leave the rolling universe behind:
> From star to star the mental optics rove,
> Measure the skies, and range the realms above.
> There in one view we grasp the mighty whole,
> Or with new worlds amaze th' unbounded soul.

As is typical of the style, Wheatley's couplets are syntactically closed and complete, an effect which the rhyme underscores. This is not just language organized into twenty-syllable units but thought itself proceeding by rhymed lines. The remarkable rhetorical ascension of this passage is conducted in stages exactly two lines long – at least until the penultimate line finishes one movement and the final line opens a startling ("new") vista.

Two other specialized couplet forms were developed quite early in English poetry, though neither has been very common since about the sixteenth century. One is called fourteeners because that is the normative number of syllables in each of the rhymed lines; we can also call them iambic heptameter couplets. As we noticed in Chapter 2, this is the meter of George Chapman's translation of Homer's *Iliad*. Published in sections from around 1598, this was the first complete English version of Homer's epic. (Chapman also translated the *Odyssey*, though for that he used heroic couplets.) Here are the opening lines of his *Iliad*'s Book I:

> Achilles' baneful wrath resound, O Goddess, that impos'd
> Infinite sorrow on the Greeks, and many brave souls los'd   [loosed]
> From breasts heroic; sent them far to that invisible cave
> That no light comforts; and their limbs to dogs and vultures gave: ...

You can hear (especially in the first couplet) that the seven-foot line tends to fall apart into a tetrameter and a trimeter – though Chapman (as in the last couplet here) controls the tendency skillfully throughout the poem's thousands of lines. When it does, the effect is of a ballad quatrain printed as just two lines – why not help the reader's eye help the reader's ear by printing it as four lines? – and this may be a reason why fourteeners are not often used these days. Yet A. E. Stallings returns to the form in her recent translation of *The Nature of Things* by the Roman poet Lucretius (*c*.99–*c*.55 BCE):

> Life-stirring Venus, Mother of Aeneas and of Rome,
> Pleasure of men and gods, you make all things beneath the dome
> Of sliding constellations teem, you throng the fruited earth
> And the ship-freighted sea – for every species comes to birth
> Conceived through you, and rises forth and gazes on the light. ...

Besides deploying promoted stresses to keep the measure feeling flexible, Stallings varies the position of her caesurae so as to avoid the ballad-stanza trap. A similar form has the odd name **poulter's measure**, apparently because people who sold poultry would give customers fourteen eggs in a second "dozen": the form alternates hexameter and heptameter lines. Here is the opening of a poem by Queen Elizabeth I (1533–1603):

> The doubt of future foes exiles my present joy,
> And wit me warns to shun such snares as threaten mine annoy;
> For falsehood now doth flow, and subjects' faith doth ebb,
> Which should not be if reason ruled or wisdom weaved the web.

This couplet too fell out of favor. Its sound is intriguing at first, but eventually ungainly and tiring. It can sound like short measure printed in two lines rather than four, since the hexameter tends to break in half and the seven-foot line readily breaks as four feet plus three. But the heptameter can also break as three plus four. In theory, this ambiguity might be handled in such a way as to provide variety in a long poem.

Many other stanzas are not shorter but longer than the primal quatrain. The **rime royal** (or **rhyme royal**) is a stanza of seven iambic pentameter lines rhymed

ababbcc

The name comes from the fact that King James I of Scotland (1394–1437) wrote a poem in this stanza, but it was invented a little earlier by Geoffrey Chaucer. Chaucer used it most notably in his Trojan War epic, *Troilus and Criseyde* (which became one of Shakespeare's main sources for his play *Troilus and Cressida*). Many other poets adopted the stanza in the centuries after Chaucer. Four well-known poems in rhyme royal are "They Flee from Me" by Thomas Wyatt (1503–1542), Shakespeare's "The Rape of Lucrece," the proem of Milton's "On the Morning of Christ's Nativity," and Wordsworth's "Resolution and Independence" – though Milton and Wordsworth extend the stanza's last line to an iambic hexameter. Sir John Davies (1570–1626) used rhyme royal for his wonderful poem called "Orchestra, or a Poem of Dancing." Here is the second rhyme-royal stanza (out of 131), in which he offers an account of Homer's inspiration to write the *Odyssey*. (I have modernized some spellings and glossed a few unfamiliar words in the margin.)

Homer, to whom the Muses did carouse	[drink]
A great deep cup with heavenly nectar filled,	
The greatest, deepest cup in Jove's great house,	[Jupiter, Zeus]
(For Jove himself had so expressly willed)	
He drank of all, ne let one drop be spilled;	[nor]
Since when, his brain that had before been dry,	
Became the wellspring of all Poetry.	

One recurring pleasure of this stanza is the way alternating rhyme gives way to couplets. This progression lends the whole stanza a forward momentum, simultaneously letting each stanza close in a satisfying way and helping a series of them to build a narrative.

Borrowed from Italian (as the language of its name implies), **ottava rima** is (as the name says) a stanza of eight lines, rhymed

ababab c c

In English the lines are usually iambic pentameters. Though only one line longer than rime royal, the ottava rima has quite a different shape: three pairs of lines alternately rhymed, capped by a couplet. This is less the structure of a narrative than of a joke. And indeed, the most famous English poem in this form, Lord Byron's *Don Juan*, is full of jokes:

Brave men were living before Agamemnon [//|x/|xx//|x/x]
 And since, exceeding valorous and sage,

A good deal like him too, though quite the same none;
   But then they shone not on the poet's page,
And so have been forgotten: – I condemn none,
   But can't find any in the present age
Fit for my poem (that is, for my new one);
So, as I said, I'll take my friend Don Juan.

(As you can deduce from the rhyme, Byron pronounced "Juan" as two syllables, not one as in Spanish.) In many two-syllable and even three-syllable rhymes, Byron often drives his stanza to comically desperate ends. The effect is a combination of slapstick with brilliant wit. Yet poets have also found in ottava rima a very different music. W. B. Yeats used the stanza in three of his greatest poems: "Among School Children," "Sailing to Byzantium," and "The Circus Animals' Desertion," the last a meditation on the often elusive sources of his own art. It ends:

Those masterful images because complete
Grew in pure mind, but out of what began?
A mound of refuse or the sweepings of a street,
Old kettles, old bottles, and a broken can,
Old iron, old bones, old rags, that raving slut
Who keeps the till. Now that my ladder's gone,
I must lie down where all the ladders start
In the foul rag and bone shop of the heart.

Here and at the ends of the two other poems listed, Yeats brings the stanza to a high resonance – increased if anything by the shift to off-rhyme in the third pair ("complete / began / street / can / slut / gone") followed by the sharp finality of "start / heart."

Sir Edmund Spenser invented a stanza for his epic *The Faerie Queene* (an extended allegory understood as starring Queen Elizabeth) which we now call Spenserian stanza. It's a long stanza of nine lines which rhymes as tightly as many Italian and French forms (it may be a further development of the ottava rima) but with the striking difference that after eight iambic pentameters it closes with an iambic hexameter:

a b a b b c b c c(6)

Though the stanza always maintains its reference to Spenser, who looms very large in the history of English verse, its imposing size and rigorous rhyme scheme have appealed to many later poets. One example is Percy Shelley's elegy for John Keats, "Adonais" (1821). Shelley may have chosen the form partly in tribute to Keats's own use of it in poems such as "The Eve of St. Agnes." (This may remind us of Auden's use in his elegy for Yeats of a stanza Yeats had notably used. This is a way in which poems and poets sometimes invoke each other even without explicit mention.) Here is perhaps the most famous of the fifty-five stanzas of "Adonais" (ll. 460–468):

> The One remains, the many change and pass;
> Heaven's light forever shines, Earth's shadows fly;
> Life, like a dome of many-coloured glass,
> Stains the white radiance of Eternity,
> Until Death tramples it to fragments. – Die,
> If thou wouldst be with that which thou dost seek!
> Follow where all is fled! – Rome's azure sky,
> Flowers, ruins, statues, music, words are weak
> The glory they transfuse with fitting truth to speak.

Shelley exploits all the grandeur implicit in the form. Other poets besides Keats and Shelley were using the stanza during this period. A little earlier it may have been the influence of the Spenserian stanza (as well as Milton's example) that encouraged Wordsworth, in "Resolution and Independence," to end his rhyme royal stanzas with a hexameter. A little later Tennyson adopted the Spenserian stanza for his poem "The Lotos-Eaters," which recounts a story from Homer's *Odyssey* about the temptations of ennui. This is a kind of cross-pollination or grafting that goes on frequently among poetic forms. It's more useful to think of it this way than as a matter of fashion. Each of the poems listed shows a poet thinking anew through a known form.

Three more forms borrowed from other literary traditions have enough currency in English to be worth mentioning. In all three cases the form resides not entirely in the stanzas themselves but in special relations among stanzas. **Terza rima** is simply **tercets** (three-line stanzas) joined by **chain rhyme**:

a b a   b c b   c d c   d e d …

Its attraction for poets derives partly from its association with Dante Alighieri (1265–1321) – his *Divine Comedy* is in terza rima – and partly from the attractive push-and-pull of the rhymes. (The obvious formal puzzle is how to end the poem. Dante closes each Canto of his poem with an abab quatrain in which the forward-looking rhyme of the second line is capped off by the fourth.) The **pantoum** (or **pantun**), often vaguely thought of as a Malaysian form, became popular in French and then English poetry beginning about 200 years ago. It's in quatrains; the lines may be any length, and they don't usually rhyme; instead the second and fourth lines of each quatrain are repeated exactly as the first and third lines of the next quatrain. There's some similarity to terza rima – they're both chain forms – but the standard way to end a pantoum is to use the poem's first and third lines as the second and fourth of its final quatrain, not capping the form off but making it circular. Good examples accessible online include "Parent's Pantoum" by Carolyn Kizer (1926–) – she ends in a complicated, non-standard way – and "Hotel Lautréamont" by John Ashbery (1927–). Finally the **ghazal** (in English usually pronounced something like "guzzle") is a very old Arabian and Persian form increasingly popular in English poetry in the past fifty or a hundred years. The poem is always in two-line stanzas (generally five to twelve of them) all syntactically separate, every stanza ending with the same word. (The stanzas are often called "couplets," but they don't rhyme with each other.) The stressed syllable before every refrain-word rhymes throughout the poem; the lines all have the same number of syllables; the poem's first line also ends with the refrain-word; and some form of the poet's name is traditionally embedded in the final pair of lines. Some poets ignore some of these rules. Aga Shahid Ali (1949–2001), the American poet born and educated in Kashmir, helped popularize the ghazal in English. His anthology of English examples by well over a hundred poets is called *Ravishing DisUnities* (Wesleyan, 2000) to emphasize that the two-line stanzas in each poem strive to be as centrifugal as possible: as divergent in theme or topic or tone as the poet can manage. Since the poet is also an individual writing at a particular moment, some kind of unity seems bound to assert itself. This simultaneous conflict and resolution, apparent randomness incorporated by or within the moment of writing, has proven attractive to recent poets.

In Chapter 2 we discussed the importation into English poetry of Classical forms, particularly the hendecasyllabic and the Sapphic stanza. Some poets in English have found success with other Latin and Greek forms:

the **choriambic** line: / x / xx / / xx / / xx / x /

the **Alcaic** stanza:　　/ / x / / / xx / x /
　　　　　　　　　　　/ / x / / / xx / x /
　　　　　　　　　　　/ / x / / / x / /
　　　　　　　　　　　/ xx / xx / x / /

the **elegiac couplet**, roughly a hexameter followed by a pentameter.

As noted in Chapter 2, the standard practice is to replace the long and short syllables of Classical languages with the stressed and slack syllables characteristic of English. Sometimes this "translation" becomes complicated. In Latin the first line of the elegiac couplet is a dactylic hexameter in which each of the first four feet is allowed to be either a dactyl or a spondee, the fifth is always a dactyl, and the sixth is (almost) always a spondee. The pentameter second line of the couplet is not like the English iambic pentameter but runs more or less like this:

$$/ xx / xx / \text{''} / xx / xx /$$

(A caesura divides the line into two symmetrical halves. Inserting foot divisions here is merely confusing since each half-line ends with a kind of half-foot.) These rules are convoluted enough so that poets often approximate the elegiac couplet, calling on the tone of the Classical form without worrying excessively about the details. W. H. Auden – we have already seen that Auden could handle any poetic technique he set his mind to – is approximating the elegiac couplet in his poem "In Praise of Limestone." Here are the first ten of its ninety-three lines. (The odd number results, despite the couplets, from his ending the poem with an isolated hexameter.)

> If it form the one landscape that we, the inconstant ones,
> Are consistently homesick for, this is chiefly
> Because it dissolves in water. Mark these rounded slopes
> With their surface fragrance of thyme and, beneath,
> A secret system of caves and conduits; hear the springs
> That spurt out everywhere with a chuckle,
> Each filling a private pool for its fish and carving

> Its own little ravine whose cliffs entertain
> The butterfly and the lizard; examine this region
> Of short distances and definite places: ...

Recognizing the imitation Auden is pursuing helps us to hear his lines as alternating six and five feet – and in turn hearing the feet helps us recognize the elegiac couplet. We might scan the first lines this way:

```
x x  /  |  x  /  | /   x  |  x  / |  x x /  |x   /
If it form the one landscape that we, the inconstant ones,
x    x / |x  x  /  |x   /  |  / |x   /  x
Are consistently homesick for, this is chiefly
x  /  |x  x /  |  x  /|x   /  |x   /  |x   /
Because it dissolves in water. Mark these rounded slopes
x    x / |x   / |x   x   /  | / |  x /
With their surface fragrance of thyme and, beneath,
```

None of the substitutions in this scansion is out of bounds in English iambics, but the frequent anapests, the odd emphasis placed on small words by the interrupted syntax, and the occasional bare stress, together push the iambic meter well into the background in our sense of the lines' conversational movement.

More information about all the forms mentioned here and descriptions and definitions of many others are easy to find. The most authoritative catalog of forms is *The Princeton Encyclopedia of Poetry and Poetics*. The Fourth Edition (2012) weighs in at 1,200 pages (though it has been kept surprisingly inexpensive). Beyond lists of forms this volume contains extended essays on the poetries of many nations and cultures and thorough definitions of literary terms from "accent" to "zeugma." A number of smaller poetry handbooks and lists of examples are available, notably John Hollander's *Rhyme's Reason* – Hollander invents examples of all the forms he lists – and Lewis Turco's *The Book of Forms*. Finally, while online sources are not always reliable they are plentiful and can be useful if you remember to cross-check them.

A Stanza at Work

Ottava rima, the "In Memoriam" stanza, Sapphics, and other named stanza patterns are *received* forms. Some poet invented each one, though in many cases we don't know who or when. Afterwards another poet can choose to fulfill the same stanzaic contract. But in other cases poets make up their own stanza forms for each poem either from pieces of known forms or from scratch. Two poems by George Herbert (1593–1633) will help us explore in more detail how poets make, choose, and use a particular stanza to organize a poem beyond the level of individual lines.

Herbert's were all Christian devotional poems. The collection published right after his death, *The Temple*, had a very wide audience and a number of his poems are still sung as hymns. Most of the poems in *The Temple* have one- or two-word titles that name various theological concepts or rituals. One is called "Matins," the service of morning prayer in the Anglican Church. (Herbert's original title is "Mattens," which was one common spelling at the time. Some of his words are unfamiliar now. I have modernized the spelling and I'll gloss words that may give trouble.) For this poem Herbert created a small but expansive stanza that feels like a morning stretch:

```
        x  / | x  / |  x     /
        I cannot ope mine eyes,              [open my]
    x   / | x  / |x  / |x  /
    But thou art ready there to catch
    x    / |  x   / |  x    /| x(/)
    My morning-soul and sacrifice:           [prayer]
  x   /|  x   /  | x  / | /   / |x  /
  Then we must needs for that day make a match.
```

(The poem will give us four more stanzas.) "Thou" in the second line is God: the poem is Herbert's greeting on this next of the days made by God. His tone is joking: I can't get up so early that you aren't already there, so I guess we're stuck with each other. But "thou art ready" more seriously suggests the poet's loving reliance on God's presence. This is a prayer of thanksgiving (*The Book of Common Prayer* speaks of a "sacrifice of praise and thanksgiving"), not of terror at God's justice or doubts about the poet's own worthiness, though these themes are both explored elsewhere in *The Temple*. Herbert's invented term "morning-soul" proclaims this spirit.

In this first stanza we notice a pattern of line lengths. We expect – if only because we can glance ahead down the page (when there's no commentary to break up the poem!) – that this will be repeated in the poem's four further stanzas: the indentations emphasize the pattern. The stanza begins with an iambic trimeter and then expands through two tetrameters to a pentameter that feels especially final and satisfying.

The Pentameter as Replete

If the iambic pentameter does give a particularly gratifying sense of closure, why? One reason is simply that by Herbert's time it had become so dominant a line in English verse that arriving at it feels like coming home. A second reason, which possibly even underlies the first, is that *five* has a special role within any regime of rhythm based on four, which includes a large proportion of Western musical and poetic rhythmic regimes: four-beat measures in popular songs, quatrains in poems, and so on. When four is the complete set, five is the complete set *capped.* Try saying "*one*, two, three, four, *one*, two, three, four." Then replace the second "*one*" with "*five*" and leave the following "(two, three, four)" silent. You should feel a tiny touch of triumph on "five!" We'll look a little further into these rhythmic phenomena in Chapter 5, Song.

It's also worth observing that the four lines of Herbert's first stanza are divided asymmetrically by the sense and syntax. The colon at the end of the third line marks off the following final line as a complete clause ("Then we must needs for that day make a match"), one that states a logical conclusion to be drawn from the three lines preceding. The stanza is an uneven array of three lines plus one. Those first three are in turn divided, though less sharply, by the comma that separates the short clause of the first line ("I cannot ope mine eyes") from the longer coordinate clause that follows ("But thou art ready there to catch / My morning-soul and sacrifice"). The syntax expands just as the sequence of metrical lines does.

Herbert's second stanza again divides itself unevenly but in the opposite direction:

x / | x / |x   /

My God, what is a heart?

/ x | x / |x   / | x   /

Silver, or gold, or precious stone,

x   / | x   / | x (/) |x /

Or star, or rainbow, or a part

x / | /   / | x / |x (/) | x   /

Of all these things, or all of them in one?

119

I've scanned the first line with a stress on "is" rather than "what." Herbert's question looks at first as though he is asking God (the opening "My God" is an address, not an exclamation) for a definition of "heart." In a way that may be what the whole poem does, but here the question turns out to be a narrower one: What is a heart made of? A stress on "is" shows Herbert saying in effect, I thought I knew about hearts but mine is now in such a state that I'm not sure. Certainly the precious materials he goes on to name are the materials of wonder. Waking into God's day has exalted the poet into awe at his own heart – also made by God, after all.

The reversed asymmetry of this second stanza after the steady rising of the first one makes for a change in mood, though not a downward turn. The poem has shifted playfully toward a tone of scholarly inquiry. The stanza's opening line poses a question to which the next three propose five specific possible answers followed by an indecisive a-little-of-everything (the faltering moment is delicately dramatized by the line break in the middle of the phrase) followed in turn by the most all-inclusive response. If the logical structure is that of a pedantic query-and-answer, the dramatic rhythm turns out to be just as steadily expansive as in the opening stanza, reconfirming the emotional theme announced by the metrical enlargement from three to five feet.

In his third stanza – in the center of the poem – Herbert redivides the four-line stanza more evenly. At first the opening line seems almost identical to that of the previous stanza:

> x   / | x (/)|x /
> My God, what is a heart,
>   x   / | x   (/) |x / | x   /
> That thou shouldst it so eye, and woo   [examine]
> /   x |x / | x / | x /
> Pouring upon it all thy art,
> x / | x   / | x   / | x   / |x /
> As if that thou hadst nothing else to do?

(In the original the first word of the third line is spelled "powring." This adds to the statement of God's generosity a suggestion of the "power" that underlies the gift. "Art" adds yet another aspect to this indirect portrait of God's many attributes.) But here the second line ("That...") introduces a relative clause that extends the syntax of the first line and so alters what looked like a repeated question. Now Herbert marvels not at himself (as made by God) but at God's willingness to focus infinite attention on so finite a bit of creation. Through this shift in syntax the first two lines are bound together and the last two lines balance the others with what is logically a kind of footnote.

Kinesthetics Revisited

Again, words like "balance" and "expansion" should invite you to literal kinesthetic responses. In Herbert's first stanza, his first three lines draw us forward and the fourth makes us pivot. In his second stanza, the opening question catches us up short with a mock catechism and in the next three lines we wander among alternatives. The third stanza invites us to stand with our hands out weighing its two halves. Ezra Pound says not only that "poetry begins to atrophy when it gets too far from music" but also that "music begins to atrophy when it departs too far from dance."

The equal syntactical division of the third stanza is repeated and strengthened in the fourth. This time a colon at the end of the second line marks the balance point even more clearly:

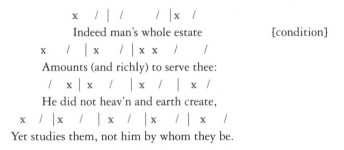

```
      x   / | /     / |x  /
      Indeed man's whole estate              [condition]
   x   /  | x   /  | x x   /     /
      Amounts (and richly) to serve thee:
    /   x | x   /   | x  /   |  x  /
      He did not heav'n and earth create,
   x  / |x  /   | x  /  | x   /  | x    /
   Yet studies them, not him by whom they be.
```

("He" is stressed because it refers to "man" in direct contrast to God.) Thus Herbert has given us two (oppositely) asymmetrical stanzas and then two symmetrical ones. (*What will he do in the fifth and last?* we wonder.) In these third and fourth stanzas the poem's simple alternating rhyme scheme, abab, reinforces the symmetrical division.

This stanza seems to digress somewhat. He no longer focuses on himself or his heart (as a representative of the heart of any of God's creatures) but on "man" in general. The poem turns from celebrating God's munificence to lamenting our human error when we ignore God the Creator in favor of the things created. This was a familiar theological theme in Herbert's time. (The theme was taken up later in the seventeenth century by a growing scientific culture that treated nature as a book worth studying for its own sake as well as for its evidence of God's work.) Here Herbert's lesson seems a little out of place, a pat religious homily intruding on what had been a personal exultation. In that sense the stanza's trim syntactical symmetry may seem thematically even *too* fitting; for a moment it threatens to render the poem static.

Herbert's last stanza counteracts the digression by turning back to his own desire to face God directly. Keeping this focus is not easy (as the poem's middle stanzas show), and he asks for help in resolving the conflict between praising God's work and praising God:

> /   x| x / | x   /
> Teach me thy love to know;
> x   x   /   / | x   / | x   /
> That this new light, which now I see,
> x   / | x   / | x   / | x   /
> May both the work and workman show:
> /   x| x / | x   (/) | x   / | x   /
> Then by a sunbeam will I climb to thee.

You might scan the last line differently, giving to the second half of the compound "sunbeam" the stress it seems to want (the original said "sunne-beam") and removing the promoted stress on "will." If so, this probably means that you are responding, quite appropriately, to the line's joyful play with sound: all the long vowels in "by," "-beam," "I," "climb," "thee." Through this play, as through the sublimely childish image of climbing a sunbeam, Herbert sheds the fourth stanza's theological severity and returns to the simplifying delight of the poem's beginning.

Of course this stanza also answers the formal puzzle Herbert established by dividing his first four stanzas into 3 + 1 lines, then 1 + 3, then twice into 2 + 2. Here at the end he isolates *both* the stanza's first and last lines syntactically. The singular first line that made the first stanza asymmetrical and the singular last line that made the second stanza asymmetrical are here combined to make the whole stanza symmetrical – like the third and fourth but with the difference that the new symmetry contains the asymmetries of the first two stanzas. It isn't difficult to feel that this sequence, which encompasses the whole poem, duplicates the rising or expanding movement that Herbert established in the first place by inventing his trimeter-tetrameters-pentameter stanza. The verb "to amount" was a synonym for "mount" or "rise," so the fourth stanza's phrase "Amounts (and richly)" serves as the poem's motto for itself.

It's especially interesting to watch the same poet bringing the same kind of attention to bear on the choice of a quite different stanza for a different poem. *The Temple*'s second poem with the title "Justice" (it's usually referred to as "Justice (II)") has a more complicated emotional trajectory than "Matins": it begins with an address to "dreadful Justice." The stanza is more complicated as well, as is indicated even in the way the lines are indented. We'll examine some details of Herbert's handling of this stanza after looking at the whole poem, which gives you a chance to think about these questions first without interference. (Again I have modernized the spelling.)

```
  /    / | x   / | x   / | x   /  | x   /   x
  O dreadful Justice, what a fright and terror
                x    / | x   /
                Wast thou of old                          [in the past]
                x    / |  x  / x
                When sin and error
        x   /  | x    /  |  x    /  | x   /
        Did show and shape thy looks to me,
        x    /    |   x    / |  x /| x    /
        And through their glass discolor thee!
  /  x  | x   x    /   / | x    /   | x   /
  He that did but look up, was proud and bold.


  x    / | x (/) | x   / | x       /    | x   /
  The dishes of thy balance seemed to gape,        [scale]
                x     /|  /   /
                Like two great pits;
                x   /  | x    /
                The beam and scape                        [parts of a scale]
```

/ x | /   / | x / | x   /
Did like some tort'ring engine show: [machine; appear]
x / | x / | x / | x   /
Thy hand above did burn and glow,
/ x | x / | x / | x / | x /
Daunting the stoutest hearts, the proudest wits.

x / | x   / | / / | x / | x /
But now that Christ's pure veil presents the sight,
x / | x /
I see no fears;
x / | x /
Thy hand is white,
x / | x   / | x (/) | x /
Thy scales like buckets, which attend
x / | x / | x (/) | x   /
And interchangeably descend,
/ x | x / | x (/) | x   / | x /
Lifting to heaven from this well of tears.

x   / | x / | x / | x   / | x /
For where before thou still didst call on me,   [constantly]
x / | x   /
Now I still touch
x   / | x   /
And harp on thee.   [dwell on]
/   / | x (/) | x   / | x   /
God's promises have made thee mine;
/   x | x / | x / | x /
Why should I justice now decline?
x / | x (/) | x / | x / | x /
Against me there is none, but for me much.

The first stanza recalls the fear of divine retribution that (for Herbert) characterizes the Old Testament idea of justice. Our fear of it so distorted or "discolored" justice (this part is all in past tense) that even to glance up in its direction was audacious. No wonder, says the second stanza, evoking images of Hell with its "pits" and "torturing engine." With the third stanza we turn to the

New Testament dispensation in which mercy supplants justice, or rather makes it attractive rather than terrifying. Here Herbert shifts to present tense. The "veil" refers to Christ's sacrifice which gives us a path to salvation "through the veil, that is to say, his flesh" (Hebrews 10:20).

We're accustomed to the image of Justice as carrying a scale – not the doctor's scale that indicates weight with a simple number but the older kind with two balance pans. (Herbert calls them "dishes" at the beginning of the second stanza. In the third stanza he uses "buckets" as a simile for the same things, here called "scales" – which might be confusing, except that we do refer to the device both as "a scale" and as "a pair of scales.") Indirect or punning reference to the scales runs through the poem's language even when the image isn't immediately present. Words like "descend" and "Lifting" – which hinge across the line break at the end of the third stanza – vividly show us scales not in calm equilibrium but rocking perilously back and forth. In the penultimate line "decline" (to go down, or to turn down) makes the joke a last time and most seriously: to reject justice would be foolish – since Christ has promised that salvation is possible – but also blasphemous: at the gate of the Christian heaven you don't say "No thanks." Divine justice consists of weighing one thing *against* another; you can weigh heavy or weigh light but you can't not weigh. The poem's last line saves the day but remains aware of how precarious the sinful soul's condition is.

If the stanza in "Matins" repeatedly acts out the soul's expansion into the gift-space of God's new day, in this poem about "Justice" the stanza shows a soul chastised and then recovering. In this case Herbert's invented stanza begins with a bold iambic pentameter, then shrinks to two dimeters, works its way up through a pair of tetrameters, and finally climbs back to pentameter. Just as the whole poem begins with the "dread" of Old Testament justice and ends with the New Testament's "promise" of justice transformed by mercy, so the stanza's form dramatizes a repeated rise from abjection to redemption.

The rhymes in the "Justice (II)" stanza underscore the drama sketched by the line lengths: abaccb. The 'c' rhyme joins the two iambic tetrameters into a couplet, a unified last effort on the way back to pentameter. The widely separated 'b' rhymes surprise us by linking that final pentameter back to the first of those terror-shrunken dimeter lines. This relation between the second and sixth lines necessarily changes in later stanzas, but infernal "pits" are the just destiny of "the proudest wits" (stanza 2) and "I see no fears" prepares us for "Lifting to heaven from this well of tears" (stanza 3). Herbert links the sound-similarity of rhyme

125

with a similarity of sense also in the poem's very first rhyme, "terror / error," the only two-syllable rhyme in the poem. It summarizes the dire situation from which the poem works to arise, and the rhyme reminds us that it's our sin ("error") that made us contemplate justice with "terror."

The final pentameters of the four stanzas display a pattern that may not be incidental. The first three of them begin with trochaic substitutions but the last does not. The settled regularity of the poem's final line is another signal that at least for the moment the soul has achieved peace.

"Matins" taught us to notice how Herbert uses syntax to divide the lines of his stanza among clauses. In "Justice," too, the stanzas are not all divided the same way – that would give the stanza a stiffness that might have immobilized the poem. In fact no two are divided the same:

    1st: 2 + 3 + 1
    2nd: 2 + 2 + 2
    3rd: 2 + 4
    4th: 1 + 2 + 1 + 1 + 1

This little chart points to an overall variation in the amount of syntactical fragmentation in the six-line unit. It calls particular attention to the least fragmented, stanza 3, and the most fragmented, stanza 4. These seem to be two different ways in which Herbert heightens feeling in these climactic (Christian, past-tense) stanzas. The long, almost unbroken syntactical run in stanza 3 from "Thy hand is white" all the way through "Lifting to heaven from this well of tears" produces an energetic vitality reminiscent of "Matins," though here the feeling is more fraught. The final stanza's many self-contained lines, on the other hand, including all of the last three, give a sense of solid, hard-won confidence. They are three strokes of a triumphant bell, the last longer and surer than the previous two.

Whole-Poem Forms

Among the forms that poets adopt, many rest on the kinds of stanzaic building blocks we have been examining. A poem in quatrains, for instance, may need twelve or 200 lines to get its work done; the poet repeats the stanza three times or fifty times. In contrast, some other poems complete a single formal pattern without repeated parts, or with a specific mixture of parts of different kinds. We can call these **whole-poem** forms, since we can't be sure about the form until we've read the whole poem.

One very familiar whole-poem form is the **limerick**. It's a very old form, but in the past century or two it has become especially popular for light verse. It's one kind of poetry made up by many people who don't make up other kinds. An apparently anonymous limerick that circulated on the Internet for quite a while, though it's surely much older, jokes about the form's association with bawdy themes:

> A bather whose clothing was strewed
> By breezes that left her quite nude
> Saw a man come along,
> And unless I'm quite wrong,
> You expected this line to be lewd.

The form always rhymes aabba – a pleasingly closed structure. Its first, second, and fifth lines are three beats or feet long and the third and fourth just two, which heightens the punch-line effect of the longer last line. In recent uses the lines are almost always in some form of triple meter – call it anapestic trimeters and dimeters, though the first slack syllable is often dropped and an extra slack often ends lines so that the two-syllable rhymes can add to the comic effect. But the same form long precedes its dirty-joke reputation:

> Hickory, dickory, dock
> The mouse ran up the clock
> The clock struck one
> The mouse ran down
> Hickory, dickory, dock.

Many of the whole-poem forms that have attracted poets writing in English in the past two centuries are originally French or Italian, and are often long and elaborate: for instance, the **ballade**, the **rondeau**, and the **virelai**. (Details and examples of all these forms are easy to find online.) Another of these, the **chant royal**, begins with five eleven-line stanzas all rhymed

a b a b c c d d e d E

– where the capital letter indicates a **refrain** line, a whole line repeated exactly at the end of every stanza. The form ends with a short **envoi**, which means "a sending-forth" (as a diplomatic envoy is sent) and is traditionally the poet's instruction to the poem (rather like a carrier pigeon) to go find the poet's beloved and speak the poet's love. In the chant royal the envoi is rhymed

d d e d E

The heavy burden of rhyming in these Romance-language forms makes them especially challenging in English. The challenge is tamed to some degree by refrain lines. The **triolet**, for example, has a very high proportion of repetition:

A B a A a b A B

Here is one by Thomas Hardy:

> How great my grief, my joys how few,
> Since first it was my fate to know thee!
> – Have the slow years not brought to view
> How great my grief, my joys how few,
> Nor memory shaped old times anew,
> Nor loving-kindness helped to show thee
> How great my grief, my joys how few,
> Since first it was my fate to know thee?

(Though many of these Romance lyric forms are conventionally put into iambic pentameter when they're imported into English, the triolet is usually in tetrameters as Hardy's is.) The challenge of forms with refrain lines – this is more true in poems than in songs, where refrains reinforce the listener's feeling of certainty and orientation – is to make each instance of the refrain act as a rediscovery: something known before but transformed when encountered anew. This keeps the form from feeling mechanical. Hardy makes this happen partly by changing the syntactical function of his repeated clause, "How great my grief, my joys how few," in each of its three occurrences: first as an exclamation, then as the object of the speaker's "view," then as something that nothing has been able to "show thee." Treading the internal round of his feeling, he keeps stumbling upon the same bitterness. This refrain's shift from exclamation to rhetorical questions counters the form's static circling with a kind of progression, though not one that leads out of his self-absorption.

In some modern periods English poets have turned to poetic traditions from other than the Romance languages. In the past century or so Japanese forms have been particularly popular. The **haiku** – at its simplest a single tercet whose lines are five syllables long, seven syllables, and five – may be second in popularity only to the limerick. Similarly, the **tanka** has lines of five, seven, five, seven, and seven syllables. When these forms are brought into English they are usually stripped of the elaborate conventions that surround them in their original cultural context. Traditionally, for instance, haiku always contained a reference to a season of the year, usually a highly stylized reference. Gregory Corso (1930–2001) produced this striking but extremely un-Japanese haiku, section V of his "Mexican Impressions":

> In the Mexican
> zoo they have ordinary
> American cows

Two more Romance-language forms are worth describing because so many poets in English have used them in the past century or so. The **villanelle** is always nineteen lines long, divided into five tercets and a quatrain. It uses just two rhyme sounds, but also has an elaborate pattern of repetition of *two* refrain lines on the first rhyme, labeled A^1 and A^2 in this scheme:

$$A^1 \, b \, A^2 \quad a \, b \, A^1 \quad a \, b \, A^2 \quad a \, b \, A^1 \quad a \, b \, A^2 \quad a \, b \, A^1 \, A^2$$

Poets including Dylan Thomas ("Do Not Go Gentle into That Good Night"), Theodore Roethke ("The Waking"), Elizabeth Bishop (1911–1979) ("One Art"), and recently many others, have been attracted by the form's emphasis on recurrence, which can be adapted to themes of cyclical regularity, meditative absorption, accumulating joy or grief, or time's combination of perpetual return and inexorable forward motion. The villanelle resists narrative, though the poet can take that, too, as a challenge. Somewhat similar effects accompany the **sestina**, a thirty-nine-line form in six stanzas of six lines each with a three-line envoi. In this case rhyme is replaced by repetition: the lines in the six stanzas all end with

129

the same six words, but the order of those words rotates from stanza to stanza in a consistent pattern of permutation. Designating the six end words by numbers, we can graph those six stanzas this way:

```
- - - 1   - - - 6   - - - 3   - - - 5   - - - 4   - - - 2
- - - 2   - - - 1   - - - 6   - - - 3   - - - 5   - - - 4
- - - 3   - - - 5   - - - 4   - - - 2   - - - 1   - - - 6
- - - 4   - - - 2   - - - 1   - - - 6   - - - 3   - - - 5
- - - 5   - - - 4   - - - 2   - - - 1   - - - 6   - - - 3
- - - 6   - - - 3   - - - 5   - - - 4   - - - 2   - - - 1
```

(Notice that a hypothetical seventh stanza would return to the original order.) The three-line envoi conventionally uses all six words, usually in the original order, three at the ends of lines and the other three internal to the lines. Elizabeth Bishop again provides a famous example, called simply "Sestina," which you can easily find online.

Whole-Poem Forms: The Sonnet

One whole-poem form or family of forms, the sonnet, has maintained an uncanny popularity for centuries. It's a poem in fourteen lines of iambic pentameter (though there are exceptions to both basic rules, suggesting that poets know how common and instantly recognizable readers will find this form). People sometimes write whole cycles of sonnets, such as the **crown of sonnets** in which the last line of each becomes the first line of the next. By investigating its use in just two poems we can ask why a poet might choose this form for a wide range of purposes.

We have already seen a sonnet: Wordsworth's "Composed Upon Westminster Bridge," which was the extended example of iambic pentameter at the end of Chapter 1. Wordsworth follows one of the two most common patterns, distinguished primarily by their rhyme schemes: his is an **Italian sonnet**. The form was perfected (though not invented) by Petrarch (1304–1374), and this version is also sometimes called the **Petrarchan sonnet**. Here is the pattern of Wordsworth's rhymes:

abba abba cdcdcd

These rhymes mark the poem as having two main parts: the octave (from the Italian word for "eight," *otto*) and the sestet (*sesto*, "six"). The rhyming of the sestet can vary; a common alternative is cdecde. In any case, however, this kind of sonnet almost always maintains the sharp division into these two unequal parts. Often this formal division is accompanied by a shift in tone or topic. An octave may present a problem and the sestet its resolution, for example.

In a moment we'll explore an Italian sonnet by Edna St Vincent Millay (1892–1950). First, though, the topic of whole-poem forms gives us a chance to notice something that is not talked about very often: the information we receive visually about a poem before we even begin to read it. (You may remember the first page of Chapter 1, where a similar point is made with regard to prose and verse.) Just turning a page, even before we begin reading, can introduce us to several features of the event we're about to engage in:

We see that it's probably a poem, not an advertisement or a news story. The poem is all one unit without stanza breaks. Its width suggests that if it's metrical its lines will be approximately iambic pentameter in length. (In English sonnets are usually in iambic pentameter, though tetrameter and hexameter sonnets turn up from time to time.) We can anticipate that the whole experience of reading the poem once will probably take us about a minute. When we commence having that experience we will retain an approximate, proportional sense of how much is over and how much is yet to come. When we tune the radio to a popular-music station we expect to have experiences around three minutes long, while in a concert hall where one of Gustav Mahler's symphonies may be on the program we expect to be immersed in music for considerably longer, and at a festival in

Morocco we may be living in music's continuous midst for days. How we hear each seconds-long span of the music – for instance, on what time-scale we listen for *repetitions* – will change depending on these initial expectations. How we watch a scene in a standard two-hour movie differs according to whether we're fifteen minutes or a hundred minutes into the experience. It's always worth asking yourself what you know about a poem before you begin to read it and tracking how that evolves as you do read it.

Here is Millay's sonnet in a more readable form:

```
  /   x | x  /|  x  /| x  (/)| x  /
```
I, being born a woman and distressed   a
```
  x /|   x  /|   x   /| x (/)|x  /
```
By all the needs and notions of my kind,   b
```
  x    /|   x (/)|   x  /|x (/)|x  /
```
Am urged by your propinquity to find   b
```
  x   / |x  /| x   / |x / | x  /
```
Your person fair, and feel a certain zest   a
```
  x  / |  x   / |x   /|  x (/)|x    /
```
To bear your body's weight upon my breast: a
```
  /  / | x (/) |x  / | x /  | x /
```
So subtly is the fume of life designed,   b
```
  x   / |x(/) |x  / |  x    / | x   /
```
To clarify the pulse and cloud the mind,   b
```
  x    /|  x  /|  x  /|x  /|   x /
```
And leave me once again undone, possessed.   a
```
  /    / |x  / |  x  /|x  x  /   | / x
```
Think not for this, however, the poor treason   c
```
  x  x   /   / |x / |   x  /|x x    /
```
Of my stout blood against my staggering brain,   d
```
  x (/) |x  / | x  (/) | x   / | x  / x
```
I shall remember you with love, or season   c
```
  x   / |  x  / |x  /|  x  /| x  /
```
My scorn with pity, – let me make it plain: d
```
  x  / |  /   /| x /|x /|x    / x
```
I find this frenzy insufficient reason   c
```
   x  / |x  / |x  (/) |  x  / |x /
```
For conversation when we meet again.   d

Sonnets have been associated with love poetry for so long – at least since Petrarch – that Millay can take advantage of this tradition to make what is from one angle a joke about what love poems are expected to say, and from another angle a declaration of modern feminist independence. The two impulses are related. The poem takes a stand against what is expected both of its genre and of its author's sentiments.

Like Wordsworth, Millay has adopted the strictest rhyme scheme for her sestet: cdcdcd. This is unusual in English because it's difficult. English is a language poor in rhymes, at least as compared with Italian.

Rhymes in Different Languages

Italian, like other Romance languages, is a more strongly **inflected** language than English. Partly for this reason, its words end in a fairly small number of ways, so that two words chosen at random have a good chance of rhyming. There are probably *no* unrhymable words in Italian, while in English we have many. One well-known group comprises the color-words "orange," "purple," and "silver," but there are also no full rhymes for "woman," "music," "olive," "oblige," "problem," "empty," and dozens of others. When poetic forms are imported from a rhyme-rich language like Italian or French into a rhyme-poor language like English the poet is faced with increased difficulty in fulfilling the contract of the form's rhymes.

Rhyming the sestet as cdecde (or another similar variation) is one step easier because it allows one more rhyme sound and requires only two rhyme-words for each sound as opposed to three. (The octave requires four for each of its two rhymes.) The poet may choose the most stringent variation simply as a sign of maximum engagement with the subject, and Wordsworth's "steep / hill / deep / will / asleep / still" – the one disyllable "asleep" helps shape the series – gives that general feeling. In Millay's case, taking on the extra, maximal challenge of rhyme may make a more direct gesture of self-assertion. Her 'c' rhyme ("treason / season / reason") is the only so-called feminine rhyme in the poem; aside from any additional irony in that term, she uses the two-syllable endings to stretch out these three lines in preparation for the sharp jab of the 'd' rhymes that follow: "brain / plain / again."

While the Italian sonnet almost always maintains a sharp split between octave and sestet, it need not divide the two halves of the octave at all. Both Wordsworth and Millay use syntax not to mark off but to bridge the gap between quatrains (between lines 4 and 5):

> This City now doth, like a garment, wear
> The beauty of the morning ...   (Wordsworth)

> ... and feel a certain zest
> To bear your body's weight ...   (Millay)

One reason to do this is simply to increase the unity of the octave and so strengthen the shift we feel at the turn into the sestet. (That point in a sonnet, between lines 8 and 9, is called the **volta**, Italian for "turn.") But the rhymes of the Italian octave – two quatrains of *rimes embrassées* which rhyme with each other, too – can also be heard as a series of rhymed couplets offset from the quatrain boundaries:

a bb aa bb a

Wordsworth takes full advantage of this possibility, and his couplets are tightly bound by syntax:

> ...Dull would he be of soul who could pass by
> A sight so touching in its majesty:

> This City now doth, like a garment, wear
> The beauty of the morning; silent, bare,

> Ships, towers, domes, theatres, and temples lie
> Open unto the fields, and to the sky; ...

Millay is less insistent on this parsing of the octave, but she exploits it increasingly through the three opportunities the form provides, culminating in the couplet,

> So subtly is the fume of life designed,
> To clarify the pulse and cloud the mind,

which sounds almost like an aphorism by Pope or Samuel Johnson (1709–1784): "Nor Light nor Darkness bring his Pain Relief, / One shews the Plunder, and one hides the Thief." The rigorous formal proportions of the couplet make its wit, and the wit of the form makes the irony of the observation poignant. Who would "design" such an apparently self-defeating system? Millay's careful balance of "clarify" and "cloud" (governing the wild "pulse" and the hapless "mind") sharpens the question.

The octave/sestet division of the Italian sonnet may help explain what might otherwise be mysterious: the sonnet's astonishing longevity. It would be difficult to find any poetic form above the level of the line, except for the simplest stanzas such as quatrains, that has lasted for 700 years. The sonnet's popularity has waxed and waned – there were few in the eighteenth century but the Romantics brought them back with enthusiasm (Wordsworth wrote 400 of them) – but sonneteers abound even now. Why? It seems that we strongly prefer temporal shapes that are somewhat skewed toward their ends. We like narratives to be climactic, not anti-climactic. If a lyric poem has no narrative it still has an internal structure, a plot of statement, and this too is most satisfying when it has a climactic shape rather than either a symmetrical or a front-loaded contour. The Italian sonnet, then, is a *form* that encourages the poet to make a *structure* we are likely to find pleasing.

The other major kind of sonnet is the **Shakespearean** or **English sonnet.** (Shakespeare wrote 154 of them; Surrey (1516–1547) and Sidney had created this variety earlier in the sixteenth century.) This form is constructed on a different rhyme scheme from the Italian:

abab cdcd efef gg

The first thing to notice is that only two rhyme-words are required for each of the seven rhymes, which fits it better to English.

Sonnet Variants

Partly because it has been around so long, variations on the sonnet are numerous. Edmund Spenser wrote sonnets in a form halfway between the Italian and the English:

abab bcbc cdcd ee

> Like Shakespeare, he ends with a couplet and divides the first twelve lines into quatrains. However, he uses rhyme to link those quatrains somewhat as Petrarch links the two halves of his octave.

The second and more important feature of the Shakespearean form is its tendency to fragment into three separate quatrains and a couplet. The dividing point between octave and sestet *can* still mark a major turn in the poem, but the form does not insist on it in the same way as in the Italian. In some of Shakespeare's sonnets the couplet seems almost an afterthought. The final couplets of the "procreation sonnets," numbered 1 to 17 – "But were some child of yours alive that time, / You should live twice, in it and in my rhyme," for example – are nearly interchangeable. One of his sonnets (126) does without the couplet entirely. In many other cases, of course, Shakespeare uses the couplet to clinch the whole poem, like the punch line of a joke or the "Q.E.D." at the end of a mathematical proof.

Millay wrote somewhat more Shakespearean than Italian sonnets. Here is a poem from her first book, *Renascence* (1917):

```
x (/) | x    / | x    / | /    / |x x  /
If I should learn, in some quite casual way,                a
   x  / | x   / |  /  x |x  / |x  /
That you were gone, not to return again –                   b
  /  x  |  x /  | /   x |x / | x   /
Read from the back-page of a paper, say,                    a
  /   x |x /  | x (/)|x / | x    /
Held by a neighbor in a subway train,                       b
  /  x | x / | x x    / / |x (/)
How at the corner of this avenue                            c
x   / | x  / | | / x | x / | x  /
And such a street (so are the papers filled)                d
x / | x x   /  |  x  / |x  (/) |x /
A hurrying man – who happened to be you –                   c
x   / | x  / | x  / | x  (/)|x  /
At noon to-day had happened to be killed,                   d
```

```
x    x      /    / | x / | x   /  | x   /
I should not cry aloud – I could not cry                    e
x   /  | x     /  | x    /   | x   /  | x   /
Aloud, or wring my hands in such a place –                 f
x   /  | x   /   | x   /  | x  /  | |  /    /
I should but watch the station lights rush by              e
   x   x    /    / | x /  | x (/) | x   /
With a more careful interest on my face,                   f
x    / |  x  / | x     /  | x   / | x /
Or raise my eyes and read with greater care               g
   /   x | /   / | x   (/) | x   / |  x   /
Where to store furs and how to treat the hair.            g
```

Line 5, the beginning of the second quatrain, continues the sentence – in fact the whole poem gains power by confining itself to a single sentence – but the topic turns. The first quatrain was about the imagined way in which she receives news of the death while the second imagines the event itself. The third quatrain and the couplet go on to say how she would react to the news. In content, then, Millay retains something of the Italian sonnet's internal structure: her octave establishes the situation and her sestet responds to it. The turn into the final couplet ("Or ...") is not a sharp turn but a gentle shift within the sestet's continued response, focusing more and more closely on her surroundings and so acting out the shocked dissociation of her imagined self. The unity of the couplet with the quatrain preceding it retrospectively reinforces the octave/sestet division, while the final rhyme of "care" and "hair" both emphasizes the triviality of the advertising her eyes are fixed upon and then allows "care" – sustaining the burden suggested by "careful" in the twelfth line – to break free of the implied phrase "hair-care" and reverberate with its whole sense of mental suffering.

These two poems of Millay's, whose forms she selected from the narrow range of traditional kinds of sonnets, demonstrate as clearly as George Herbert's invented stanzas the attentiveness with which poets fit a form to the poem they want to write – or explore a form to find out what (else) it may have to say. Perhaps the poet could tell us which of these is an accurate description of the history of a particular poem, but if the poem is successful we cannot. The poem and its form seem to be molded simultaneously out of the same stuff.

Lines and Sentences

At the beginning of this chapter, before examining rhyme and stanzas we noticed in passing that lines of verse participate also in a different kind of structure, the sentence. We have seen that the lines and rhymes of which poems are built can become fairly complex. The sentences of which the poem is *simultaneously* composed are differently so. In the first place, syntax is a system *more* complex than any meter or rhyme scheme. The few hundred pages of this book contain just about all you're likely to need to know about how lines are constructed and combined, but a complete review of the rules that govern English sentences requires far more than a thousand pages much denser than these.

Comprehensive English Grammars

Two examples are Randolph Quirk *et al., A Comprehensive Grammar of the English Language* (Longman, 1985), and *The Cambridge Grammar of the English Language* (Cambridge, 2002), at 1,779 and 1,860 pages respectively.

At the same time, however, only specialists are likely to consult those books, since they are precise records of what every native speaker of English *already knows* about how to make and understand sentences because we learned syntax unconsciously during a crucial early period of our lives.

While poetic forms such as the anapestic tetrameter and Herbert's "Justice" stanza are – whether the poet receives or invents them – imposed on the poem's language more or less arbitrarily, sentences are almost inevitably part of all speaking and writing. (When we speak many of our sentences are fragmentary and interrupted, but at each moment of speaking we are in the midst of a sentence we *could* finish.) Poets, like all speakers and writers, can manipulate syntax within these rules embedded in the language in a huge number of ways, but can't break them without the reader noticing that something has gone seriously odd – and probably wrong – with the poem's language. To put this another way, the poet is inevitably always *somehow* managing a relation between the poem's lines and its sentences.

The most basic relation is accumulation: unless the poem's sentences are unusually and regularly short, lines *build up* sentences. This sounds simple, but it's something like the art of building walls out of natural stone (rather than bricks). Let's look at a few poems to see how the line-by-line assembly of lines into sentences controls the pacing and meaning of the poem. To avoid distraction, we'll use unrhymed lines, specifically unrhymed iambic pentameters (blank verse).

Most of the **dramatic monologues** of Robert Browning rely on a spiky, flexible pentameter that can extend (in the case of *The Ring and the Book*) for thousands of lines. As the term implies, these poems are speeches by a single character (not the poet) which construct a sense of that person in relation to others – particularly the person the speaker is addressing if any – and to their situation. Gathering these functions of drama into a poem requires finesse. When we're in a situation we don't say "I am sitting on the balcony at evening talking with my wife": we speak from inside the situation. The poem, on the other hand, needs to set the scene, not assume it. Here is the opening of Browning's poem (1855) named "Andrea del Sarto" after the Renaissance painter (1486–1530):

> But do not let us quarrel any more,
> No, my Lucrezia; bear with me for once:
> Sit down and all shall happen as you wish.
> You turn your face, but does it bring your heart?

The first line's "any more" characterizes, without talking about it directly, the time immediately preceding the speech. (We guess who speaks from Browning's title, a shortcut to identification which makers of dramatic monologues often employ.) "Lucrezia" in the second line tells us whom the speaker addresses and we conclude without much trouble that this is his wife. Their relation is summarized neatly if not happily by the relation between "quarrel" in the first line and the more abject "bear with me" in the second, and "for once" adds testiness to the plea. In the third line "sit down" suggests that he is sitting already and asking her to join him, a request he bolsters with an open-ended promise of compliance. The fourth line is the poem's second sentence. It changes the subject or at least the emotional register of the speech. Notice how important "but" is in the middle of the line. Until then we might think that "You turn your face" indicates that she turns away; no, she turns toward him, but this merely sends him back into what appears to be his habitual doubt.

Once we turn our attention to sentences an old question may come back to us: why verse? In Browning's second line the opening "No" doesn't just repeat the negative "do not let us…"; the emphatic repetition embodies a small turn in the speaker's tone of voice, the beginning of his pleading. At the end of the line the colon represents a pause between the generalized request and the specific one. These are points that articulate the dramatic movement of this crucial opening passage. Though some of this dramatic effect would be present without line breaks, the turns and separations of verse – particularly at the ends of lines – make the representation of the scene stronger and more immediate. They push us gently away from a sense that we are reading toward a sense that we are listening to a man speak.

A different kind of dramatic or narrative accumulation happens at the start of Keats's fragmentary epic, "Hyperion." A little background that would have been familiar to Keats's readers: preceding the Greek gods was a generation of Titans. Saturn was their king and Hyperion their sun-deity. The poem takes up their story just after these Titans have been defeated by the next generation. Saturn's place has been taken by Jupiter (to use the Latin name Keats would have favored; Zeus in Greek) and Hyperion's by Apollo. Keats deals in *scenes*: he is acutely interested in drama, an interest that Browning adapts differently in his monologues a few decades later. Here are Keats's opening two sentences:

> Deep in the shady sadness of a vale
> Far sunken from the healthy breath of morn,
> Far from the fiery noon, and eve's one star,
> Sat gray-hair'd Saturn, quiet as a stone,
> Still as the silence round about his lair;
> Forest on forest hung about his head
> Like cloud on cloud. No stir of air was there,
> Not so much life as on a summer's day
> Robs not one light seed from the feather'd grass,
> But where the dead leaf fell, there did it rest. …

This is a place of dejection and isolation. Though the word "alone" does not appear, we're aware that Saturn's immobility and his solitude are so linked that the simile "as a stone" seems almost literal. Saturn is almost reduced to a statue of himself.

One function of lines in this passage – a function of verse, that is – is to slow down the action (there explicitly *is* no action) and our observation of the scene. Keats's first three lines are all adverbial phrases: we haven't gotten to a subject or verb yet but are amassing details of the setting. The keynote of that setting is the series "Deep," "Far sunken," and "Far from …," all of which Keats places at the beginnings of lines. The fourth line gives us the sentence that has been delayed: "Sat gray-hair'd Saturn, quiet as a stone." The sounds of the words bind the line tightly together: the three or four 's' sounds, the 'n' that closes both "Saturn" and "stone," even the light 't' at the ends of "Sat" and "quiet" and in the middle of "Saturn" and the 'r' buried in "hair'd" and "Saturn"; and the play of vowels that ranges from the near-pun on "Sat / Saturn" to the series that runs from the short 'a' sounds at the beginning through the long 'i' in "quiet" down to the deep 'o' of "stone." Aside from the pleasure such highly organized sound gives – the line feels good to say – it also helps mark off the line as a unit. A sentence and a story are going on, but this moment concerned with Saturn and the stone excerpts itself and invites us to linger. If we remember Keats's passage at all we're likely to remember whole lines.

Keats's lines are also remarkable in their sequence for the shifts of scale that they enact. The first three lines lead us down and in to find Saturn in line 4 and then focus us (as we may even imagine his eyes to be focused) on "a stone." Line 5 glances up and outward: though "Still as the silence" seems to continue the focus of "quiet as a stone," the phrase "round about" widens our view. The camera zooms out. The following lines extend the zoom to "Forest on forest" and even "cloud on cloud." The next lines – the poem's second sentence – zoom back in again but with a difference. We are now not quite in the scene with Saturn because "as" puts us into a simile, a parallel to the actual situation. ("Like" at the beginning of line 7 enacted a similar shift from scene to superimposed image, but very lightly.) Line 8 speaks of "a summer's day," not "the summer's day" in which Saturn may be sitting; we don't know the season where Saturn is. Keats has shifted us momentarily to another world – possibly the English world in which Keats and his expected reader live – and in this world he brings our attention to extremely small detail, in part by means of the emphatic meter of line 9:

/   / | /   / | /   x | x / | x   /
Robs not one light seed from the feather'd grass

The next line (the last of the quoted passage) closes off the second sentence with another sharply etched image. It's worth noticing that most of the sentences end at the ends of lines. This large-scale congruence is the norm, and though he departs from it (as in line 7) he doesn't do so often. This contributes to our general impression that lines construct sentences.

Tennyson, in his monologue "Ulysses," is less concerned with scene than Browning or Keats and more concerned with argument or rhetoric. What his opening sentence accumulates are not details to represent a setting or register a relation between characters but grounds for a case:

> It little profits that an idle king,
> By this still hearth, among these barren crags,
> Matched with an agèd wife, I mete and dole
> Unequal laws unto a savage race,
> That hoard, and sleep, and feed, and know not me. ...

This is a speaker who already knows where he wants to go: away. The end of his argument (seventy lines later) is a foregone conclusion. The basis for Ulysses' discontent – after the grand tragedy of the Trojan War that he has survived – is encoded in his adjectives, one or two per line: "idle," "still," "barren," "agèd" (though it seems churlish to complain about Penelope's age when she has waited twenty years for her husband despite a houseful of suitors), "Unequal," and "savage." These grievances are interestingly distributed among things he can do nothing about (the "barren crags"), things that may be beyond his control but are part of his heritage of kingship (the "savage race" on his island of Ithaca), and things he might best take up with himself such as the "Unequal laws" he promulgates. (Is there any reason why "a savage race" should *require* "Unequal laws"?)

In the first line "an idle king" seems to be the subject of a clause. (The first word, "It," is formally the subject of the sentence, but "It ... profits" is more a stub than a real clause.) In the third line Tennyson surprises us with "I," which takes over as the clause's subject. This makes "an idle king" a phrase in apposition, a temporary displacement of the subject from the personal "I." Between these two points, a line and a half act (much as in the Keats passage) to delineate bits of a scene, though here the details aren't merely shown but are conscripted to support a general indictment. The first two line breaks coincide with the logic of the speech; then a break comes in the middle of line 3 (a strong caesura after "wife") followed by the new clause "I mete and dole." These verbs are transitive (more frequently "mete out" and "dole out"), and since we're expecting direct objects we haven't yet heard this line pushes forcefully into the next. This lends extra emphasis to the start of that fourth line and helps make Ulysses' culminating complaint itself sound savage.

The suspension of the verbs "mete and dole" at the end of a line also prepares us for the harsh catalog of actions by the "savage race": "That hoard, and sleep, and feed, and know not me." This in turn prepares us for the famous last line of the poem, in which Ulysses enunciates his own determination

> To strive, to seek, to find, and not to yield.

These sound like the grand ambitions that proclaim a grand character, and the line is sometimes quoted in isolation with that tone in mind. But on the one hand, it is noticeable that at the end of the poem Ulysses has not actually *done* anything, and on the other hand, the parallel between his list of verbs and the list of verbs he attributed to the subjects of his kingdom in line 5 calls into question the majesty of the conclusion. The parallel is highlighted by the isolation of both lists as separate lines of verse.

Another poem cast as an argument but also dependent on scene-making is one that Adelaide Crapsey (1878–1914) wrote while being treated in a sanatorium in Saranac Lake, New York, for the tuberculosis that would kill her about two months later. Its title captures both the scene and the argument: "To the Dead in the Graveyard Underneath My Window."

Adelaide Crapsey

Crapsey is not very widely known but she is mentioned with respect by a number of critics. She has been seen as a pioneer of Imagism, the free-verse movement at the root of modernist poetry in English, though she may not have been aware of the movement since it was still very new when she died. She wrote about 200 poems. She was the inventor of the *cinquain* (sometimes "American cinquain" to distinguish it from earlier five-line stanzas), an intriguing whole-poem form of just five short lines: one foot, two, three, four, and one again (usually iambic). She also wrote part of what promised to be an unusually rigorous *Study of English Verse* and clearly thought carefully about form. As one critic says, Crapsey saw her cinquain as "the most condensed metrical form in English that would hold together as a complete unit" (O'Connor, "Adelaide Crapsey: A Biographical Study," unpublished MA thesis, Notre Dame, 1930, pp. 26–27).

(The poem's apologetic subtitle, "Written in a Moment of Exasperation," does little to reduce the defiance of her tone.) Here are the first eleven of the poem's forty-eight lines:

> How can you lie so still? All day I watch
> And never a blade of all the green sod moves
> To show where restlessly you toss and turn,
> And fling a desperate arm or draw up knees
> Stiffened and aching from their long disuse;
> I watch all night and not one ghost comes forth
> To take its freedom of the midnight hour.
> Oh, have you no rebellion in your bones?
> The very worms must scorn you where you lie,
> A pallid mouldering acquiescent folk,
> Meek habitants of unresented graves. ...

If Tennyson's Ulysses displays a certain lassitude (which distresses him), this speaker inveighs loudly against lassitude. The strength of the poem rests not on the vociferousness of its rant as such but on the vigor of her control over the lines' accumulation. After a first line that (with the title) efficiently establishes her tone and situation, she gives us a line whose material derives (reasonably, after "I watch") from sight: "And never a blade of all the green sod moves." Then the source of her language shifts from what she senses directly to what she knows ("To show where restlessly you toss and turn") or fantasizes ("And fling a desperate arm or draw up knees") or even, through an empathic imagination spurred by awareness of her own imminent mortality, enters into: "Stiffened and aching from their long disuse." The next pair of lines (again "I watch...") recapitulates and ends the first sentence. Then she expresses her response in a closed, single-sentence line: "Oh, have you no rebellion in your bones?" This gives her solid footing for the diatribe to begin in earnest: "The very worms must scorn you ..." We would feel less sympathetic to her contempt if she weren't so aware of the dead's passivity as a danger she herself needs to avoid.

In all of these cases, whatever the developing purpose of the poem it is very much one line at a time that the poet discovers that purpose and discovers it to us. From this perspective the metrical line is not a form to be filled or a contract to be fulfilled. It is a generator. What it generates among other things are the parts of sentences.

We call lines that *finish* sentences or clauses **end-stopped lines**. (The extreme case is a series of lines that *are* complete sentences.) In the clearest instances the line ends with a mark of terminal punctuation: a period, question mark, or exclamation point. But lines can be end-stopped to varying degrees. The following pentameters – four of several hundred from "Esthétique du Mal" by Wallace Stevens (1879–1955) – are all more or less end-stopped, though only two end in periods:

> ...Lie sprawling in majors of the August heat,
> The rotund emotions, paradise unknown.
> This is the thesis scrivened in delight,
> The reverberating psalm, the right chorale. ...

Though the second and fourth lines don't complete clauses, their little bouquets of noun phrases, all **appositives** with little syntactical urgency, feel self-contained. They resist the forward momentum of the sentence, which wants to complete itself, and of the reader, who wants to get on with the poem. To one extent or another, lines of verse always impede this onward urge – they want us to stop and savor them – and end-stopped lines resist it most strongly.

Conversely, the syntax may carry more strongly across the break from one line to the next. When this forward impetus feels stronger than the call to pause we say that the line is **enjambed**. (The term comes from French, in which *jambe* means "leg"; a homelier English version of the term is "run-over lines.") Just as lines can be end-stopped in a range of ways and to varying degrees, the same is true of **enjambment**. The two complement each other: the less end-stopped a line is the more it enjambs into the next. The relation of the lines to sentences becomes less a continuous accumulation than a contrary movement in which one line is modified or even contradicted by the one that follows.

The greatest power of enjambment is to revise our understanding retrospectively. Yeats's "No Second Troy" begins with the apparently mild rhetorical question,

> Why should I blame her that she filled my days ...

We all prefer our days to be full rather than empty, and if there is a person who fills them the ordinary response would be gratitude. When the poem continues, however,

> With misery, ...

we recognize that we are in a different story from the one we might have expected. (On the other hand, since the situation was loaded enough to call forth a poem it may never have been *likely* that the poem would continue unruffled in the vein of that first line.)

Terms of Enjambment

It's inconvenient that we don't have terms for the bits of language on either side of a strong enjambment, which would make it easier to talk about them. The French speak of something like Yeats's "With misery" as being *en rejet* ("in rejection" as it were). But in French critical vocabulary what precedes the break is conversely said to be *en contre-rejet* only if it's less than half of its line. Since the operative language setting up Yeats's enjambment is his whole preceding line, even this awkwardly foreign term won't fit.

Not only does our sense of the poem's speech change as we go forward, but the new line also makes us reconsider the line that came before. If the rhetorical question might have the casual sound of

/   x | x   / | x   (/) | x   / | x   /
Why should I blame her that she filled my days

the more fraught, actual question might sound more like this:

x   / | x   / | x ...
Why should I blame her that she filled my days

Each of the four questions that the whole poem comprises has this same ambiguity of stress, as each question veers between resigned reflection and embittered complaint:

Was there another Troy for her to burn?
x   (/) |x / |x   / | x (/) |x   /   (no, of course not)
/   x |x / |x   / | x (/) |x   /   (well, there was me)

Yeats's poem takes an unusually abrupt turn at this line break, but enjambment often entails at least some degree of retrospective revision or correction. Millay's sonnet "To Elinor Wylie" (a poet three years younger than Millay who died in 1928) declares at the beginning of its sestet,

> Yet here was one who had no need to die

which is a startling thought, until the next line completes it:

> To be remembered.

To speak of the enjambment as "correcting" the previous line wouldn't be accurate. The excessive wish – she needn't have died *at all* – though contrary to what we know of human mortality, hangs in the air even after the notion is rationalized by the next line. The mental revision prompted by enjambment doesn't *cancel* our previous impression. In poems meanings are never canceled. Though the prior hypothesis is marked "revised," its implications continue to haunt the speech that follows. Within Millay's restrained regret that Wylie died so young lurks an outcry against death itself.

Even our earlier examples of apparently steadily accumulating blank-verse lines include instances of enjambment. We already noticed how the verbs at the end of one of Tennyson's lines push toward the object which is delayed till the next line:

> ... I mete and dole
> Unequal laws unto a savage race

Crapsey's "exasperated" address to the dead first shows their restless arms and legs and then in the next line startlingly transports itself into the feeling in those limbs:

> ... And fling a desperate arm or draw up knees
> Stiffened and aching from their long disuse ...

What shifts at the line break is the point of view: from the imagining watcher into the body being watched.

In Wordsworth's long blank-verse autobiographical poem *The Prelude*, an early passage (lines 41–47 of Book First, "Introduction: Childhood and School-Time") turns on subtle but crucial enjambments. He begins by remembering the feeling of a "gentle breeze":

> For I, methought, while the sweet breath of heaven
> Was blowing on my body, felt within
> A corresponding mild creative breeze,
> A vital breeze which travelled gently on
> O'er things which it had made, and is become
> A tempest, a redundant energy,
> Vexing its own creation.

This sentence traverses quite a distance: from the sensation of breeze on his cheek through the idea of a force inside himself that resembles the breeze (in its continuous motion, for example) to a proposition that this internal force has actually created the world inside him and even the world outside as it is available to his senses. How does the poet cover so much ground so fast (in less than fifty words)? Part of the technique depends on the tiny words "within" and "on." When we encounter "within" at the end of the second quoted line we await – across the line break – an object of the preposition. The likely objects would have to do with the wind or the "breath of heaven" proposed as its source ("within / The breeze"? "within / Heaven's lungs"?). But we get no object. We revise our understanding: "within" is used absolutely, so what he felt was within *himself*. This effects the first major transition in the passage. Two lines later something similar happens with "on": this preposition too turns out to have no object and must mean "onward." This opens the way for the next line to begin enumerating all the territory the breeze (internal and/or external) has covered or will cover, and this turns out to be cosmically large. At the end of that line "become" initiates an enjambment of a more usual but effective kind: hesitating for a moment between lines we speculate what such an interior "breeze" might "become" and are startled at the sudden power of "A tempest."

Enjambment is a force or pattern that depends on lines by definition but does not depend directly on meter. Therefore it remains when meter is subtracted from the poem's methods of controlling its own rhythmic unfolding. For this reason we will return to enjambment in the next chapter, Free Verse.

Let's look at one final example of sentences and lines and their interaction. "The Labyrinth," by Edwin Muir (1887–1959), is spoken by Theseus, the ancient Greek hero who killed the Minotaur. The monster (half man, half bull) was confined in a vast maze for rather complicated family reasons. Theseus is remembering a later part of the story when he has (with the help of a thread given him by Ariadne) worked his way out of the labyrinth yet finds himself haunted by its twists and turns. The poem's opening sentence, thirty-five lines long, wonderfully enacts this labyrinthine quality of the hero's experience. Here is its beginning:

> Since I emerged that day from the labyrinth,
> Dazed with the tall and echoing passages,
> The swift recoils, so many I almost feared
> I'd meet myself returning at some smooth corner,
> Myself or my ghost, for all there was unreal
> After the straw ceased rustling and the bull
> Lay dead upon the straw and I remained,
> Blood-splashed, if dead or alive I could not tell
> In the twilight nothingness (I might have been
> A spirit seeking his body through the roads
> Of intricate Hades) – ever since I came out ...

The opening line is a dependent clause promising at least one more clause to complete the sentence, but that is only the first of many delays and twists. The second line pauses to describe his state of mind. The third continues that description but then follows it with a further qualifying clause ("so many [that] I almost feared..."). Each succeeding line presents us with another hesitation, another kink in the path, another parenthesis experienced as a detour. The phrase "since I came out" is repeated several times to comb out the ever-entangling narrative. Not until after another dozen lines do we get the actual subject and verb of the sentence: "There have been times when I have heard my footsteps / Still echoing in the maze ..." Even then the exit from this sentence is many lines away, and even the sentence's end denies exit: "all seemed a part / Of the great labyrinth." Muir's skill in holding this sentence together – a reader may feel overwhelmed but never gets lost – is aided greatly by one initial decision he made: the whole poem is in iambic pentameter. The unifying, recurring, ever-varying experience of the lines is the main thing that sustains our journey.

4

Free Verse

Many of the poems from the past hundred years that you'll encounter – probably a majority – are written in **free verse**.

"Free Verse" as a Name

The name "free verse" is too widely used to be ignored, but it's unfortunate. It suggests liberation from constraints such as meters inherited from previous poetry, but it doesn't acknowledge the control over its own form and structure that any verse needs to exercise in order to do its job of guiding the reader's attention (as well as the poet's).

The name began as a translation of the French phrase *vers libre*, which referred to late nineteenth-century verse that abandoned the syllable counting that had long governed French poetry more strictly than accentual-syllabic meters like iambic pentameter ever ruled English verse. (We saw in Chapter 2 why syllabics, like accentuals, are more brittle than meters that count both syllables and stresses.) All that "free verse" really means is "nonmetrical verse" – verse whose prosodic control is not characterized by a numerical rule. This more accurate name, though, is too awkward to have caught on. It also retains the disadvantage of being a purely negative label – a subtler form of the problem with the more popular term "free verse."

Verse: An Introduction to Prosody, First Edition. Charles O. Hartman.
© 2015 John Wiley & Sons, Ltd. Published 2015 by John Wiley & Sons, Ltd.

There was important nonmetrical English poetry before 1900: the Psalms in the King James Bible, William Blake's "prophetic books," and most essential for the future of free verse particularly in America, the poems of Walt Whitman (1818–1892). Predominantly, though, free verse is a phenomenon of the twentieth century and after. When it began to be popular among poets just before World War I it aroused fierce controversy. ("These men are the Reds of literature!") The underlying anxiety did have *some* rational basis. Centuries of tradition in the writing and critical discussion of verse had assumed that "meter" and "prosody" and "poetry" all overlapped without sharp distinctions. Take away meter, the argument went, and you take away the poetry. But nonmetrical poems kept being written and read – more and more throughout the century – and this suggests that we should reframe the question: when you discard meter what remains? What kind of prosody, what control over the reader's rhythmic attention, might replace foot-based meter?

The most fundamental answer is that in the absence of meter rhythm remains. The free-verse poet can highlight and manipulate the manifold components of rhythm as meticulously as the poet working metrically – even, some would argue, more subtly. We'll investigate this aspect of free verse as we go along.

Lines Are Still Lines

Those who dismissed free verse as "prose cut into lines" – a charge frequently raised in the 1920s and 1930s – were implying that meterless writing inevitably collapses into rhythmic vagueness, so only the content of the language could support its claim to be poetic. Content, as we'd still agree, is only a small part of what makes a poem a poem. Of course this argument ignores the rhythmic animation and coherence that prose can achieve – no reader thinks of *The Great Gatsby* or *Ulysses* or *Gravity's Rainbow* as rhythmically lax or inattentive. But an even stronger answer to the charge against free verse as prose pretending to be poetry stems from what we discovered in the previous chapter about enjambment. "Prose cut into lines" is no longer prose. What happens at the point of cut is just as potentially vivid and sense-altering as what happens at the ends of metrical lines. The effect can even be more intense because the absence of meter foregrounds the poet's decision – arbitrary but therefore expressive – to end the line just there, not a syllable earlier or later.

Here are the words of a short poem by William Carlos Williams (1883–1963), written before 1923, called "Landscape with the Fall of Icarus." ("Brueghel" is Peter Brueghel the Elder (1525–1569) whose painting of the same title emphasizes how marginal even great catastrophes are to the daily lives of farmers and merchants.) Here, though, the words are printed as prose without Williams's line breaks:

> According to Brueghel when Icarus fell it was spring a farmer was ploughing his field the whole pageantry of the year was awake tingling near the edge of the sea concerned with itself sweating in the sun that melted the wings' wax unsignificantly off the coast there was a splash quite unnoticed this was Icarus drowning

It's highly unlikely that Williams wrote his poem by composing this prose text and then cutting it into lines. But he revised his poems painstakingly and his revisions often concentrated on experiments with line breaks. The typewriter, a fairly new invention at the time, gave him a control over the appearance of his verse that earlier poets had had to leave to publishers. This helped Williams during the 1920s to develop many of the techniques that free-verse poets have depended on ever since.

When you read the prose version, the giveaway that something is missing is the absence of punctuation. One way Williams used line breaks was as a kind of master punctuation mark – a mark that's available only to writers of verse – which could replace other kinds of punctuation. From the run-on sentences of the prose you might be able to predict some of the line breaks in Williams's actual poem:

> According to Brueghel
> when Icarus fell
> it was spring
>
> a farmer was ploughing
> his field
> the whole pageantry
>
> of the year was
> awake tingling
> near

> the edge of the sea
> concerned
> with itself
>
> sweating in the sun
> that melted
> the wings' wax
>
> unsignificantly
> off the coast
> there was
>
> a splash quite unnoticed
> this was
> Icarus drowning

The line break at the end of the first stanza acts in part as a replacement for a missing period or semicolon or colon. Yet there are also surprises, line breaks (or non-breaks) you may have been less likely to anticipate. One is the last break: "this was / Icarus drowning." This clause would never be divided by punctuation in prose, but the line break acts as a dramatic pause revealing the last two words as the compressed climax of the scene: Icarus is not just "falling" but has struck the water and is "drowning." The line isolates this climactic event just as Brueghel's tiny representation of Icarus's legs isolates him in the painting. Earlier the sea is characterized as "concerned" – not for Icarus but "with itself." Williams uses a line break to focus attention on the distinction. Conversely, while in prose we would expect a comma to separate the two adjectives "awake" and "tingling" Williams juxtaposes them within one line. This not only links the two ("tingling" becomes a delicious semi-synonym for "awake") but also foreshadows the surprise of "sweating." This word is bewildering if we try to make it refer immediately to the "sea" or the "year." Rather, it goes all the way back to "the farmer." By dissolving a little of the syntactic glue that holds the poem's sentence together line breaks paradoxically enable connections across wider stretches of language – in this case between two points nine lines apart. Similarly, by isolating the unusual adverb "unsignificantly" as a line Williams lets us see how the word applies equally well to the melting of Icarus's wings that precedes it and the splash "off the coast" that follows.

Perhaps the main surprise is how short Williams's lines are. If we *only* used line breaks to replace obviously missing punctuation the whole poem could have been just six or eight lines long:

> According to Brueghel when Icarus fell it was spring
> a farmer was ploughing his field
> the whole pageantry of the year was awake tingling
> near the edge of the sea concerned with itself
> sweating in the sun that melted the wings' wax unsignificantly
> off the coast there was a splash quite unnoticed
> this was Icarus drowning

Williams's far shorter lines focus our attention intensely on the halts and lurches of the language, sometimes even isolating single words.

Early poems by Williams helped establish one modern style for free verse. When the lines are much longer than Williams's the line break recedes somewhat as the chief shaping force of the poem's rhythm. For example, here is Walt Whitman's "The Dalliance of the Eagles," published in 1880:

> Skirting the river road, (my forenoon walk, my rest,)
> Skyward in the air a sudden muffled sound, the dalliance of the eagles,
> The rushing amorous contact high in space together,
> The clinching interlocking claws, a living, fierce, gyrating wheel,
> Four beating wings, two beaks, a swirling mass tight grappling,
> In tumbling turning clustering loops, straight downward falling,
> Till o'er the river pois'd, the twain yet one, a moment's lull,
> A motionless still balance in the air, then parting, talons loosing,
> Upward again on slow-firm pinions slanting, their separate diverse flight,
> She hers, he his, pursuing.

Every line is more or less end-stopped: it's a syntactical unit whose completeness is marked by punctuation. Some lines even combine several clauses or phrases. No line break interrupts the syntax on any scale smaller than that of the phrase, as Williams's frequently do.

Still, no one would mistake Whitman's verse for prose. During the first half of the poem the density of the language's rhythm increases noticeably. In comparison with ordinary speech or most prose, Whitman's language is marked by strong, clear contrasts between the stressed syllables and the unstressed ones around them.

(It does the opposite of mumbling.) Consequently, though of course we can't scan this free verse as if it were made of metrical feet we can easily record where the speech stresses fall. From the second line to the fifth there's a thickening:

   /   / /   /   /   /   /

Skyward in the air a sudden muffled sound, the dalliance of the eagles, ...

   / /   /   / /   /   / /   /

Four beating wings, two beaks, a swirling mass tight grappling, ...

Within this overall crescendo of stresses we notice continual variations in rhythm – try speaking "The clinching interlocking claws" aloud – in a way we would not in prose. After the quickened pulse of this fifth line ("Four beating wings ...") the rhythmic variations continue to uncoil, dominated by all the present participles ("tumbling turning clustering loops") that are a signature of this poem's language. After the eagles finish mating in midair – an astonishing moment when as far as we can tell time stops ("A motionless still balance in the air") – the poem's rhythm relaxes somewhat, though even at the end ("She hers, he his, pursuing") it's denser than any usual speech.

Bad Verse and Prose Cut into Lines

Of course there are plenty of bad free-verse poems that don't capture or keep our rhythmic attention. The lines don't do enough work as lines, and the fact of verse becomes no more than an annoying intrusion. It's reasonable to dismiss such poems as "prose cut into lines." The real question is what resources the poet can bring to bear that do make us hear the lines' rhythms as necessary.

Whitman, then, within the larger shape of each line focuses our awareness on rhythms at a smaller scale. As we saw in earlier chapters, metrical verse can do this as well, but the unpredictability of free verse can sharpen our hearing for rhythm. At the same time, Whitman's long lines send our attention outward toward the poem as a whole as an act of *framing*. Just as a photographer moves through the world with a portable frame and selects a rectangle for viewing later and elsewhere, the poet singles out an experience to show us. The poem's language, like what it represents, is framed in several ways at once: by the poem's overall shape, by the lines, and by the sentence which runs throughout the poem. Or so says the punctuation – though as we follow the sentence from its introductory line (the only place where Whitman's "I" speaks directly, another sort of frame for the experience) to the period at the end we never actually encounter a main clause. If the "sudden muffled sound" in line 2 looks like a subject, it never gets a verb. Instead the poem dissolves into noun phrases, prepositional phrases, and those ubiquitous present participles ("a swirling mass tight grappling"), full of energetic activity but never resolving into actual statement. In this way Whitman balances the narrative (and sexual) rise and climax and fall of the eagles' action against his own silence as the observer for whom the event ends but never exactly finishes. Williams, too, undermines the straightforward progress of his sentence (or sentences?) in "Landscape with the Fall of Icarus," and his clipped lines make the fragmentation of syntax even more evident. In both cases lines both collaborate with syntax and counter it.

Let's look in more detail at what kinds of work line endings and the lines they define can do in the absence of meter. In 1938 W. H. Auden wrote a poem called "Musée des Beaux Arts" – the title means "Museum of Fine Arts" and refers to the one in Brussels. That's where Brueghel's "Landscape with the Fall of Icarus" hangs, and as you'll see, Auden works his way toward talking about the same painting as Williams. If you print out Auden's words as prose, hand the passage to several people, and ask them to divide it into lines of verse, the average of their responses will look much like this:

> About suffering they were never wrong, the Old Masters:
> how well they understood its human position;
> how it takes place while someone else is eating
> or opening a window or just walking dully along;
> how, when the aged are reverently,
> passionately waiting for the miraculous birth,
> there always must be children
> who did not specially want it to happen,
> skating on a pond at the edge of the wood:
> They never forgot that even the dreadful martyrdom
> must run its course anyhow in a corner,
> some untidy spot
> where the dogs go on with their doggy life
> and the torturer's horse scratches its innocent behind on a tree.

157

> In Breughel's *Icarus*, for instance:
> how everything turns away quite leisurely from the disaster;
> the ploughman may have heard the splash,
> the forsaken cry,
> but for him it was not an important failure;
> the sun shone as it had to on the white legs
> disappearing into the green water;
> and the expensive delicate ship
> that must have seen something amazing,
> a boy falling out of the sky,
> had somewhere to get to and sailed calmly on.

Let's consider this poem briefly before we turn to the one Auden actually wrote. It sounds like a lecture. The syntax is more elaborate than in ordinary speech, the statements about "the human condition" and "the Old Masters" are very grand, and at the same time the diction is lightened by fussy but casual phrases ("anyhow," "some untidy spot") that a chatty lecturer might include to put his audience at ease. It sounds very practiced, too. We might guess that the speaker is some sort of guide in the museum pointing out and explaining various paintings to a tour group. In fact, the poem seems to exemplify exactly the attitude it talks about: in the presence of epic calamities that aren't theirs people remain preoccupied with their own affairs. (As we saw in relation to Williams's poem, this is what the painting itself seems to say.) In a sense, this mirroring is what we expect poems to do. We admire poems whose "content" (what is said) is reinforced by being replicated in their "form" (how it's said). The poem doesn't just say something but enacts it at the same time. But this poem (which is *not* Auden's) demonstrates the *limits* of that virtue. What it enacts after all is bland indifference in the face of mythic drama. However appropriate, this duplication of tedious content by tedious manner leaves the verse feeling weary and dull.

Now let's turn to Auden's real "Musée des Beaux Arts":

> About suffering they were never wrong,
> The Old Masters: how well they understood
> Its human position; how it takes place
> While someone else is eating or opening a window or just walking
>   dully along;
> How, when the aged are reverently, passionately waiting

For the miraculous birth, there always must be
Children who did not specially want it to happen, skating
On a pond at the edge of the wood:
They never forgot
That even the dreadful martyrdom must run its course
Anyhow in a corner, some untidy spot
Where the dogs go on with their doggy life and the torturer's horse
Scratches its innocent behind on a tree.

In Brueghel's *Icarus*, for instance: how everything turns away
Quite leisurely from the disaster; the ploughman may
Have heard the splash, the forsaken cry,
But for him it was not an important failure; the sun shone
As it had to on the white legs disappearing into the green
Water; and the expensive delicate ship that must have seen
Something amazing, a boy falling out of the sky,
Had somewhere to get to and sailed calmly on.

The only difference lies in Auden's enjambments. The thing most wrong with the phony version is that it's *redundant*: the line breaks all come at points where the syntax already divides the words ("the ploughman may have heard the splash, / the forsaken cry").

By breaking lines in the middle of syntactical units Auden introduces new stresses into the poem. When we jump across a line break the beginning of the new line receives more stress than it might have otherwise. (The end of a line is another place where the imminent line break may increase stress. It's worth thinking about how our bodies prepare for a jump across a gap and react on landing.) In Chapter 1 we discussed "contrastive stress," the habit of speech by which we emphasize oppositions ("What do *you* want to see?"). To take an example from the world of baseball, we say,

       /   /
Chicago White Sox, Chicago Cubs

We don't say,

             /   /
Are you a fan of the Chicago White Sox or the Chicago Cubs?

That question is bewildering in the real world of the American major leagues. And if someone asks,

/

Do you like the Chicago White Sox?

we hear the person referring to something that doesn't exist, so that we might sarcastically reply, "No, I prefer the Denver White Sox." (There are no Denver White Sox.) Enjambments take advantage of this process of contrastive stress. By introducing unexpected emphasis a line break can suggest a contrast that might not otherwise be apparent.

As we read the clause "How well they understood its human position," we're likely to focus on "well" and perhaps "position," the beginning and end of the syntactical unit. But when we read "how well they understood / Its human position," we stress "human" ("Its" is too modest to accept stress). This makes us ask, "human" as opposed to what? One answer might be "animal," and indeed we get dogs and horses later in the stanza. Is Auden claiming that animals don't suffer? Not at all – only that human suffering is different from that of animals, perhaps because of its (as far as we can tell) unique imaginative component. Thinking about how and why we're in pain complicates our pain. Also, the sufferings referred to in this stanza have to do with "martyrdom," death for the sake of a religion, which animals never choose for themselves and never inflict on each other. Through the implied contrast with animals Auden narrows and sharpens the meaning of "suffering" in his first line. The enjambment helps to define a word that was vague or abstract. As the version with lazy line breaks does not, Auden's poem makes us think about what "suffering" means.

Moving in another direction we might hear "human" as opposed to "divine," since this part of the poem is concerned with Christian notions of martyrdom that revolve around the Crucifixion and Christianity has for centuries debated the divinity and humanity of Jesus. This poem suggests that Jesus had to be human in order for his suffering and sacrifice to be redemptive. How does this ancient theological issue come into the poem? It's introduced through a contrast between notions of human suffering and the divine, which arises from unexpected stress on the word "human," which in turn arises from the line break.

160

We might call this function of line breaks *semantic*: it changes or refines the meaning of a word. The same kind of thing happens in the enjambment at the well-known ending of a poem by James Wright (1927–1980), "A Blessing":

> Suddenly I realize
> That if I stepped out of my body I would break
> Into blossom.

The word "break" first seems to imply injury or destruction – stepping outside one's body could mean dying – but when the full phrase is completed we realize that "break" can also mean something about *opening*. We break into a wall safe or into show business or into song.

Returning to Auden's poem we might hear some of his other line breaks as semantic in this way. In "waiting / For the *miraculous* birth, there always must be / *Children* who did not specially want it to happen" (emphasis inferred), we may think about whether the births of these indifferent children are less "miraculous" than that of Jesus. Also, he will become a Savior with a revolutionary attitude toward children (see Mark 10:13–15, for example): we have to become like children to enter heaven.

Most of Auden's enjambments, though, and most enjambments in most poems, serve as pivots or fulcrums for less elaborate turns of thought. "[T]he ploughman may / Have heard the splash" – or he may not, and in any case doesn't trouble to turn and look at it, since "for *him* it was not an important failure," though it was for Icarus. "[T]he sun shone / as it *had* to" – though it has just melted Icarus's wax wings and in effect drowned him. Many line breaks act simply to inject a note of wonder into a discourse which, as we saw earlier, is otherwise slightly too dreary to celebrate the vision it announces:

> ... the green
> Water
> ... must have seen
> Something amazing

We might also turn for a moment from the lines' ends to the lines themselves. For many free-verse poems, one consequence of abandoning meter is increased variety in the lengths of lines. Even when we first glance at Auden's poem on the page, we may notice its longest line:

> While someone else is eating or opening a window or just walking
> dully along;

Poetic versus Printed Lines

When lines become long enough, the simple principle we used to define verse in Chapter 1 – that the right-hand margins of the lines are chosen by the poet, not imposed by the mechanical constraints of printing – can become slightly muddled. When the printer must break a verse line into two or more typographical lines the custom is to indent the run-over part by some standard margin. Since indentation of certain lines is *also* a device that poets sometimes use deliberately, ambiguous cases are possible. Fortunately they're not frequent, and various contextual cues can help. A single indented line, for instance, as in Auden's poem as printed here, is almost certain to be a run-over line. A poet's formal choices, including typographical choices like indentation, typically occur more than once.

The tedium that infected the whole poem when it was divided at the points of least resistance is here confined to one line. The bland list of ordinary actions acts out that tedium, but only for a moment, turning it into a kind of joke. We might also notice the shortest line –

> They never forgot

– which hardly seems to be pulling its weight as a line. Yet in order to comprehend it we need to track what "They" refers to. We look back to the "Children" and "the aged" before them, but they're not the ones who don't forget. Instead the reference goes all the way back to "the Old Masters" at the beginning of the poem. In this way Auden makes us, consciously or not, review the stanza's whole first half, which creates a momentum that we carry into the second half of the stanza after this pivot point.

Types of Free Verse

Free verse is so ubiquitous in modern and contemporary poetry and so diverse that a tempting clarifying move would be to specify its various kinds. This is what a background in meter suggests that we do: there are iambics and anapestics and trochaics, and iambics can be pentameters or tetrameters, and so on. Yet the question of what kinds of free verse exist or are possible has never been very satisfactorily answered and, for reasons we'll consider, perhaps never will be.

Still, some of the kinds of variations that we have already seen suggest a simple schema:

Line ends \ Lines	short	long
enjambed		
stopped		

If we could fill the four lower-right boxes with the name of poets or individual poems we'd have a label for the *style* of each free-verse poet or poem. Though we may suspect from the outset that the chart oversimplifies the real situation of readers and poets, we can certainly find examples of the four categories that these two intersecting dimensions generate.

The poem we saw earlier by Whitman, "The Dalliance of Eagles," like most of his poems, is made of long lines largely end-stopped. An even clearer example is "Come Thunder" by Christopher Okigbo (1930–1967), in which he foretells the Nigerian civil war in which Okigbo himself would soon serve and be killed. (The ellipses are in Okigbo's original.)

> Now that the triumphant march has entered the last street corners,
> Remember, O dancers, the thunder among the clouds …
> Now that laughter, broken in two, hangs tremulous between the
>   teeth,
> Remember, O dancers, the lightning beyond the earth …
>
> The smell of blood already floats in the lavender-mist of the
>   afternoon.
> The death sentence lies in ambush along the corridors of power;

> And a great fearful thing already tugs at the cable of the open air,
> A nebula immense and immeasurable, a night of deep waters –
> An iron dream unnamed and unprintable, a path of stone.
>
> The drowsy heads of the pods in barren farmlands witness it,
> The homesteads abandoned in this century's brush fire witness it:
> The myriad eyes of deserted corn cobs in burning barns witness it:
>
> Magic birds with the miracle of lightning flash on their feathers ...
>
> The arrows of God tremble at the gates of light,
> The drums of curfew pander to a dance of death;
>
> And the secret thing in its heaving
> Threatens with iron mask
> The last lighted torch of the century ...

Only a few of these lines are absolutely end-stopped in the sense that their ends coincide with the ends of sentences. But the ellipses at the ends of other lines mark them as sentence fragments that will not continue in the next line. We know not to anticipate enjambment. More important, until the last three every line is a complete clause or at least (as in lines 8 and 9) a self-contained noun phrase appended to a sentence already well under way. The free-standing integrity of the lines is largely responsible for the stately tone which makes us respond to the dignity of the poem's prophetic assertions. This solemnity is balanced and enlivened by the vivid imagery contained within these closed utterances: "the secret thing in its heaving."

Long lines have a natural tendency toward being end-stopped. When a poem fills its lines beyond medium capacity and at the same time suspends our syntactical understanding at the end in preparation for the next line, it makes extra demands on us. Some poets, though, take advantage of this added labor to expand our sense of the poem's scope. Robinson Jeffers (1887–1962), an early Californian poet who celebrated vigor and fortitude, sometimes begins a new syntactical project at the end of the line. Here is his posthumously published poem "Vulture" (1963):

> I had walked since dawn and lay down to rest on a bare hillside
> Above the ocean. I saw through half-shut eyelids a vulture
>   wheeling high up in heaven,

And presently it passed again, but lower and nearer, its orbit
    narrowing, I understood then
That I was under inspection. I lay death-still and heard the flight-
    feathers
Whistle above me and make their circle and come nearer.
I could see the naked red head between the great wings
Bear downward staring. I said, "My dear bird, we are wasting time
    here.
These old bones will still work; they are not for you." But how
    beautiful he looked, gliding down
On those great sails; how beautiful he looked, veering away in the
    sea-light over the precipice. I tell you solemnly
That I was sorry to have disappointed him.
To be eaten by that beak and become part of him, to share those
    wings and those eyes –
What a sublime end of one's body, what an enskyment; what a life
    after death.

The poet lies "death-still," but line endings like "I understood then / That I was under inspection" and "gliding down / On those great sails" make us feel the huge unmoving internal energy with which he watches and welcomes the circling bird. "Homage to the Empress of the Blues" by Robert Hayden (1913–1980), his 1948 celebration of Bessie Smith, uses enjambment less aggressively than Jeffers, but even more pervasively:

Because there was a man somewhere in a candystripe silk shirt
facile and dangerous as a jaguar and because a woman moaned
for him in sixty-watt gloom and mourned him Faithless Love
Twotiming Love Oh Love Oh Careless Aggravating Love,

    She came out on stage in yards of pearls, emerging like
    a favorite scenic view, flashed her golden smile and sang

Because grey laths began somewhere to show from underneath
torn hurdygurdy lithographs of dollfaced heaven;
and because there were those who feared alarming fists of snow
on the door and those who feared the riot squad of statistics,

    She came out on stage in ostrich feathers, beaded satin,
    and shone that smile on us and sang.

165

Each line is a sizable gesture of image. At the same time, the firm syntactical frame ("Because ...") keeps us aware of the larger sentence that unfolds through each four-plus-two-line stanza. This elaborate syntax of logical certainty also highlights the apparent illogic of the statements. How could the existence of the man in the "candystripe silk shirt" and the white policemen's "fists of snow" on the door cause Bessie Smith's resplendent appearance on stage? By making us ask this question the poem sketches all the circumstances of her world, to which her elegance is one part of her response as the power of her singing is another. While Jeffers's enjambments emphasize the poem's still-living onward drive, Hayden's enjambments emphasize how taut and broad his sentences must be to contain Bessie Smith's presence.

When we turn from long-line to short-line free verse, we would expect much more enjambment. Fully end-stopped short lines are quite possible, but they seem to be associated with special effects. "Chronic Meanings" (1993) by Bob Perelman (1947–) is an exceptionally clear example. Here are the fifth and sixth stanzas out of seventeen:

> On our wedding night I.
> The sorrow burned deeper than.
> Grimly I pursued what violence.
> A trap, a catch, a.
>
> Fans stand up, yelling their.
> Lights go off in houses.
> A fictional look, not quite.
> To be able to talk.

(One problem with this example in the context of this chapter is that the lines are actually metrical, though the meter is an unusual one: Perelman counts not syllables or stresses but words, five per line.) The poem is an elegy for Leland Hickman (1934–1991), a poet and editor who died during the AIDS epidemic. Each line is end-stopped by force, as it were. The sentences don't continue past the line break because they are terminated before they can complete their work of statement, just as Hickman's life was cut off prematurely. In her poem with a structurally related topic, "Anorexic" (1980), Eavan Boland (1944–) uses severely curtailed lines to image the speaker's pathological self-denial. The first stanza announces both her method and her theme:

> Flesh is heretic.
> My body is a witch.
> I am burning it.

In the second stanza she relents enough to break a clause in two:

> Yes I am torching
> her curves and paps and wiles.
> They scorch my self-denials.

The poem sometimes returns to ruthlessly end-stopped lines ("I am starved and curveless. / I am skin and bone. / She has learned her lesson."), though in the last dozen of the poem's forty-six lines Boland takes advantage of enjambment to build momentum toward an ending. A poem similarly concerned with renunciation is "Stanzas, Sexes, Seductions" by Anne Carson (1950–), which begins with this stanza:

> It's good to be neuter.
> I want to have meaningless legs.
> There are things unbearable.
> One can evade them a long time.
> Then you die.

Carson's language of self-rejection is less direct and more fanciful than Boland's, so that we retain more sense of the conflict as paradoxical – who is doing the rejecting of the self? – rather than starkly antagonistic. Her final stanza, like Boland's, uses enjambment, but it also diminishes the coherence of the syntax so as to enact the war of the language-embodied mind with itself. ("Themselves" refers again to the legs.)

> Rocking themselves down,
> crazy slow,
> some ballet term for it –
> fragment of foil, little
> spin, little drunk, little do, little oh, alas.

All these examples of end-stopped short-line free verse feel exceptional. This reminds us that the more usual method is to use short lines not to truncate syntactical development but to play against it and therefore highlight it. Enjambed short-line free verse may be the most common of the four kinds our chart provides for. The first example in this chapter showed Williams developing strategies commonly used by poets ever since. Even earlier, before World War I, poets such as Ezra Pound and H. D. (Hilda Doolittle (1886–1961)) were developing a style of poetry called Imagism of which free verse was a central and consciously revolutionary feature. H. D.'s "Oread" (the title means "a mountain nymph" and identifies the poem's speaker) is a famous example from 1914:

> Whirl up, sea –
> Whirl your pointed pines
> Splash your great pines
> On our rocks,
> Hurl your green over us,
> Cover us with your pools of fir.

The poem is punctuated as a single sentence. Internally, though, the sentence is organized as a series of imperatives: "Whirl up ... Whirl ... Splash ... Hurl ... Cover ..." The sentence functions as a container, but syntax doesn't work as a driving force the way it does in Auden's "Musée des Beaux Arts" or Hayden's "Homage to the Empress of the Blues." That role of propelling the language forward is transferred instead to the chain of images succeeding each other as sensory impressions do. This is how the poem achieves its strange mixture of tones, at once static and ecstatic. The division of these images into quick lines makes an essential contribution to this effect.

By 1924 we can see H. D. introducing into free verse techniques more familiar in metrical verse, especially rhyme. Here is her meditation on Helen of Troy, "Helen" (1924):

> All Greece hates
> the still eyes in the white face,
> the lustre as of olives
> where she stands,
> and the white hands.
>
> All Greece reviles
> the wan face when she smiles,
> hating it deeper still

when it grows wan and white,
remembering past enchantments
and past ills.

Greece sees unmoved,
God's daughter, born of love,
the beauty of cool feet
and slenderest knees,
could love indeed the maid,
only if she were laid,
white ash amid funereal cypresses.

Rhymes bind the lines closely – most lines rhyme with other lines. The pattern is unpredictable, however, rather than a pre-established rhyme scheme of the kinds we saw in Chapter 3. In the context of free verse a couplet like the first two lines of the second stanza comes as a kind of bonus, a deliberately added gesture of design. By the same token, this method lets H. D. suggest rhymes we might not hear in a traditional metrical context: "hates" and "face" in the poem's first two lines, for example, and "feet" and "knees" in the last stanza.

The lines in this kind of enjambed short-line verse can also center on ideas or statements rather than on images, as in "The Map of Places" (1928) by Laura Riding (1901–1991):

The map of places passes.
The reality of paper tears.
Land and water where they are
Are only where they were
When words read *here* and *here*
Before ships happened there.

Now on naked names feet stand,
No geographies in the hand,
And paper reads anciently,
And ships at sea
Turn round and round.
All is known, all is found.
Death meets itself everywhere.
Holes in maps look through to nowhere.

Riding's syntactical rhythm builds outward through enjambment as her argument mounts, and then returns to end-stopped lines that help make her conclusion sound logically water-tight. In general she rhymes her lines even more tightly than H. D., in couplets – though the first stanza's "are / were / here / there" is a series of tantalizing off-rhymes and the first two lines announce that we can't assume rhyme at all.

The best success of our four-cell chart is that it groups poems like H. D.'s and Laura Riding's and also encourages us to hear the *difference* in how they sound. Yet the most useful thing to do with the chart is to watch what goes wrong with it as a guide to free verse. By thinking about the limitations of the two-dimensional schema we can develop some methods of reading that are more useful than labels.

The first limitation is that these categories aren't the binary choices that a table wants them to seem. Line length, for example, varies continuously along a spectrum. Between Williams's shortest line in "Landscape with the Fall of Icarus" –

near

– and Auden's longest in "Musée des Beaux Arts," the one about "eating or opening a window," there's a difference of one versus twenty-two syllables (to take just one simple way of measuring length). Though a line couldn't very well be zero syllables long, there's no reason one can't be even longer than Auden's. Some of the lines in "Howl" by Allen Ginsberg (1926–1997) exceed a hundred syllables and in a normal edition occupy half a dozen lines of print. A majority of free-verse poems are made of lines that average somewhere between these lengths – often not far from the iambic tetrameter or pentameter norm of metrical verse – but substantial deviations from the average aren't uncommon. Predictably, then, it turns out to be impossible to draw any sharp boundary between "long-line" and "short-line" verse. Trying to fill in boxes in the chart we'd find ourselves with countless borderline cases and unclassifiable outliers.

Not only is line length a continuously variable property of lines, but many poems more or less drastically *mix* the length of lines. This short poem by Langston Hughes, "The Negro Speaks of Rivers," first published in 1921, shows how such a mixture can work prosodically – that is, how the poet uses changes in line length to control the poem's movement:

I've known rivers:
I've known rivers ancient as the world and older than the flow
        of human blood in human veins.

My soul has grown deep like the rivers.

I bathed in the Euphrates when dawns were young.
I built my hut near the Congo and it lulled me to sleep.
I looked upon the Nile and raised the pyramids above it.
I heard the singing of the Mississippi when Abe Lincoln went
        down to New Orleans, and I've seen its muddy bosom
        turn all golden in the sunset.

I've known rivers:
Ancient, dusky rivers.

My soul has grown deep like the rivers.

(It's worth thinking about how we know that the second and seventh of these ten lines *are* lines, broken in print merely because of the narrowness of the page.) These lines are all completely end-stopped, being closed off with terminal punctuation except for the two dramatic colons. This closure reinforces our sense of each line as a sentence, a statement, and of the sequence of them as an expanding series of oratorical gestures. The right-hand margin of Hughes's poem is – or would be if we could print it on wide enough paper – a direct visual graph of the poem's rhetorical story-line of rise and fall.

Hughes' technique of widely varying line lengths is essential to this particular poem. (It's not his usual method in other poems.) Other poets may use patterns of line length to create large-scale developments from short, inward lines to long, expansive ones or vice versa. Most free-verse poems not surprisingly tend to keep line length roughly constant. This gives them a basic kind of unity. Hughes trades in this unifying line-to-line consistency for the different, larger-scale unity of his line lengths' ebb and flow. This overall coherence is reinforced on a more local level by the syntactical closure of his lines. Every poem needs both disparity and wholeness, and most poems offer both on every level, so that readers, even while being stimulated and disconcerted by changes and surprises, feel the poem's integrity, not only at the end when they can contemplate the poem as a single entity, but also from moment to moment. From this perspective, Hughes simply found an unusual way to combine all these demands. It's a method he adapted from the speaking style of the African American preachers who were his contemporaries (as James Weldon Johnson also did around the same time), and it registers a relation to oratory and heightened speech quite different from that of Williams or even Auden with his more obvious rhetorical bent.

When we turn from the long-line/short-line dimension of our chart of free-verse styles to the end-stopped/enjambed dimension we find an even more radically continuous spectrum to dispute the proposed binary division. Obviously the percentage of enjambed lines can vary from zero on up, not only from poem to poem but from one part of a poem to another. Beyond that, enjambments themselves vary in "strength." Some line breaks cut into the syntax more sharply than others. At one extreme, the opening lines of "How It Is" by Maxine Kumin (1925–2014) are completely end-stopped; there's no enjambment at all at the end of either line:

> Shall I say how it is in your clothes?
> A month after your death I wear your blue jacket.

(The next lines in the poem do introduce enjambment.) One step further, the weakest, least disruptive enjambment is one that divides the sentence between complete clauses, as in the opening of Randall Jarrell's "The Death of the Ball Turret Gunner" (1945), which represents the tail-gunner in a World War II bomber as a doomed embryo:

> From my mother's sleep I fell into the State,
> And I hunched in its belly till my wet fur froze.

Jarrell parcels clauses into lines, but the comma and "And" are his only gestures toward enjambing the sentence.

When a poet breaks the line between phrases rather than clauses, we feel a stronger sense of syntactical momentum carrying us on down the poem's page. This is probably the most common kind of enjambment in free verse. The opening stanza of "Hawk" by Mary Oliver (1935–) is a very spare example of this kind of "phrasal" verse:

> This morning
> the hawk
> rose up
> out of the meadow's browse

The first line is – though we won't know this for certain until the next line – an adverbial phrase which modifies the whole sentence and sets the poem in time. The second is a simple noun phrase, the subject of the sentence. The third is a verb phrase that initiates the hawk's action (and introduces action into the poem). The fourth is a prepositional phrase that places the action in space and in the speaker's field of view. ("[B]rowse" is used here as a noun referring to the plants that animals eat, which draw them to the place where the hawk hunts them.) There are many kinds of phrases, some (such as noun phrases) presenting more of an impression of completeness than others (such as prepositional phrases introducing a new sentence and obviously anticipating it). Correspondingly, there are innumerable kinds of enjambment even on this single level of syntactical division.

When lines are broken *within* phrases the poem's language becomes agitated and urgent. If we're reading with the necessary attention, the momentum of the syntax doesn't make us ignore the line breaks. Rather, the two forces – continuity in the sentence, isolation of the line – are set sharply against each other. These enjambed lines from "Oranges" by Gary Soto (1952–) emphasize the fluidity of the sentence (or rather sentence fragment) running through the lines despite interruptions:

> December. Frost cracking
> Beneath my steps, my breath
> Before me, then gone,
> As I walked toward
> Her house, the one whose
> Porch light burned yellow
> Night and day, in any weather.

The first line break fractures a participial phrase. The noun phrase that ends the second line is complete but obviously anticipates some kind of verb – which in fact we don't get: the line break marks a gap in which we must supply something like "going" or "moving." "[T]oward / Her house" is a prepositional phrase divided between lines, and "whose" is a relative adjective that belongs to a phrase not completed until we get "Porch light" in the next line. These enjambments momentarily suspend the sentence and represent the eager, halting steps of memory as it pieces together the eager, halting experience being recounted.

In contrast, "I Know a Man" by Robert Creeley (1926–2005) the line breaks splinter syntax so violently that we're almost surprised to find that by the end of the third stanza a kind of sentence has been produced, which the last stanza answers in the voice of a second speaker:

> As I sd to my
> friend, because I am
> always talking, – John, I
>
> sd, which was not his
> name, the darkness sur-
> rounds us, what
>
> can we do against
> it, or else, shall we &
> why not, buy a goddamn big car,
>
> drive, he sd, for
> christ's sake, look
> out where yr going.

Even beyond the fragmentation of noun phrases ("his / name") and prepositional phrases ("against / it"), Creeley highlights the written transcription of speech not only by his shorthand-style contractions ("sd," "yr") but by the ultimate enjambment, a break within the word "sur-/rounds."

Just one step less extreme than Creeley's intra-word line break is a break that detaches a **clitic** – a word like "the" which never stands alone – from the main word it depends on. Dividing these is a highly disruptive move which foregrounds the presence of the poet as *writer*, so poets use it only in rare contexts, as at this moment in the middle of John Ashbery's long poem "Self-Portrait in a Convex Mirror" (1975), a poem that offers a virtual catalog of enjambment types:

> The backing of the looking glass of the
> Unidentified but precisely sketched studio. ...

Even stranding a conjunction like "and" at the end of the line is likely to create a kind of melodramatic *over*-emphasis which poets avoid.

Enjambment is usually described, as here, in terms of the syntactical unit which is interrupted: a break between phrases is less strong or sharp than a break within a phrase, for example. More subtly, when we read the end of a line and before we go on to discover what syntax the line break *will turn out to have interrupted*, we can ask what kind of syntax the line *before* the break seems to have or might have. The first lines of two poems by Elizabeth Bishop demonstrate how this question illuminates our sense of the movement of the poem we're beginning to read. "At the Fishhouses" (1947) begins,

> Although it is a cold evening,

The line is a complete clause, but it's not just the comma at the end that tells us that the sentence will continue. The first word, "Although," makes the clause a dependent or subordinate one and tells us that this first clause ("it is a cold evening") will make the next clause surprising. (It will turn out to be "down by one of the fishhouses / an old man sits netting.") The opening line, then, announces that the poem's sentences will provide a rigorous structure for all the sensory information and thought the poem offers. The line teaches us something about how to read the rest of this poem, with what kinds of expectation. By the end Bishop's long sentences will encompass large and striking statements about the nature of "knowledge." The syntactical regimen established from the beginning is a fundamental part of what allows her to arrive there.

In contrast, here's the first line of "The Fish" (1940):

> I caught a tremendous fish

Though it has no terminal punctuation this clause could easily be a sentence by itself. This reduces the syntactical momentum. The following lines can add copious detail, but at the moment there is no further *statement* to be made. This turns out to reflect the whole poem's structure, in which the poet looks long and closely at the fish but takes no action until the last line: "And I let the fish go."

In all free verse – in all verse in fact – the degree to which a particular line *could* stand on its own syntactically is an important element in how it contributes to the ebb and flow of the poem's movement.

The terminology of syntactical constituents (prepositional phrase, conjunction, and so on) may be unfamiliar territory to you. This is unfortunate but not a disaster. Just as scansion is a helpful aid, so are grammatical terms. Still, we saw in Chapter 1 that the point of listening closely to a metrical line is not to scan it but to hear it, and something similar is true of syntax. Specifying the syntactical details of an enjambment can make its effect easier to describe to someone else – in an essay for example – but the important point is to hear how the enjambment works. Even without the terminology you can track your feeling for how the poem is moving forward and how each line's moment within it wants to linger. The ends of lines are the places where your double sense of continuity and separation are likely to play against each other most vividly.

Free Verse, Prose, and Syntax

Robert Frost famously said that "writing free verse is like playing tennis with the net down." (He first said it in an address at Milton Academy in 1935, during the controversy over free verse, but repeated it later. The gibe is almost as often quoted as Frost's poems.) The verse we've been examining here shows that the game of language is still played across a net even more essential to the game than meter: the syntax of sentences. Enjambment is only the most obvious way free verse can not only keep that net taut but even raise it.

We began by disputing the old charge that free verse is "prose cut into lines." Yet some free verse does maintain a close relationship with prose. The poems of D. H. Lawrence (1885–1930) are not always easy to distinguish from his prose. This is a whole poem called "Things Men Have Made" (1929):

> Things men have made with wakened hands, and put soft life into
> are awake through years with transferred touch, and go on glowing
>   for long years.
> And for this reason, some old things are lovely
> warm still with the life of forgotten men who made them.

If commas were added to the ends of the first and third lines and these two sentences were given as a speech to a character in a novel, it's hard to feel that we'd miss the line breaks. Setting this utterance apart as a poem still makes the basic difference of framing it, of course. But internally the language doesn't seem to care deeply that it's in lines.

A very different relation to what prose makes us think of as "normal" sentences is evident in poems by Samuel Beckett (1906–1989) such as this opening stanza from 1961 (the poem has no title except its first line):

> what would I do without this world faceless incurious
> where to be lasts but an instant where every instant
> spills in the void the ignorance of having been
> without this wave where in the end
> body and shadow together are engulfed
> what would I do without this silence where the murmurs die
> the pantings the frenzies towards succour towards love
> without this sky that soars
> above its ballast dust

We can trace one or probably two sentences here but they're deliberately tortuous. Probably the "where" in the middle of the fourth line begins a clause parallel to the "where" clause that begins the second line; probably in the third line "the ignorance" is the object of "spills." The four instances of "without" are probably all coordinated though they fall at different points in their lines. The lines, then, are deliberately interlinked with syntax in ways our study of enjambment has made familiar. But in the high-temperature vessel of this poem the syntax itself has been half-dissolved. (Beckett, one of the twentieth century's masters of prose, uses similar techniques in his novels and stories.)

Throughout this chapter we've seen how free verse can retain the sentence norms of prose and counterpoint them with line breaks in various ways. Beckett's alternative suggests that free verse can also take advantage of the heightened attention that poems generate to disrupt syntactical norms, which in turn lets us focus more intensely on their operation. Poetic language whose sentence structures are fragmented may come to resemble the language of speech or of thought or of dreams, rather than of prose.

Prose and Speech

Prose and speech are sometimes mistakenly confused. In Molière's play *The Bourgeois Gentilhomme* (*The Middle-Class Nobleman*) the title character, suddenly rich enough to take the lessons in fine language that will fit him for his new social station, learns that "I've been speaking prose for forty years without ever realizing it!" Molière is making fun of the teacher's pedantic assertion that "there are regrettably only two forms in which you may express yourself: poetry and prose." But prose is a *written* form and so quite separate from speech. Normal prose offers a highly formalized and rationalized version of the language of speech. This is most obvious in the rigorous system of modern punctuation; no one speaks a semicolon, though highly literate people may speak with a consciousness of the hierarchical organization of syntax that semicolons indicate. When that version of syntax is loosened, one direction in which it may go is toward speech. This is what happens in Robert Creeley's poem "I Know a Man," discussed earlier – though as verse it's still a written *imitation* of speech.

Syntax never disappears: it's built into language just as fundamentally as vocabulary, though we're usually far less aware of it. The almost invisible essentiality of syntax becomes clearer when we try to track our understanding of a small segment of Beckett's poem: "where to be lasts but an instant where every instant / spills in the void the ignorance of having been..." When we encounter "spills" we guess that it's a verb (not the noun in "please wipe up those spills") because we come to it from a clause that begins "where every instant." It's true that "every instant" *might* be an adverbial phrase – the spilling happens at every instant – but because "instant" was treated as a noun just a moment ago ("an instant") we try taking it as a noun here. If "every instant" is a noun phrase, what is its function? Since there's no earlier verb to conscript this phrase as a direct object, we predict that it will function as a subject governing some verb yet to come – and "spills" supplies the verb. If "spills" is a verb, we don't yet know whether it will have a direct object (it might work either as in "he spills the milk" or as in "the milk spills out") but we know that it either will or won't – that as a verb it will be either transitive or intransitive: these are categories that English syntax enforces. Next, after a prepositional phrase that specifies where the spilling takes place ("in the void") we get another noun phrase, "the ignorance," which has nothing else to attach itself to, so our best bet is to go back to "spills" and take "the ignorance" as its direct object. We're too avid for syntax to be willing not to attach the phrase "the ignorance" to anything at all, and if we don't hear it as an object we'll hear it as a new subject.

Tortuous as all this may sound, we do these calculations without thinking about them because our language-ready brains are always *parsing* the verbal input they receive. We can't turn off the automatic questioning that our parsing brains do. Rather, the poem can raise it to the level of conscious curiosity. In Theodore Roethke's villanelle "The Waking," for example, one of his refrain lines is: "I learn by going where I have to go." A sentence needs a verb and a verb is either transitive or intransitive. If "learn" is transitive then its object is the clause "where I have to go" (which "I learn by going"). But "learn" may be intransitive. If so, then "I learn" whatever it is that I learn (no object specified) "by going where I have to go." Roethke has encoded two distinct sentences in one line of nine words. The prose we read is usually designed to make our parsing task as easy as possible, but poems are sometimes interested in working our parsing muscles harder than that. One result may be that we marvel at how rich an intelligence we are granted simply by the fact of having language. More immediately, it gives the poet a way to say two things at once and make us think about the relation between them.

Gertrude Stein (1874–1946), another great experimentalist of language, scrutinizes sentences in similar ways in both her prose and her poems. Here is the beginning of section XV (out of 162) from her book-length poem *Stanzas in Meditation* (1932):

> Should they may be they might if they delight
> In why they must see it be there not only necessarily
> But which they might in which they might
> For which they might delight if they look there
> And they see there that they look there
> To see it be there which it is if it is
> Which may be where where it is
> If they do not occasion it to be different
> From what it is. ...

Unlike Beckett's verse, this firmly resists being parsed into complete sentences. Adding punctuation would be much more difficult and wouldn't help. Instead pieces of potential sentences seem to pile up and overlap. The chain of false starts, recommencements, and tentative turns displays what the rationalized syntax of most prose smooths over and conceals: the rhythm of thinking. As the poet John Ashbery says, comparing Stein's poem to the late novels of Henry James,

> If these works are highly complex and, for some, unreadable, it is not only because of the complicatedness of life, the subject, but also because they actually imitate its rhythm, its way of happening, in an attempt to draw our attention to another aspect of its true nature. Just as life is being constantly altered by each breath one draws, just as each second of life seems to alter the whole of what has gone before, so the endless process of elaboration which gives the work of these two writers a texture of bewildering luxuriance – that of a tropical rain-forest of ideas – seems to obey some rhythmic impulse at the heart of all happening.

At the same time, the repetition of words and phrases entailed by this project gives Stein's verse the additional auditory coherence of almost continuous rhyme and assonance.

This field of syntactical dislocations that Beckett and Stein explore – this dethroning of the sentence though not of syntax – has become part of the toolkit available to more recent poets too. The method of "Elegant Endings" by Richard Blanco (1968–) is clear from his first few lines:

> A foggy night, a long silver train, someone's hand
> pressed on the glass, crystallized breaths eclipsing
> a face in a window slowly moving past someone left
> with smoke clinging around their feet – that ending.
> Or the one with the glass shells of runway lights –
> cobalt, carmine, and jade dotting a stretch of tarmac
> below a plane lifting someone into the hull of night.
> Or maybe …

These "endings" are familiar to us from the final shots in countless movies. Just as those generic, detachable cinematic moments float free within our consciousness of "the movies," the poem presents them as isolated noun phrases. Timothy Donnelly (1969–) begins the first section of his poem "Three Panels Depending on the Heart" (2003) with a different array of fragments, not only noun phrases but partial verb phrases and clauses as well:

> Because I could forever, my theatrical body
> doubled over the bathtub estranged, a volcano;
> might continue clenched in this arrangement

> of numb white tile, white fixture, unfeelingly
> learning, a bent apprentice to the pitch
> of the wave of what mourning tows me along. ...

This is close to the method we saw in Stein's verse but put to a more imagistic use. Even the opening unfinished dependent clause, though it has no actual content ("could" what?), gives us the picture of an anguished gesture. The loaded words "I" and "forever" are largely responsible. The incompleteness of the clause itself helps verify the disconsolate stance. How far such shards of charged language can go in making a poem come across whole is an inquiry poets continue to pursue.

In Stein's poem we saw how the lens of verse can bring into focus both the potentialities of syntax and the intensities of sound in words. These are separate properties of language which happen to be produced by the same technique of writing. Examples like this and others we've examined suggest one final limitation of the two-dimensional chart we tried out in the previous section. The chart tracks just two features of poetic language: the length of lines and the way their ends interact with syntax. Yet some of the ways free verse – when written with enough attention to all the nets available – can encourage poets to write and readers to read involve more aspects of language than these two. In the first three chapters of this book we saw how a meter abstracts and organizes a few elements out of the rich, continuous, and inclusive field of linguistic rhythm. At its best and most characteristic free verse takes on a relation to the details of language that is more diffuse than that of metrical verse but therefore potentially more comprehensive. Good metrical verse always urges us to look beyond the meter; good free verse gives us no alternative.

How Free Is Free Verse?

In Chapter 2, as we investigated the various different systems of meter that poets have used in English, we noticed that from a perspective inside one of those systems any verse that lies outside it looks nonmetrical. From the point of view of iambic meter accentual verse and syllabic verse both seem defective or incomplete. For that matter, if syllabic meter is our norm most iambic pentameter looks irregular. In this peculiar sense, almost any verse might be considered nonmetrical, and when we say that a poem is in "free verse" we mean that it follows no known metrical system. Yet some free verse seems to lie very *near* the boundary of some familiar metrical territory. These poems make the problem of classification messy and difficult but they may also enrich it in ways that help us both in reading the poems themselves and in thinking about how different kinds of verse are related.

Dylan Thomas's "In My Craft or Sullen Art" (1946) seems like a good example of syllabic verse. It begins:

> In my craft or sullen art
> Exercised in the still night
> When only the moon rages
> And the lovers lie abed
> With all their griefs in their arms, ...

Every line is seven syllables long and the stress patterns shift freely and clearly from one line to the next just as we saw in Thom Gunn's "Considering the Snail" in Chapter 2. But the last line of the poem's first stanza – "Of their most secret heart." – has only six syllables. Is this a mistake? A design that escapes us? A deliberate imperfection like the ones woven into Navajo rugs to keep the human design open to a wider spirit universe? These questions are not answered but further complicated by the last line of the second (and final) stanza, "Nor heed my craft or art," and also – canceling any thought of a last-line-of-a-stanza rule – another six-syllable line within that stanza: "On these spindrift pages." Probably all we can say is that the poem is in seven-syllable lines except where it isn't. When free-verse lines are roughly the same length, which is most often true, some approximation to syllabic meter is almost inevitable. Thomas's poem may simply come unusually close to that metrical norm.

The same is true of accentual meter. Poetic language tends to be rhythmically denser than most speech and stress is almost unavoidably prominent in English verse. It follows that many poems in free verse stay fairly close to a constant number of stresses per line. As we saw in Chapter 2, accentual meter – for this very reason – must maintain an exceptionally clear norm to be recognized as metrical. By this measure not very many modern English poems are definitely accentually metrical. Yet many poets' free verse does sustain a relatively consistent line length of three to four stresses, or two to three, or occasionally four to five or more.

The poems of Philip Levine (1928–) often seem to be measured this way. Here are the opening stanzas of his "You Can Have It" (1991):

> My brother comes home from work
> and climbs the stairs to our room.
> I can hear the bed groan and his shoes drop
> one by one. You can have it, he says.
>
> The moonlight streams in the window
> and his unshaven face is whitened
> like the face of the moon. He will sleep
> long after noon and waken to find me gone. ...

The first line has three main stresses, though we hear a fourth if we stress both words in the loaded phrase "comes home." The next line is still more definitely a three-stress line, but the third line has at least four and the next is easier to hear with four than three. The second stanza opens with another pair of clear three-stress lines and the next line is almost as definite. The last of the lines quoted here ("long after noon and waken to find me gone") must have four stresses and probably five or even six. These variations don't defeat expectation, because the poem never established a clear (metrical) expectation. They do give us, in a way different from meter, an intriguing experience of variety within general consistency or constancy emerging from variety.

In Levine's narrower poems such as "For the Poets of Chile" (1976), the stresses tend to be more prominent and more unambiguous in number. This poem's first dozen lines include only a few that don't read easily as having two accents:

> Today I called for you,
> my death, like a cup
> of creamy milk I
> could drink in the cold dawn,
> I called you to come
> down soon. I woke up
> thinking of the thousands
> in the *futbol* stadium
> of Santiago de Chile,
> and I went cold, shaking
> my head as though
> I could shake it away. ...

In the fourth line it would feel odd to withhold stress from "drink" or "cold" or "dawn." Near the end of this passage the line "and I went cold, shaking," though we may emphasize only "cold" and "shaking," might have a third accent on "went." When we perform this line internally or out loud, if we're inclined to deliver it as two clear stresses it's largely because of the context of predominantly two-stress lines from which we come upon it: habit normalizes what we hear. The near-regularity may help us notice how both lines rely on the same word, "cold."

Again, when lines are longer their measure by number of accents becomes less definite. In Levine's "The Simple Truth" (1994) it may not be meaningful to identify any base number of accents:

> I bought a dollar and a half's worth of small red potatoes,
> took them home, boiled them in their jackets,
> and ate them for dinner with a little butter and salt. ...

Yet it's always evident that Levine is attending closely to these questions of measure, whether he adheres to an accentual norm or not. He makes this explicit in his 1988 poem, "A Theory of Prosody":

> When Nellie, my old pussy
> cat, was still in her prime,
> she would sit behind me
> as I wrote, and when the line
> got too long she'd reach
> one sudden black foreleg down
> and paw at the moving hand,
> the offensive one. The first
> time she drew blood I learned
> it was poetic to end
> a line anywhere to keep her
> quiet. After all, many morn-
> ings she'd gotten to the chair
> long before I was even up.
> Those nights I couldn't sleep
> she'd come and sit in my lap
> to calm me. So I figured
> I owed her the short cat line.

> She's dead now almost nine years,
> and before that there was one
> during which she faked attention
> and I faked obedience.
> Isn't that what it's about –
> pretending there's an alert cat
> who leaves nothing to chance.

The poem says nothing about beats or accents or metrical approximations or about anything usually identified as "prosody." If its lines are rigorously constrained, it says, the cause is the phantom cat. The cat's principle isn't an auditory one nor even visual in the sense in which for human readers (and writers) a poem has a visible shape – it concerns the action of the poet's hand. The "Theory" posits a field of impatience which the cat exercises and the poet ought to. The rule of the line is: don't go on too long. We might identify "too long" as anything over three accents, but this may or may not be a relevant measure of the amount of "attention" which – for this poem – is right. All that's sure is that "obedience" to the line's true limits, whatever they are, is essential. Certainly Levine's lines never just run out of steam. We feel each one push up hard against that invisible barrier at the right-hand margin, a barrier the poem teaches us to see as policed with sharp claws.

The most important and complex frontier of free verse lies along the border it shares with the accentual-syllabic meter dominant for so long in English poetry. The flexibility of that metrical regime, too, makes its boundaries less definite than those of meters with simpler foundations. Many free-verse poems play near this border or cross and recross it.

Vers Libéré

There's no widely accepted name for the kind of free verse that depends on and takes advantage of approximations to meter. The French term *vers libéré* – not *vers libre*, free verse, but "freed" verse – is sometimes borrowed, but it's misleading. Just as *vers libre* specifically signifies liberation from the strict syllable counting of classical French verse, *vers libéré* refers even more specifically to some nineteenth-century French poets' abandonment of rules about alternating masculine and feminine rhymes. The need for these particular freedoms is inherently less urgent in English, which has rarely paid much attention to such fixed rules.

T. S. Eliot's poems typically use this method. He declared that "No verse is free for the man who wants to do a good job." In a 1917 essay, "Reflections on 'Vers Libre'," he gives a clear explanation of the effect that he and others after him sought:

> We may therefore formulate as follows: the ghost of some simple metre [which is how he has described iambic pentameter] should lurk behind the arras in even the "freest" verse; to advance menacingly as we doze, and withdraw as we rouse.

(An "arras" is a curtain hung in front a wall, typically for the sake of warmth in a cold stone castle, which can conceal people, secret doors, and so on. In this passage both "ghost" and "arras" oddly recall *Hamlet* – Hamlet's dead father and the arras behind which Polonius hides and is killed by Hamlet's sword-thrust through it.) This image is very different from the feeling we have in reading William Carlos Williams's poems. The difference is deliberate on both sides.

Many of Eliot's lines fail any test for metricality, but in reading them we hear echoes from the repertoire of metrical tunes. He manipulates our recognition of meter without adopting the meter itself. Accustomed as we are to the various sounds of iambic pentameter, we can often hear his shorter lines as familiar fragments. Here are a few lines from "The Hollow Men" (1925) matched with quite standard scansion patterns we might find in blank verse:

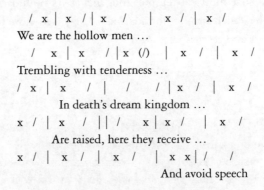

In this poem Eliot also mixes in occasional full pentameters:

> The supplication of a dead man's hand
> Under the twinkle of a fading star

Sometimes he divides a pentameter between lines which our ears easily recombine:

<pre>
 /   x | x   / | /   / | x   / | x   /
Lips that would kiss / Form prayers to broken stone.
</pre>

In longer lines in other poems Eliot sometimes uses a recognizable iambic pentameter but adds a further fragment to the end. Here are two separate lines from "Gerontion" (1920):

<pre>
 /   x | x   / | x / | x   / | x (/)
History has many cunning passages, contrived corridors ...
 x   / | x x / | x / | x / | x   / x
In memory only, reconsidered passion. Gives too soon ...
</pre>

("History" might have three syllables, "memory" only two; these hypothetical scansions are inherently uncertain.) Occasionally a long line seems to contain two overlapping pentameters:

<pre>
              / | x   / | x   / | x x   / | x   /
    x   / | x / | x   / | x   / | x   /
In fractured atoms. Gull against the wind, in the windy straits ...
</pre>

Such strategies are possible only because we're so used to these metrical patterns that we recognize them even when the other lines in their vicinity aren't metrical.

A more extended passage from "Burnt Norton," the first of Eliot's *Four Quartets* (1943), shows how he uses closer and more distant echoes of meter to shift our sense of a metrical background into and out of focus:

> Words move, music moves
> Only in time; but that which is only living
> Can only die. Words, after speech, reach
> Into the silence. Only by the form, the pattern,
> Can words or music reach
> The stillness, as a Chinese jar still
> Moves perpetually in its stillness.

187

> Not the stillness of the violin, while the note lasts,
> Not that only, but the co-existence,
> Or say that the end precedes the beginning,
> And the end and the beginning were always there
> Before the beginning and after the end,
> And all is always now. Words strain,
> Crack and sometimes break, under the burden,
> Under the tension, slip, slide, perish,
> Decay with imprecision, will not stay in place,
> Will not stay still ...

Part of the rhythmic effect in this passage comes from the repetition of "words" and "only," with smaller eddies of "music," "reach," "beginning," "end," and the plays on "still(ness)." But Eliot's main underlying means of control is to modulate among metrical approximations. The second line comes closest to a regular pentameter:

$$/ \quad x \mid x \quad / \mid x \quad / \mid \quad x \quad x / \mid x \quad / \quad x$$

Only in time; but that which is only living

With this tune established in our minds we're likely to justify the next line as metrical, though with an unusual defective foot at the end (the internal rhyme helps):

$$x \quad / \mid x \quad / \mid \quad / \quad / \mid x \quad / \quad \mid \quad /$$

Can only die. Words, after speech, reach

The sixth line is similar and the thirteenth line pushes this metrical variation even farther by ending with two defective feet:

$$x \quad / \mid x / \mid x \quad / \mid \quad / \quad \mid \quad /$$

And all is always now. Words strain,

In a thoroughly metrical context this line would feel out of place. Here, though, while the pentameter is close enough to the surface of the passage to make us hear the line as scanned, from the outset we've been prepared for lines that won't scan at all ("Words move, music moves"). Instead, that opening line of the passage presents a self-contained rhythm expanding from the spondaic "Words move" by adding a slack syllable ("music moves"), as the next line ("Only in time") adds another.

Other lines follow the "Gerontion" model:

/   x | x / | x   / | x(/) | x   /
Into the silence. Only by the form, the pattern

Later in the passage, as more unstressed syllables accumulate the lines depart more definitely from iambic pentameter. Although we can hear the eighth line as another pentameter-plus-a-fragment –

/ | x   / | x (/) | x   / | x /
Not the stillness of the violin, while the note lasts

– the twelfth line approaches if anything an anapestic norm:

x   / | x   x / | x   x   / | x   x   /
Before the beginning and after the end.

What was unstably iambic has flipped over into a different meter. Yet the line after that begins with three clear iambs again: "And all is always now." By both establishing a role for iambic pentameter and denying it supremacy Eliot achieves a firm control that still leaves plenty of room for surprise and dynamic expression.

Robert Hayden found the method of Eliot's verse valuable in his explorations of African American history and experience. Here is the first stanza of "A Ballad of Remembrance" (1948):

> Quadroon mermaids, Afro angels, black saints
> balanced upon the switchblades of that air
> and sang. Tight streets unfolding to the eye
> like fans of corrosion and elegiac lace
> crackled with their singing: Shadow of time. Shadow of blood.

The first and last of these lines would be difficult to scan in a convincing way. In between them, though, all three lines would be at home in any blank-verse poem. There aren't even many metrical substitutions aside from initial trochees and a spondee or two, until the two adjacent anapests loosen the fourth line in preparation for the fifth line's expansion beyond the limits of pentameter. Similarly, section III of Hayden's "Beginnings" shows how the modified expectations of this kind of verse let him establish a loose pentameter norm and then break it with the forceful rhythms of his short last line:

> Greatgrandma Easter, on my father's side,
> was a Virginia freedman's Indian bride.
> She was more than six feet tall. At ninety could
> still chop and tote firewood.

We respond to the metrical pace of the first three lines, perhaps unconsciously because of the many substitutions (especially anapests), and then respond differently to the dense rhythms of the last line, which seem to imitate the actions as he names them. The couplet rhyming helps keep the lines from acting too centrifugally.

Eliot's not-quite-metrical verse, as well as his allusions and his way of constructing long poems (such as "The Waste Land") by juxtaposing disparate materials, helped Hayden locate the methods he needed to handle his ambitious poem "Middle Passage" (1941). Its third section uses the story of the schooner *Amistad* which was first uncovered by another poet, Muriel Rukeyser (1913–1980), in her biography of the chemist Willard Gibbs (whose father was involved on behalf of the slaves in the trial following the boat's grounding). The opening stanza of this section of the poem, in its whole sound, recalls Eliot:

> Shuttles in the rocking loom of history,
> the dark ships move, the dark ships move,
> their bright ironical names
> like jests of kindness on a murderer's mouth;
> plough through thrashing glister toward
> fata morgana's lucent melting shore,
> weave toward New World littorals that are
> mirage and myth and actual shore.

If we're not sure how to scan the first line, the second line dismisses the question with its self-contained rhythm of repetition. The short third line might or might not remind us of an iambic trimeter, but the following line rings clear as a pentameter. The next lines move a little away from pentameter and back toward it, while the final line concentrates more on its four strong stresses than on any accentual-syllabic norm.

As William Carlos Williams gave poets one set of tools for dismantling the dominant meter, so Eliot gave other poets techniques for taking new kinds of liberties with the meter while relying on fragments of its tune. Gwendolyn Brooks (1917–2000) worked in both metrical and nonmetrical verse, but some of her most important poems toy with the boundary. "The Lovers of the Poor" (1960) is about a hundred lines long, and if statistical preponderance were the point we would have to call it an iambic pentameter poem. Yet if a large majority of its lines scan easily others refuse the treatment. Brooks is careful to begin with nonmetrical or metrically problematic lines rather than letting steady pentameters seem to disintegrate unaccountably. Here are the first lines of the poem (the opening word "arrive" continues the sentence which the title "The Lovers of the Poor" is revealed as having begun even before we knew we were embarked on a sentence):

> arrive. The Ladies from the Ladies' Betterment League
> Arrive in the afternoon, the late light slanting
> In diluted gold bars across the boulevard brag
> Of proud, seamed faces with mercy and murder hinting
> Here, there, interrupting, all deep and debonair,
> The pink paint on the innocence of fear;
> Walk in a gingerly manner up the hall.
> Cutting with knives served by their softest care,
> Served by their love, so barbarously fair.
> Whose mother taught: You'd better not be cruel!
> You had better not throw stones upon the wrens!
> Herein they kiss and coddle and assault
> Anew and dearly in the innocence
> With which they baffle nature. Who are full,
> Sleek, tender-clad, fit, fiftyish, a-glow, all
> Sweetly abortive, hinting at fat fruit, ...

If we wanted five feet from the opening line we would need a bizarre fourth paeon (x x x /) in the middle. The third line can probably be scanned only with an initial anapest followed by a bacchius, which would normally be enough to rule out any iambic pentameter. By the time we reach the sixth line –

$$x \quad / \quad | \quad / \quad x \quad | \; x \, / \, | \, x \; / \; | \; x \quad /$$
The pink paint on the innocence of fear;

– the pentameter has hit a stride which later lines will only occasionally disrupt completely:

Their money with their hundred flawless rose-nails seems...

Seen as iambically metrical, many of the poem's lines are exceptionally friendly to anapests, especially in pairs. Brooks also enjambs strongly: the exuberant fun she has at the Ladies' Betterment League's expense overruns the hurdles of line and meter. Yet if the meter operates *as* a hurdle it also serves as a springboard. Using thoroughly nonmetrical verse throughout the poem could make Brooks's satire feel too easy or too viciously like "stones upon the wrens." The meter gives her voice a framework and her high-handed treatment of it displays mastery, never carelessness.

In her later sequence "In the Mecca" (1968) – "the Mecca" is the name of a housing project in Chicago – Brooks's verse is much more distinctly nonmetrical, as in this brief passage from the middle of the poem:

> Death is easy.
> It may come quickly.
> It may come when nobody is ready.
> Death may come at any time. Mazola
> has never known Pepita S. but knows
> the strangest thing is when the stretcher goes! –
> the elegant hucksters bearing the body when the body
> leaves its late lair the last time leaves.
> With no plans for return.

The verse here recalls Hayden and Eliot. The middle of this passage focuses on a perfectly recognizable pentameter rhyming couplet. The following lines expand beyond metrical boundaries, then contract, and at the same time invent new rhythmic arrangements based on repetition.

5

Song

One kind of verse you probably run into even more often than free verse is songs. You may not even think of songs as verse, and there are good reasons for this which we'll come back to in a moment. But if you set out to write down the words of a song – for instance a recorded song you want to learn to sing – you would probably never write it as prose with the lines' ends determined only by the width of the paper.

Which Songs?

Which "songs" are we talking about? Song, as words combined with music, is a topic that covers the whole planet, all its languages, and a time-span that greatly exceeds that of written history. Practical considerations lead me to narrow my range of examples sharply. This is a book on poetry, not music, and I've almost entirely avoided using musical notation. Nor does it come with audio files or a CD. My choice is largely restricted, therefore, to songs that are either widely known in the English-speaking world because they have been very popular in recent decades, or readily accessible in various recordings on the Internet – or both.

One reason we automatically use verse to write down a song is that most songs *rhyme* in a regular way. When we think about why this is true we come to realize the different situation that language finds itself in when it's in a song rather than

Verse: An Introduction to Prosody, First Edition. Charles O. Hartman.
© 2015 John Wiley & Sons, Ltd. Published 2015 by John Wiley & Sons, Ltd.

a poem. Typically it's language we hear rather than read. This means that the *pace* of the language – the rate at which we receive it – is controlled by a performer, not by ourselves. If you're reading a poem and realize you misunderstood a word earlier in the current sentence, you can cast your eye back up the page. If you missed a word in a song someone is singing you wouldn't tell the singer to go back and repeat the word. Even listening back in a recording is more complicated than reading back in a text, and when we do it we're disturbing our reception of the work more than when reading.

This simple fact has far-reaching consequences. One is that the *density* of language is usually lower in songs than in poems. This applies to various kinds of density: the complexity of logic and narrative, the convolution of syntax, the piling up of images, and so on. Another consequence is that the language of songs tends strongly toward clear, well-marked formal features. Free-verse songs are rare. ("Potter's Field" by Tom Waits (1949–) is an example and there are others, but they stand out as strange and their unintuitive forms are inevitably part of their point – troubling the boundary between song and prose fiction, for instance.) Rhyme, especially, is a great help to the ear in making sense of a song. Rhyme is also mnemonic: an aid to remembering the words. These memory and sense-making functions support each other.

Listening is easier than reading in some ways and harder in others. Songs present challenges to our comprehension that are different from the difficulties we encounter in the language of poems. One phenomenon that displays this difference vividly is what we've come to call *mondegreens*. These are mishearings of song lyrics that we latch onto on some first listening and then often cling to.

Origin of "Mondegreen"

The term "mondegreen" was invented by Sylvia Wright in a 1954 essay in *Harper's Magazine*, "The Death of Lady Mondegreen." She recalls her mother singing to her as a child the old ballad "The Bonnie Earl O'Moray," which ends with the lines

> They have slain the Earl O'Moray
> And laid him on the green.

Wright heard the last line as "And Lady Mondegreen" and responded warmly to the tragic story of this person her own ear had invented. Her term has stuck. A Web search on "mondegreen" turns up millions of citations.

As a child someone I know heard "For he's a jolly good fellow … which nobody can deny" as "For he's a jolly good fellow … with so many candy knives." This goofy example has several things to tell us. One is that my friend's ear's interpretation was to say the least counterintuitive. Has anybody ever seen a candy knife? Even in terms of speech sound it's surprising: the "-y" in "deny" is a long way from "-ives," for instance. (The ear's error here probably originates with word boundary – "can deny" displaced by "candy knives" – which is often a challenge in hearing language. Inserting a false word boundary before a stressed syllable is common. It's easy to mishear "effect" as "a fact," "aplomb" as "a plum," and so on.) Another striking fact about what he heard is how vivid the image is. That's one sinister "fellow." Why does he need "so many" of these knives? The strangeness and the vividness – "which nobody can deny" is boring by contrast – combine in a way that may remind us of situations and images in dreams, and it's tempting to think that mondegreens like this tell us less about the song than about the psyche of the listener. The common mishearing of "'Scuse me while I kiss the sky" in "Purple Haze" by Jimi Hendrix (1942–1970) as "'Scuse me while I kiss this guy" seems like further evidence for psychological interpretations. By the same token, these possibilities of mishearing testify to how eagerly we respond to songs, how strongly they invite our imagination to lean into our listening. Songs, as intense language rushing by us, send our mechanisms of interpretation into high gear.

If we wouldn't transcribe the words of a song as prose then we must believe that the written representation of a song's lyrics ought to involve lines. Awkwardly, though, the definition of "line" that we've taken for granted in earlier chapters assumes that we're starting from a written artifact. Lines in a poem are defined *visually* by the ragged right-hand margin that we know signifies a series of choices on the part of the poet, whether those choices involve meter (the line end corresponds to the completion of an iambic pentameter, for instance) or not (the free-verse poet has ended the line where local conditions give it the richest effect). When we're writing down a song, how do we decide where to end lines? The shape of verse seems to be coming *after* the making of the song. This remains true in a sense even if we're the ones creating the song.

Still, we're almost certain to use line breaks when we put a song into written form. But how? Probably the simplest principle to use is that rhyme points define lines. The beginning of "Like a Rolling Stone" by Bob Dylan (1941–) might look like this:

> Once upon a time, you dressed so fine, threw the bums
>   a dime in your prime, didn't you?
> People call, say Beware doll, you're bound to fall, you thought
>   they were all a-kiddin' you

But if we didn't ignore most of the rhymes we might write this instead:

> Once upon a time
> You dressed so fine
> Threw the bums a dime
> In your prime,
> Didn't you?
> People call
> Say, Beware doll
> You're bound to fall
> You thought they were all
> A-kiddin' you

(Notice that this allows us to eliminate the commas. There are no commas as such in the song we hear. We'll expand on this point a bit later.) This second transcription corresponds better to our intuition of how the song works. There are two layers of regular rhyming here (aaaab ccccb) and the first transcription acknowledged only one of them.

Lines in Transcriptions

It's worth noticing that the "official" transcription of Dylan's song on bobdylan. com presents the opening words in these two lines:

> Once upon a time you dressed so fine
> You threw the bums a dime in your prime, didn't you?

This way of notating the song emphasizes different characteristics of the language – the cascade of what are now *internal* rhymes may remind us of writing like Jack Kerouac's in *On the Road*, which is surely one of the ancestors of Dylan's song. But the official version has the disadvantage of obscuring some regularities in the lyrics that our ears naturally pick out and actively depend on. When we come to the topic of overall form in a song, similar concerns will affect how we treat larger structures like stanzas.

Something to notice about Dylan's rhymes here is that they aren't exact, full rhymes. "Fine" doesn't *quite* rhyme with "time." In song, slant rhymes are sometimes but not always important to distinguish from full rhymes. For the same reason that rhyme is nearly universal in songs, it can be more approximate than in poems without our sensing a loosening of the notion of rhyme. Because our ears rely on rhyme to keep us on the song's track, we expect rhyme to arrive at regular intervals – these become the lengths of lines in our transcriptions – and this expectation in turn guides our hearing, so that it hardly occurs to us that "fine" sticks out from the series "time/dime/prime." On the other hand, the discrepancy between "didn't you" and "kiddin' you" is wide enough to make the pairing feel clever – a three-syllable *joke* rhyme.

The fact that "didn't you" has a rhyming mate five lines later shows that rhyme can organize our hearing of a song over fairly long stretches of time. In the original recording of the song on *Highway 61 Revisited* these two rhymes occur about nine seconds apart (and the time between them is crowded with four *different* rhymes on "-all/-oll"). Of course there are limits to how long the songwriter can expect us to retain the memory of a rhyme, but some writers like to toy with those limits. The more we're tested – at least up to the point where the test fails – the more actively engaged we feel in constructing the song as we hear it.

Lines in a song are not simply determined by the rhymes that we use to define their ends. To fit its musical context the line will also maintain a certain internal rhythmic measure. In some cases this internal measure closely resembles poetic meter. "Sisters of Mercy" by Leonard Cohen (1934–) can be scanned, when printed as text, as regular anapestic pentameter:

$$x \quad x \; / \mid x \quad x \quad / \mid x \quad x \quad / \mid x \quad x \; / \mid x \quad x \quad /$$
Oh the sisters of mercy, they are not departed or gone.

197

```
  x   x   /  |  x x   /  |  x x   /   |   x x /   |x   x  /
```
They were waiting for me when I thought that I just can't go on.
```
  x   x    /   |  x x  /  |x x  x /| x x    /   | x   x  /
```
And they brought me their comfort and later they brought me this song.
```
x  x  /  | x   x /  |x  x   /  | x     x   /| x   x  /
```
Oh I hope you run into them, you who've been travelling so long.

(Anapestic pentameter is a very rare meter in poems. In songs that do lend themselves to poetry-style scansion the selection of meters is different from the norms that prevail in metrical poetry.) Even here, though, the scansion might occasionally raise eyebrows. In the first line why is "are" stressed rather than "not"? The answer has to be that *once we have heard the song*, or if we know the waltz-time music of it, to some extent we adjust our sense of stress. We decide potentially ambiguous moments by letting the strong rhythmic expectations generated by the music dominate our reading of the words. We might also notice *expletives* that a modern *poet* would probably omit: words that are inserted in order to regularize the meter. "They" in the first line is one instance: this double-subject construction (the subject of the sentence is either "the sisters of mercy" or "they," but they refer to the same people) – though it occurs sometimes in casual speech ("My brother, he's a lawyer") – is much less common in *written* work of any kind whether poetry or prose. In the second line "that" is also an expletive: the syntactical system of English allows us to leave out the relative pronoun in sentences like this, but the song retains it for rhythmic purposes. Even the "Oh" that Cohen inserts at the beginnings of the first and fourth lines is really an expletive rather than an intensifying interjection ("Oh!").

When songs do conform to poetic meters, in other words, they usually do so by making certain accommodations. An extreme form of this adjustment strikes us when we hear the **wrenched accent** that is not uncommon in old ballads. You can hear accent being forced by rhyme and meter onto the last syllable of the last word in this stanza from "The Deceived Girl" (around 1600):

> I am a prisoner far from home,
> But if you'll only steal the key,
> I'll take you where the grass grows green,
> And make of you a great lady.

Most songs, unlike Cohen's, don't lend themselves to poetic scansion. Dylan's "Just Like Tom Thumb's Blues" begins with an anapestic pentameter just like Cohen's —

x   x   / | x   x   / | x x / | x   x   / | x   x   /
When you're lost in the rain in Juarez and it's Easter time too

— but very soon Dylan stuffs the line more full of words than the *poetic* meter can stand, though the *musical* structure maintained by the band keeps it organized:

/   /   /   /
You must pick one or the other though neither of them ought
/
to be what they claim ...

Songs' rhythms are dominated by the musical context. Though this is a large subject that belongs more to music theory than to a discussion of verse, one aspect of it comes up all the time as you listen carefully to songs. Often the main rhythmic constraint that the musical phrase places on the line is that the music provides just so many *beats* for the words to fit into. (A "beat" is much clearer – as concept and perhaps as direct experience – in music than in poetry. The down-beats you dance to are more equally spaced in time than the stresses in even the most regular reading of a poem in iambics.) The musical beats provide a *measure* for the words in a song whose solidity allows the words flexibility – even more than accentual meter allows flexible counts of syllables in poetry.

The variability can be drastic. Dylan's "Absolutely Sweet Marie" has two **bridge** sections (we'll return to this term later in this chapter) that begin with these lines:

Well anybody can be just like me, obviously ...

Well I don't know how it happened, but the riverboat
captain, he knows my fate ...

These two lines fall at equivalent positions within the song's form and are there-fore sung to the same melody and musical rhythm. Yet even visually it's obvious that the lines differ in length; on counting they turn out to be fourteen syllables versus nineteen. How does this come about? The music provides (as is often true) eight beats for the words in each of these lines. The last beat will normally be left empty so that a pause will keep one line from crowding into the next. (Dylan's "Subterranean Homesick Blues" is an example of a song that revels in crowding, since the unbroken welter contributes to the song's exhilarating feeling of a deluge of words and images. In that song the words fill almost every musical beat.) In "Absolutely Sweet Marie," of the seven beats usually available for stressed syllables the longer of these two lines fills just six:

<pre>
        /   /   /   /
Well I don't know how it happened but the riverboat captain,
        /   /
   he knows my fate
</pre>

In this line, not just the last but the last two available beats are left empty of words.

Songs and Scansion

My scansion here – just as with the Cohen song discussed earlier – depends on my hearing the song, not just looking at it on the page. In a poem we'd probably put a stress on "how" and maybe on "I" rather than "don't"; but Dylan doesn't. Scanning a poem, we diagram the hearing that the line's words themselves dictate, silent though they are, through our inner ear. Scanning a song is a different act of notating our listening to someone else's performance which is only partly represented on the page.

Surprisingly, the shorter of the two lines by *syllable* count actually fills more of the *beats*: seven. Here is how Dylan sings the line:

<pre>
      / /   / /   / /   /
Well anybody can be just like me, obviously
</pre>

This scansion again makes obvious the metrical difference between lines in songs and in poems. If this were accentual meter – a seven-stress line in a poem – we would never hear more than one accent on a single word. But that's how Dylan

200

sings the line, with the rhythmic collaboration of his musical accompaniment. He stretches "anybody" and "obviously" across two beats each. This contributes to the sarcastic tone of the line as he sings it.

The rule of thumb I offered earlier, that lines in a transcription should be broken at the points that mark rhymes, fails in the case of these two lines, and the glitch offers an important note of caution. "Riverboat captain" rhymes with "how it happened" (though the rhyme is clearer in the ear than to the eye). This might lead us to break the line into three, each two beats long:

> Well I don't know how it happened
> But the riverboat captain
> He knows my fate

But the matching "Well anybody" line contains equally strong but more chaotic internal rhymes: "anybody," "be," "me," "obviously." There's no clear way to divide this into smaller lines. More important, it's not possible to divide this line by rhyme in the *same* way as the other line. Since the two lines occupy equivalent positions within the song – the first line of what the music clearly marks as a bridge – to divide them differently would be to honor a local condition (rhymes occur sporadically even in speech, after all) at the expense of our understanding of the song's larger form. Transcriptions of songs' lyrics are most useful when they best bring out the structure of the language as shaped in part by the music that the transcription doesn't show. Rhymes define lines, but not all rhymes. In cases like these two lines it makes sense to speak of *internal rhyme* in songs, even though a strict application of the rhyme-as-line principle would logically rule out internal rhyme.

We have been noticing important differences between the language of songs and the language of poems, and we'll notice more. One reason for talking about songs in a book on *Verse*, however, is the historical continuity between poems and songs. It's too simple to say that poetry was born out of song.

Poetry and Music

A thumbnail history of poetry's age-old interaction with music that has at least some mythic validity is that after poems began to be written down poetry needed to carry musical accompaniment within itself – or on its own back like a turtle.

Poetry therefore developed a version of "meter" quite distinct from the performed pulse of music. Having to reinvent the drum in a silent medium led poetry to devise self-contained linguistic structures like the Latin dactylic hexameter and the English iambic pentameter. Of course these rhythmic patternings still *could* be sung whenever music was added back to the mix. But as we saw in this book's first three chapters, a meter embodied only in written verse can adequately control our rhythmic understanding of poetry's language in more or less silent reading.

Rather, poetry and song, as we understand those terms now, developed from a common ancestor much as humans and chimpanzees did. Before the two separated – which required at least the invention of writing – people performed and listened to events involving words and music for many thousands of years. They need not have thought of the words and the music as having categorically separate existences. Of course they could make (what we call) music by drumming or playing on flutes, and they used words for all the functions that make us the species we are. But when they put language to the kinds of uses that fall in the general territory of (what we call) poetry – praise, prayer, celebration, boasting, lament – it undoubtedly came naturally to them to shape their words musically by (doing what we call) singing them. It's not entirely surprising, therefore, that songs can show us some things about poems that we might not otherwise notice.

Words and Notes

We've been considering how language functions in songs in terms of general pacing and challenges to the listener's comprehension. But this is only one aspect of the transformation of words that takes place when they are wedded to music. Not only rhythm but melody, instrumentation, tempo, vocal style, and every other musical aspect of a song influences how we hear its words, whether the words get our primary attention (as in Dylan or Cohen) or not (as in Heavy Metal).

One way to think about how words behave in a marriage with music is to consider the challenges that a lyricist faces in fitting syllables to the notes of a melody. Of course many songs are written the other way around, but that approach – musically *setting* the pre-existing words of a poem – is a branch of musical composition, not our central concern here. For us it's more useful to think about a song like the Beatles' "Yesterday": we know that the melody came to Paul McCartney (1942–), reportedly in a dream, and several months went by before he found the right lyrics. In the meantime, as is common practice he gave the song a provisional or "working" title and dummy words. After all, the writer who begins from a melody continues work on the song by singing it, and it seems to be more natural to sing words, no matter how nonsensical, than to keep singing "da da da." In this case, the working title and first line that he kept repeating was "Scrambled Eggs."

"Scrambled Eggs" couldn't last, if only because the topics it suggested would not match well with the melody's mournful tone. Yet "scrambled eggs" did satisfy some requirements of song lyrics so basic that we rarely think about them. In the first place, the number of syllables matches the number of notes in the song's opening musical phrase.

Words and Notes: Melisma

It isn't strictly required that notes and syllables be identical in number. Extending a syllable over more than one note is called **melisma**. The "Gloria" near the end of each verse in the Christmas carol "Angels We Have Heard on High" is an extreme example: sixteen notes for that word's first syllable. Still, the *norm* in songs is one note per syllable.

On this basis, "scrambled eggs" works better than "peanuts" or "teriyaki," and we can feel confident that neither of those alternatives occurred to McCartney. Beyond that we know he would not have considered "hibiscus" or "diploma": not only the number of syllables but also the stresses of the phrase have to match the melody. (Wrenched accent defies this rule.) In the three-note opening of "Yesterday" the first and perhaps third notes are emphasized much more strongly than the second, and "scrambled eggs" satisfies this pattern.

Furthermore, many other three-syllable candidates are eliminated without ever being seriously considered because they don't make up a complete phrase. "Thank You For" would not have served even as a working title. There's a

In Barry Miles's biography McCartney is quoted as summarizing all these constraints in terms of the possibilities they left for active consideration:

> I remember mulling over the tune "Yesterday," and suddenly getting these little one-word openings to the verse. I started to develop the idea ... da-da da, yes-ter-day, sud-den-ly, fun-il-ly, mer-il-ly and Yes-ter-day, that's good. All my troubles seemed so far away. It's easy to rhyme those a's: say, nay, today, away, play, stay, there's a lot of rhymes and those fall in quite easily, so I gradually pieced it together from that journey. Sud-den-ly, ... another easy rhyme: e, me, tree, flea, we, and I had the basis of it.

An account of the songwriting process in terms of elimination leaves open the question of how the writer comes up with words that *don't* defy any of the constraints. This may be impossible to explain. (McCartney just speaks as though it's easy.) Yet a great many people, when presented with a melodic phrase, find that they can quickly think of a number of sets of words – maybe no better than "Scrambled eggs" – that satisfy all the conditions of syllable count and stress and phrasal closure and phonetic ease ("Tell me more," "Tannenbaum," "Candy cane" ...). After that the writing process becomes a matter of deciding which candidate phrases say something that feels worth saying and follow each other with enough logical or narrative continuity to add up to a sufficiently coherent whole statement. How much high-level continuity a song's words need is partly determined by style and musical genre.

This brings us to a deep connection between songs and poems. When a poet is working in meter, the meter or a particular rhythmic realization of it becomes a kind of *tune* for which sets of words then somehow suggest themselves just as they do for a musical phrase. As Ezra Pound says (in an early review of T. S. Eliot):

> Treatises full of musical notes and of long and short marks have never been convincingly used [for poetry]. Find a man with thematic invention and all he can say is that he gets what the Celts call a "chune" in his head, and that the words "go into it," or when they don't "go into it" they "stick out and worry him."

Perhaps not all metrical poets think of their work this way, but surely *no* poet thinks of the job as gluing a stressed syllable onto an unstressed syllable, gluing on another unstressed one after that, and so on. This analogy can be extended equally well to free verse. In this case the "tunes" aren't metrical, but they are rhythmic "tunes" nonetheless, related to the "tunes" of stress and pace native to all our speech. We might also find that the **intonation** patterns of speech play a role somewhat like the musical role of pitch organized as melody. The pitch patterns of speech vary continuously, unlike the discrete pitches in most music, but there's an obvious common ground.

We can get a closer look at the matching of words and notes in song by considering extreme forms of it. Tom Lehrer (1928–), whose day job is as a mathematician, has accomplished some admirable technical feats as a songwriter. One section of "When You Are Old and Gray" (beginning with "An awful debility") manages to rhyme on "-ility" – in lines just seven syllables long, of which that suffix takes up three – sixteen times in a row while remaining completely coherent. From this craft perspective, his masterpiece may be "The Elements." The project in this case is not just fitting words to a pre-existing melody – the melody is taken from "The Major-General's Song" in Gilbert and Sullivan's *Pirates of Penzance* – but using pre-existing words as well, since the lyric consists (until the very end) almost entirely of the names of the chemical elements. Here's the first stanza:

> There's antimony, arsenic, aluminum, selenium,
> And hydrogen and oxygen and nitrogen and rhenium,
> And nickel, neodymium, neptunium, germanium,
> And iron, americium, ruthenium, uranium,
> Europium, zirconium, lutetium, vanadium,
> And lanthanum and osmium and astatine and radium
> And gold and protactinium and indium and gallium
> And iodine and thorium and thulium and thallium. ...

Rhyming is not the main challenge here because so many element-names end in "-ium." Continuing the alphabetical order hinted at in the beginning of the first line would have made the task impossible. As it is, Lehrer had to sort through the list of names – obviously he had to use *all* of them – and distribute them among his lines while the lines' shape was dictated by Sir Arthur Sullivan's melody. Even while solving this like an especially dense word puzzle, Lehrer contrives a few lines like the one above about thorium, thulium, and thallium, and this later on:

> And cadmium and calcium and chromium and curium.

The alliterations add an extra element of glee, as do the other consonances, asso-nances, and alphabetical order. The pleasure a *tour de force* gives us is increased when the master tops his own mastery.

Another angle on the lyric craft of songwriting is provided by deliberate subversions. Like the norms of metrical verse, the norms of songwriting can be defied or undermined for comic or satiric effect. The opening song on the debut album by the Roches (Maggie, Terre, and Suzzy) is called "We." It's a half-serious, half-sardonic self-introduction. The Roche sisters are skillful singers, as is evident in their *a capella* three-voice reduction of the "Hallelujah" chorus from Handel's *Messiah*. Their songs are often self-deprecating in a way that seems characteristic of their time: *The Roches* came out in 1979, and their next album was called *Nurds* (1980). The opening song on the first album, "We," introduces this tone along with the three singer-songwriters themselves. Here is its first stanza:

> We are Maggie and Terre and Suzzy
> Maggie and Terre and Suzzy Roche
> We don't give out our ages
> And we don't give out our phone numbers
> Give out our phone numbers
> Sometimes our voices give out
> But not our ages and our phone numbers

Even on the page some of the comedy is apparent in the corny play on "give out" and the awkward repetitions. This is the comedy of pretended incompetence – as if they didn't know any better as songwriters – here enlisted to support an intri-cate comedy of girlishness. On hearing, the tone is much clearer, especially in the last line: through rhythm and emphatic extension of the melody the music strongly emphasizes the final syllable – which can't take it ("num-BERS"?) and laughably breaks under the strain. The same comic disaster strikes elsewhere in the song, as when almost every stress is displaced in these lines:

> /   /   /   /
> We come from deepest New Jersey
> /   /   /   /
> But now we live in New York City

207

Another stanza, a satire on self-promotion and celebrity, begins with "Who have we worked with?" The line's perky tone (Let us show you our credentials!) is undercut by the ill-fitting, wandering melisma on "Who," a word much less important than "worked" yet spread over four syllables. When the line is followed by "Do we know anybody famous" and then "Anybody famous / Do we know anybody famous," the anxiety mounts to a degree that would be pathetic if it weren't so droll. To make comedy out of defying the norms of "good songwriting" requires knowing those norms intimately. The writers also count on our knowing these norms just as well; we're in on the joke.

The US national anthem offers examples of less well-calculated mismatches between words and notes. Francis Scott Key (1779–1843) wrote his poem "The Defence of Fort McHenry" (later titled "The Star-Spangled Banner") after witnessing a battle in the War of 1812. He published it as a poem, and it's not clear that he thought of it as sung from the outset, nor that he was the one who matched it with the British tune "The Anacreontic Song" by John Stafford Smith (1750–1836). The match is at best approximate. The poem is in fairly regular anapestic tetrameter and the tune is a slow waltz; so far, so good. Fortunately the first stanza, the only one Americans ever sing, doesn't present too many rhythmic tangles, though the melody's large range makes it notoriously difficult to sing. "Whose broad stripes" is a bacchius, but unlike the one that immediately follows it, "and bright stars," the foot at the start of the line is set to a quick rhythm that makes "broad" hard to fit in and the consonantal tangle of "broad stripes" tricky for the tongue to negotiate. Melodic contours oddly emphasize "by" in "by the dawn's early light" and "through" in "through the perilous fight." On the page these prepositions nestle innocuously within their anapests, but the tune thrusts them into inappropriate prominence. The three further, unsung stanzas raise still more daunting hurdles. To take one example of many, the last stanza begins (think of the tune of "O say can you see, by the dawn's early light"):

        x / | xx / | x   x   / | x   x   /
        O thus be it ever, when freemen shall stand

There's no reason why a word in an anapestic *poem* shouldn't cross the boundary between feet; it happens all the time in iambics too. If you try singing this line, however, you can't miss the miscalculation of "ever." (A line from the third stanza, at the same melodic position, is potentially even more disastrous: "A home and a country, should leave us no more.") Whether the oversight is Key's or not isn't certain. For what it's worth, the very different words by Ralph Tomlinson for which Smith originally composed the tune – a drinking-club song – don't fit it much better: "To Anacreon in Heav'n, where he sat in full Glee ..."

I've been emphasizing rhythmic relations between words and notes more than melodic ones. This makes sense because rhythm – stress, syllable quality, and so on – is the stronger common ground between language and music. It also fits with my intention to avoid musical notation, which only some readers will recognize. To end this section, however, I want to break that rule by pointing toward some kinds of melodic matching that help join words to tunes. The notation in this case is easy enough to read on the simple principle that notes written higher on the five-line staff are higher in pitch.

"Michael from Mountains", an early song by Joni Mitchell (1943–), is an elaborately skillful work of formal craftsmanship, though the skill is quieter than Tom Lehrer's. Mitchell's rhymes and her play with word sound, for instance, are exceptionally intricate:

> ... And umbrellas bright on a gray background
> There's oil on the puddles in taffeta patterns
> That run down the drain
> In colored arrangements
> That Michael will change
> With a stick that he found ...

Even without the music, in the first of these lines you can hear the play of "-br-," "-b-," and "-gr-." The half-buried rhymes of "drain," "arrangements," and "change" are clearer when heard than when read. This is word music above and beyond the call of duty in a song. Mitchell's word designs are so extravagant that they register for us as the singer's pleasure in her own work, which we further hear as echoing the pleasure she takes in her lover's company. Within this rich regime it may not be surprising to find her playing neat tricks with melody as well:

he takes you up streets

and the rain comes down

yel-low slick-ers up on swings

The first of these phrases translates its own word "up" directly into rising pitches. That might seem like an accident — a melodic line has to go *somewhere* after all — but once we hear the following line's pitches falling like the rain to which it refers, we know that the effect is deliberate. More subtly, the third phrase "swings" up and down. In every case the melodic line is one that will be repeated in other stanzas with other words that can't always take advantage of the line's pitch direction. Effects like this can only be local. Yet like the much more pervasive gestures of fitting words and notes together rhythmically, they contribute to our sense not only of the song's craft but of the joy of exercising that craft. It's an exuberance we can share by hearing.

Song Forms

So far we have been examining songs on a relatively microscopic level: syllables, notes, lines, musical and verbal phrases. Songs are distinct from poems also, however, on macroscopic levels of form. This isn't entirely true: many of the standard "set" forms for poems began as song forms. "Sonnet" comes from an Italian or French word meaning "little song." The term "villanelle" (though the poetic form itself may be quite modern) originated in a rustic dance. "Ballad" is a term almost equally at home in the now-separate worlds of poetry and song. Yet after the gradual separation of those worlds, poetic metrical forms, which needed to find their own feet (as it were) without the support of music, developed in directions not as congenial to song. Iambic pentameter, for example, is, as we've seen, a highly developed form dominant in English poetry, but it's only incidentally found in songs.

Song forms can be divided into a few general types — based on lines, on stanzas, or on more complex assemblages of sections — with one major adjunct available to all variants, the refrain. Here we'll review the abstract characteristics of each type and in the next sections we'll examine examples of each in more detail.

Stichic songs are collections of *lines* without any larger regularity of organization.

Why "Stichic"?

"Stichic" (which in English is usually pronounced "*stick*-ick") comes from the Greek word *stichos*, which simply means a "line" of verse. The same Greek root turns up in some other terms in poetics. **Stichomythia** ("line-talk") describes a passage of dramatic verse in which two characters spar with each other through an exchange of what in the era of stand-up comedy we call "one-liners." A **distich** is a pair of lines, a term used for lines logically bound in pairs but without the rhyme that would make us call them a "couplet," like the stanzas of the ghazals we saw in Chapter 3. The **hemistich** or "half-line" is an important prosodic unit in Anglo-Saxon verse, whose rules of accent and alliteration are formulated in terms of two-stress units that regularly pair up in units we would now usually call four-stress "lines."

This negative definition may seem puzzling. We have seen that songs, because they appeal to the ear without help from the acrobatics of the eye, depend more heavily than poems on formal elements such as rhyme. Regular rhyme, though, would make structures larger than the line. How can a song do without this kind of organization?

Popular songs do tend strongly toward stanzaic and larger forms. But epics, for example, are generally stichic. Homer's *Iliad* and *Odyssey* and Virgil's *Aeneid* are all in regular meters (the Classical dactylic hexameter) but are not rhymed. Their larger patterns are irregular, narrative ones. It was because he knew this that John Milton used blank verse (unrhymed pentameter) for his Biblical epic *Paradise Lost*. Homer's epics were performed – sung to the accompaniment of a stringed instrument – rather than written, because Homer (assuming he existed as an individual poet) lived during a time without writing. Virgil's and Milton's poems were written and published, but they consciously imitate Homer's sung epics. These very long works are organized above the level of the metrical line in many of the same ways as prose fiction: by scenes, the speeches of characters, and so on.

211

powerful tendency for musical phrases to be coextensive with verbal phrases, or more exactly, with syntactical constituents. This principle is related to the general irrelevance of punctuation to songs that we noticed earlier: matching verbal phrases to musical ones fulfills many of the duties that punctuation performs in writing. For the same reasons enjambment is relatively rare in songs. As we saw in previous chapters, enjambment requires us to process syntax across a gap of suspension (in written verse the line break), and in a song this means processing across a gap in time – a rest in the words filled by music – which is under the control of the performer rather than ourselves. When enjambment does occur in songs it tends to shift us toward a more cerebral and less directly emotional response. It can also confuse us, and songwriters sometimes use that befuddlement for particular effects. Some stanzas in Procol Harum's psychedelic song "A Christmas Camel" enlist enjambment to emphasize disorientation:

> Some Santa Claus-like face of note
> Entreats my ears to set afloat
> My feeble, sick, and weary brain
> And I am overcome with shame
> And hide inside my overcoat
> And hurriedly begin to quote
> And some Arabian sheik most grand
> Impersonates a hotdog stand

The songwriters' goal here is not to help us *follow* the lyrics but to enmesh us in hallucinatory half-perceptions.

Back once more to "Yesterday": Aside from its wrong tone, "Scrambled eggs" presented a subtler problem as a phrase to sing. The problem is underscored when we include the second line that McCartney used for working lyrics: "Oh, my baby how I love your legs." Songs almost always need to rhyme, but the "eggs / legs" rhyme doesn't lend itself to singing. The tendency is for the voice to linger over a line's last syllable. The more engaged the singer the stronger the impulse to leave room for the play of lilt and vibrato at the end of the phrase. Singers and therefore songwriters prefer to end lines with vowels or with consonants that are **continuants** like 'r' or 'n' rather than **stops** like 'g'. In this and similar ways, the virtually infinite range of possible language for a musical phrase very quickly gets filtered down to manageable proportions.

their language to us in discrete packages shaped by rhyme and repeated as many times as necessary. The main difference between stanzaic songs and stanzaic poems is that in song the music repeats in tandem with the lyric form. This means that the words in every stanza must succeed at the kinds of matching with notes that we explored earlier in this chapter. When Joni Mitchell made one intricately patterned stanza for "Michael from Mountains" she was committing herself to repeating that pattern several more times using different words. This is a little harder than maintaining a poetic metrical pattern in stanzas like those we saw by George Herbert in Chapter 3. The music sets additional conditions.

This increased formal burden on the stanzas is one motive, though not the most important, for the frequent use of refrains in songs. A refrain by definition repeats the *same* words to the same melody. It's possible, therefore, to make the matching of syllable and note especially exact and expressive in a refrain to a degree that would be more difficult to maintain in the changing words of stanzas generally.

Refrains vary a great deal in length, as a few examples from Dylan will show. In "Gates of Eden" he ends each of nine stanzas with the title phrase, altered each time by the context of a different preposition: "Heading for the Gates of Eden," "And there are no truths outside the Gates of Eden," and so on. In the very first stanza the refrain is reduced even further to a single word: "All except when 'neath the trees of Eden." This refrain is never rhymed within the song's stanzas; it's as if the repetition from stanza to stanza took the place of rhyme. (In fact the line in each stanza that *precedes* the refrain is often, though not always, unrhymed as well. Since every stanza begins with a strongly marked pair of rhymes, this suspension of rhyme adds emphasis to the refrain.) In a few songs a single-line refrain interrupts the stanza ("Turn, turn again" in "Percy's Song"), a pattern borrowed from old ballads. Sometimes a refrain line comes at the beginning of the stanza. In "A Hard Rain's a-Gonna Fall" – just as in the early ballad "Lord Rendal" which Dylan used as his model – each stanza develops its long answer to the short question with which it begins (a refrain with variations): "Oh where have you been, my blue-eyed son?"; "Oh what did you see, my blue-eyed son?"; and so on. In contrast "Mr. Tambourine Man" has a refrain about the same length as the varying stanzas themselves. Unusually, as if to emphasize the independent stature of this long refrain, Dylan sings it at the beginning of the song as well as after each stanza.

The "Verse-Chorus" Alternative

When a refrain is as fully developed as the one in "Mr. Tambourine Man," it's sometimes called a "chorus." The term "Verse-Chorus structure" is often used for songs – especially since about 1960 – in which "verses" (whose words change from one instance to the next) alternate with "choruses" (whose words stay the same). Perhaps a majority of popular songs from the past fifty years follow this pattern.

Unfortunately the competing terminologies can be confusing. In this book, partly because without audio examples or musical notation it's hard to keep formal distinctions among songs clear, I've opted for the simplest and most explicit terminology: "stanza" and "refrain." As we've noticed before, "verse" is a highly ambiguous word (and we'll need to use yet another meaning of it later in this chapter). "Chorus" can be a useful term, but in relation to song structure it's exactly synonymous with "stanza-length refrain." "Stanza" and "refrain" have the additional minor advantage for our purposes here that they are terms primarily associated with the words rather than the music of a song.

The songs listed here also suggest some of the thematic and dynamic functions that refrains can perform aside from their formal contribution. To put it very generally: while the sequence of stanzas enacts forward motion in time (and by the same token often tells a story), the refrains are moments when time stands still, moments to which the song returns again and again. If stanzas tend to narrate events, refrains tend to comment on them or stand off in some more abstract relation. (In many old ballads the refrain isn't even asked to make sense. The refrain in "Sir Lionel" just says, "Dellum down, dellum down.") In the early seventeenth-century "Blow Away the Morning Dew," the stanzas tell a little cautionary tale about country courtship, virginity, and so on. The refrain punctuates this narrative repeatedly with a purely lyric celebration of rustic life:

> And sing blow away the morning dew
> The dew, and the dew.
> Blow away the morning dew,
> How sweet the winds do blow.

Although by no means all stanzaic songs use refrains, they are a very common supplement to stanzas.

Two particular stanza forms are widespread and distinctive enough to warrant special mention. One we have already seen in Chapters 2 and 3: the ballad stanza, which has been used in songs in English for hundreds of years. The usual account of the meter in ballad stanzas is that it alternates four- and three-stress accentual lines. In a musical context it's easier to hear that the line is really always four beats long – which fits the powers-of-two structures (two, four, eight units) that are almost ubiquitous in Western popular music – but that in the second and fourth lines the last beat is habitually left empty of words. One example among thousands is a song made up sometime before Shakespeare died in 1616. It tells a familiar story of adultery and death involving one Lord Arlen, his wife, and her lover Mattie Groves, whose name is sometimes used as the ballad's title. Here are a stanza from the middle (notice the wrenched accent in the third line) and one from the end:

> /   /   /   /
> Get up, get up! Lord Arlen cried
> /   /   /
> Get up as quick as you can
> /   /   /   /
> It'll never be said in fair England
> /   /   /
> I slew a naked man!
>
> ...
>
> /   /   /   /
> A grave, a grave, Lord Arlen cried,
> /   /   /
> To put these lovers in
> /   / /   /
> But bury my lady at the top
> /   /   /
> For she was of noble kin.

Ballads are common currency in England, Scotland, Ireland, and America. In contrast, the **blues** form is native to America, the invention of descendants of African slaves probably late in the nineteenth century. (In the 1950s and 1960s British musicians became devotees of blues form and the performance style that went with it. The Rolling Stones, John Mayall, and others helped bring the blues back into popularity in the United States as part of the so-called "British Invasion.") The musical characteristics of blues – certain chord progressions, microtonally "bent" notes, and so on – are more striking than the form of the words, but there is a standard blues stanza of three lines, the second normally identical to the first and all three rhymed. Here are the opening stanzas of "Bad Luck Blues" by Ma Rainey (1886–1939):

> Hey people, listen while I spread my news
> Hey people, listen while I spread my news
> I wanna tell you people all about my bad luck blues

> Did you ever wake up just at the break of day
> Did you ever break up just at the wake of day
> With your arms around the pillow where your daddy used to lay

Individual blues stanzas migrate easily from one song (and performance, and performer) to another. As Dave Van Ronk (1936–2002), the folksinger, remarks in his memoir *The Mayor of MacDougal Street*, "blues is different. Blues is like a kielbasa … you don't sing a whole blues, you just cut off a section." The free-floating character of blues stanzas goes along with the fact that unlike a ballad, which almost always takes telling a story as its central task, a blues song is more often the expression of a state ("the blues") than a narrative.

The third and final type of structure often found in the kinds of songs we're examining does not have a conventional name, but we might call it "whole-song" structure just as in Chapter 3 we used the term "whole-poem" forms for sonnets, villanelles, and other forms not made up of repeating identical parts. After World War I, **whole-song** forms became common in show tunes and the jazz standards derived from them. Even now they show up frequently in popular songs. The most typical whole-song structure is annotated **AABA**. This means that the song has four sections – often called **strains** – in which the music is identical in the first, second, and fourth but differs in the third. The B-strain has several other names ("middle eight," "channel") but the most common name is **bridge**. The shift from the second A-strain into the bridge and back again invites the songwriter to make a transition of some kind – in tone (for example, from complaint to hope), in temporal focus (past versus present, present versus eternal), or in some other thematic dimension – and then shift back again with a new perspective. Often the music moves into a different key in the bridge. These musical and verbal shifts underscore and support each other. The moment of return from the bridge to the final A-strain is almost automatically climactic, though the climax can be handled in countless ways.

"Over the Rainbow" is often used as an especially clear example of AABA form. The Beatles' "I Want to Hold Your Hand," too, is a widely known song with an AABA form. (This is only slightly complicated by repetition of the bridge and final A-strain one more time at the end of the performance – a very common practice.) The A-strains –

> Oh, yeah, I'll tell you something …
> Oh please say to me …
> Yeah, you got that something …

– are all set to the driving, familiar tune in the key of G. The bridge – "And when I touch you I feel happy inside" – shifts down to what feels like the slightly darker key of C major. Though the tempo remains the same, the drum part and the guitar strumming both become less relentless. The lyrics, too, modulate from the "you" on which all the A-strains focus to a more inward observation of the singer's own state ("And when I touch you…").

"I Want to Hold Your Hand" also shows that AABA structure can incorporate a refrain as well. Every A-strain ends with the title line. The B-strain does not. By incorporating both the ecstatic refrain, repeated three times at the end of each A-strain, and the contrasting music and tone of the B-strain, the Beatles get about as much dramatic mileage out of the standard components of whole-song form as possible.

AABA is not as far as these whole-song forms go. Songs with two or more different bridges – AABABA, for example – are not common but Dylan's work beginning in the mid-1960s is full of them. On the other hand, A and B seem to be the only letters we need for notating these structures within the styles of music we're considering here. In other musical traditions this is not true. Scott Joplin's ragtime compositions are built of a larger number of contrasting sections. His "Maple Leaf Rag" would be notated like this: AABBACCDD. Broadway show tunes traditionally follow the AABA pattern, but precede it with an introductory passage that is less melodically developed and serves as a transition from the show's spoken dialogue into the song itself. Confusingly, this introductory section – which is usually omitted in non-theatrical recordings of show tunes – is called the "Verse." (There are countless recordings of "Body and Soul," but very few of them – a few by Billie Holiday (1915–1959) – include the Verse.)

"Verse-Chorus" Revisited

Earlier we noticed the term "Verse-Chorus structure." Now we can see how it developed from the names for parts of the show-tune structure. The AABA part – the part of "Body and Soul" or "I Got Rhythm" or "All the Things You Are" that everybody knows – becomes the "Chorus," while the preceding "Verse" is the part that everyone forgets. However, songs in "Verse-Chorus" style since the 1960s have not one but several "verses" with different lyrics, each followed by a "chorus" with repeating words. Because the terms change meaning, it's confusing to retain them, and this is why I have stuck with "stanza" and "refrain" in most contexts.

Popular music, however, when not content with stanzas (perhaps with a refrain) seems to find all the structural variety it needs within just a two-strain system, A and B.

The discussion of the following three more detailed examples will make much more sense if you find and listen to the song itself. Fortunately that is much easier to do now than it was even a few years ago.

Example: Stichic

Carl Hancock Rux (1975–) released "No Black Male Show" on his 1999 CD, *Rux Revue*. It's not hip-hop though it's very conscious of hip-hop. Parts of the track (almost eight minutes long) look with a disillusioned eye at the simultaneous self-aggrandizing narcissism of hip-hop performers and their gullible exploitation by a music and wider entertainment industry which cared little about the artists. (This is well before the developments that led to Jay-Z's triumphant declaration that "I'm not a businessman, I'm a business, man.") The track's musical background – which begins before the words, continues under them, and in one section (2:58–3:34) submerges them to inaudibility – utilizes a pared-down version of hip-hop instrumentation: a slow, steady drum part (bass drum plus snare and hi-hat played with brushes), a skeletal bass line, and a keyboard that plays long chords in a simple alternation. It's apparently played by live musicians without samples or loops.

The piece is not exactly or obviously a song: Rux, whose voice is a rich baritone, speaks the words rather than singing them. He has training as an actor as well as being a published poet. It's not surprising that he later developed the text into a theater piece. Over the subdued musical foundation supplied by his producers Tom Rothrock and Rob Schnapf, Rux speaks about 1,000 words which, unlike hip-hop lyrics, rarely rhyme. Here is one section of the text he performs (4:39–6:06):

> ...You be having these kinds of conversations
> You be sharing cigarette butts outside the Martin Beck discussing
> Chekhov's first act with Doctor West
> In a Russian vernacular, and still
> Ain't nobody paying admission to hear your dreams on Open Mic
> Night
> Of "That Great Gettin' Up Morning" when you might could maybe
> what the hell with Jesus, just
> Get across the Manhattan Bridge
> Be canonized tragically on Great Jones Place
> Yes, you be
> Dreaming of record deals and winning poetry slams
> Warning: the slam judges don't know the difference between a
> sestina and a simile
> Warning: this may be hazardous to your health
> Warning: your heroes never did this to themselves
> Warning: some of your heroes are drunk and vomiting in the
> alleyways
> Shootin' smack and countin' the metaphors on the page like
> Rosary beads, hoping for tenure track from purple lips and vodka
> spittle
> Warning: Broadway is only interested in you posthumously

219

Stichic song abounds today in hip-hop, rap, and the whole range of "spoken word" poetries. Hip-hop lyrics, sometimes improvised and usually at least pretending to be so, almost always rhyme heavily, and the crafting of them is sometimes called "rhyming." But rhyme is *so* central to these works that it often comes too thick and fast to make regular structures beyond the line. Even couplets may dissolve when the line rhymes internally. Here is a brief section of Big Daddy Kane's "Put Your Weight on It":

> Cause I leave em panickin when I start damagin
> Kickin this swift, leaves you stiff, like a mannequin
> And frozen, this is a mind explosion
> as the chosen flows in, the competition throws in
> the towel, my sharp tongue is like a license
> I strike like Mike, Tyson I be icin

The rhyme between "explosion" and "throws in" – though it exemplifies the extravagant invention prized in hip-hop – is no more important and hardly more structural in function than the intermediary rhymes on "frozen," "chosen," and "flows in." The goal is not structure but torrent. It's not accidental that one of the chief themes of hip-hop is the brag itself. As Kane boasts later in the same rap,

> Lyrics are bright and recite on the mic to excite
> delight, ignite, a bright light and a fright night
> for types who bite, to be quite like
> the man with mic swingin all tight, but can't get it right

It's not certain that "stichic" is quite the right term here. In work of this kind, as we'll see shortly in a more extended example, performance and music and breath do define lines – a transcription as prose would feel wrong – but the unit of composition may be not the line but the rhyme itself, returned to as quickly as possible and sustained for as long as possible. To have all these rhymes dictate the ends of lines on the page would make for misleading chaos. On the whole a stichic transcription is probably the best compromise.

Outside of epic and hip-hop, stichic songs are rare. By far the largest number of songs you're likely to hear are stanzaic. Like stanzaic poems, they present

> Warning: publishers aren't buying books 'bout nothin' but your
>   tragedy
> Warning: the record companies want to buy you and your
>   publishing rights with free Hilfiger gear
> For the poem your father died for
> Want to mix it to machine drum samples that drown out the verse
> Want uninformed theory 'bout revolution
> Want to edit all terse language that may offend the money people
> Want to dress you in Spandex
> Put a Glock and a blunt in your hand and stand you under a Philip
>   Morris sign at a bar mitzvah bash
> They want your black ass, not your black art

Here is another segment, the ending (6:45–7:09), which strongly echoes a passage at the very beginning, giving the whole piece a sense of orderly dramatic construction. This final section shows another way some of the words of "No Black Male Show" play out their rhythms and feelings:

> Hell no won't be no won't be no hell no won't be no won't be no
>   black male show showin' today hell no won't be no won't be
>   no show
> Hell no won't be no show no show not today hell no won't be no
>   no black male show hell no won't be no show
> No show no not today hell no
> Hell no won't be no show no
> No show
> Not today hell no
> Won't be no show
> Not today

At the risk of shifting the topic from the recording artist (Rux) to the critical writer (me) I need to call attention to the suspect qualities of these texts I'm offering. It's my own transcription; no written version seems to be available online or in print. I have probably gotten many things right: early in the first quoted segment I've capitalized and quoted "That Great Gettin' Up Morning" because I recognize it as the title of a gospel song recorded by Mahalia Jackson, Harry Belafonte, and others. (Just before the final section of "No Black Male Show" quoted here, Rux says, "Somebody said gospel is dead.") I know about

Chekhov and feel confident that "Doctor West" refers to Cornell West, the literary and cultural critic. I happen to be less familiar with Spandex and Glocks, and this puts me on notice that I may have misheard some other lyrics. These are the risks of working from audio rather than from solid print.

Deceptively solid print: the lines into which I have distributed Rux's words look plausible, but what authority do they have? How credible is my claim that "No Black Male Show" represents stichic song if it isn't sung and does without the regular rhyme that most often defines lines? Yet if it isn't a song I don't know what to call it. It isn't (originally) a theatrical monologue, since there's no theatre, just an audio recording. If it's just someone with a sharp mind and a focused point of view talking, then where does the musical background come from? Though I've put it on a page as if it were a poem in the most conventional sense, Carl Hancock Rux has never done so as far as I know. We can certainly call it poetry, but its existence for us only as sound makes us deal with the words in the same time-bound way in which we treat the lyrics of a song. Let's call it a song, then, if only as a default category. As for the lines and line breaks, because there are no rhymes that recur at all regularly, I've fallen back on a different, perhaps more elemental criterion to define lines: I've broken them where Rux takes a breath.

Some poets, most prominently Charles Olson (1910–1970), have claimed that the free-verse line is a breath unit. The claim seems to apply best to the long-lined free verse of Walt Whitman (one of Olson's strongest influences) and Allen Ginsberg (a simpatico contemporary). Many critics have been skeptical. Some have sardonically responded that in that case Whitman must have had enormous lungs. Also, when we're talking about poems we usually want to be careful not to replace the *poem* with some individual's *performance* of it. The poem's existence on the page independent of individuals is part of the poet's point in writing and printing it. To speculate about how the poet's or another reader's breathing coincides with lines seems to blur what has become an important boundary since poetry separated itself from music.

This objection is less persuasive when the text exists for us directly *as* performance. Carl Hancock Rux demonstrably *does* have big lungs. He also has an actor's training and presence and a jazz musician's ability to "look ahead" while improvising (or in this theatrical case pretending to improvise), allocating the resource of breath as it will be needed to complete the present line. Rux's longest line –

221

> Hell no won't be no won't be no hell no won't be no won't be no
>   black male show showin' today hell no won't be no won't be
>   no show

– though it's thirty-two syllables long, takes him just about six seconds to perform. The highly repetitive language – "no" is its signature, occurring nine times (plus the six additional negatives in "won't") – drives home the point: Rux rejects both the oppressions and the blandishments of hip-hop stardom. At the same time, his delivery of all these words in one breath, demonstrating not only control but prowess, mesmerizes us in a way that makes him – in this text, for this moment – register for us as a star.

    Parceling his text into units delimited by breath – which I'm calling lines and transcribing that way – gives Rux access to an arsenal of effects characteristic also of Whitman and Ginsberg. For example, he can begin or end several consecutive lines with the same word or phrase:

> Warning: the slam judges don't know the difference between a
>   sestina and a simile
> Warning: this may be hazardous to your health
> Warning: your heroes never did this to themselves …

> The law is a conquistador conjure-man the law is a
> Prime-time sit-com infiltrator the law is a
> Boilerplate best-seller the law is a …

These patterns have a long tradition as rhetorical devices: the first is called **anaphora** (repeated beginnings) and the second is called **epistrophe** (repeated endings). Rhetorical devices easily find a home in printed verse but their land of origin is heightened, persuasive speech. In a song these devices begin to create more extended structural patterns than the basic stichic form otherwise entails.

    Yet these local effects are incidental to the larger project of Rux's performed speech. Maybe to register for us as art – or just to seize our attention – speech must either invite us into the empty spaces between words and phrases or dazzle and overwhelm us. As an instance of the first strategy, printed short-line free verse typically encourages us, when we turn it back into speech by performing it internally, to hear it slowly, being drawn into the resonant intervals between lines. To inundate us instead speech has to come at us slightly too fast to grasp entirely. This is what Rux's piece does. It's not that his delivery is particularly rapid. Rather the turns of thought and expression come quickly enough to keep us on our toes. When we hear his line about slam-poetry judges who "don't know the difference between a sestina and a simile" the joke (helped by alliteration) holds us just long enough so that by the time his next line is half uttered we feel ourselves hurrying to catch up. (We catch up by listening back, as it were, to what our ears captured but our minds didn't.) Clearly this kind of effect is easiest to achieve when the language is spoken or sung. Not allowing us to linger is how it carries us along. It's this control of pace, more than the presence of (minimal) music, that situates "No Black Male Show" in the realm of song.

It's the performance (in this case recorded) that gives Rux's text the tone it has rather than other possible tones. This includes "tone" on several levels. Earlier in the piece he repeats "Not responsible for..." at the beginnings of several lines and finishes the series with the bare phrase "Not responsible" – which his voice turns into an ironic question more precisely than printed punctuation could do. On the other hand, just before the first section I've quoted he speaks a number of lines that ring changes on what we have come to call "the 'n' word." I have not quoted them, not because the passage isn't brilliant but because on the page where the words are toneless, or rather tonally ambiguous, the offensiveness of the epithet remains unmitigated. As performed, however, the lines build up a critique of the word itself that is surprisingly funny, angry, and warm-hearted all at once.

Example: Stanzaic

"Hard Times Come Again No More" is a fairly old song. The American song-writer Stephen Foster (1826–1864) wrote it in 1854. Yet it remains popular and seems to be revived in conspicuous ways whenever the theme announced by its title becomes prominent in people's minds – all too often, in short. For example, in the midst of economic crisis Bruce Springsteen featured it during his 2009 tour. At any given time a number of audio and video presentations of the song are available online.

Foster gives his song two refrains of different scope. One is a stanza four lines long, the same length as his main stanzas. Each main stanza also ends with the song's title, a one-line refrain. The same line also ends the four-line refrain stanza, which also contains yet another version of it in its second line. Here is the complete lyric:

> Let us pause in life's pleasures and count its many tears
> While we all sup sorrow with the poor
> There's a song that will linger forever in our ears
> Oh! Hard Times, come again no more
> > 'Tis the song, the sigh of the weary
> > Hard Times, Hard Times, come again no more
> > Many days you have lingered around my cabin door
> > Oh! Hard Times, come again no more
>
> While we seek mirth and beauty and music light and gay
> There are frail forms fainting at the door
> Though their voices are silent, their pleading looks will say
> Oh! Hard Times come again no more
> > 'Tis the song, the sigh of the weary
> > Hard Times, Hard Times, come again no more
> > Many days you have lingered around my cabin door
> > Oh! Hard Times, come again no more
>
> There's a pale drooping maiden who toils her life away
> With a worn heart whose better days are o'er
> Though her voice would be merry, 'tis sighing all the day
> Oh! Hard Times, come again no more
> > 'Tis the song, the sigh of the weary
> > Hard Times, Hard Times, come again no more
> > Many days you have lingered around my cabin door
> > Oh! Hard Times, come again no more
>
> 'Tis a sigh that is wafted across the troubled wave
> 'Tis a wail that is heard upon the shore
> 'Tis a dirge that is murmured around the lowly grave
> Oh! Hard Times, come again no more
> > 'Tis the song, the sigh of the weary
> > Hard Times, Hard Times, come again no more
> > Many days you have lingered around my cabin door
> > Oh! Hard Times, come again no more

This style of notation – which runs the refrain right up to the main stanza it follows while indenting the refrain to distinguish it visually – is not standard but it has the advantage of clarifying the song's overall structure.

If we stand back a little, the four-line main stanzas seem to approximate a ballad stanza rhymed abab:

> /   /   /   /
> Let us pause in life's pleasures and count its many tears
> / /   /
> While we all sup sorrow with the poor
> /   /   /   /
> There's a song that will linger forever in our ears
> /   /   /
> Oh! Hard Times, come again no more

The four-line refrain begins by reversing the pattern:

> /   /   /
> 'Tis the song, the sigh of the weary
> /   /   /   /
> Hard Times, Hard Times, come again no more

By *beginning* unusually with a three-beat line, Foster emphasizes the shift from the main stanza to the refrain.

The meter of these lyrics begins to look more complicated when we try to describe it more completely. The song is always performed slowly, which leaves room for more stress. Each line is sung to a musical phrase that is eight beats long. As is normal in music, beats 1, 3, 5, and 7 are stronger than beats 2, 4, 6, and 8. When applied to words this pattern produces the meter called *dipody* (Latin for "two feet"). It's rare in poetry that isn't closely associated with music. In dipodic verse not only do stresses alternate with slacks, but stronger stresses alternate with weaker ones. In Foster's first line "pause," "pleasure," "count" and "tears" get the strong stresses, but we can hear weaker ones as well. If we use ' for the weak stresses, the first line – its rhythms adjusted by the melody – looks like this:

> '   / '   /   /   ' /
> Let us pause in life's pleasures and count its many tears

One weak stress is displaced by the music from "life's" to "in." This is similar to kinds of accommodation between metrical and rhythmic forces that we saw in the iambic pentameter, though here the metrical control is transferred out of the words into the music. Other lines in the song show a further, limited range of accommodations.

> ### Poetry, Song, and Stress
>
> If you're musical, you may notice that something about this scansion looks backwards. The first strong downbeat in the line isn't at its beginning as musical habit leads us to expect, but on "pause." The secondary stress on "Let us" is really an upbeat or **anacrusis**. For the same reasons, the beginning of the second line, "While we," belongs *musically* to the line before it. (This is parallel to a line that puzzled us in Chapter 2 from Thomas Hardy's "The Robin," and may help justify the somewhat tortuous explanation supplied there.) To put it simply, music tends to emphasize beginnings (ONE two THREE four), while lines of verse emphasize ends, especially through rhyme. So a notation appropriate to the lyrics is often out of phase with the notation of the music.

Another weak stress appears to be missing from the line. The fifth of the musical beats supporting every line in the main stanza is left without a syllable:

$$\text{/ \quad / \quad / \qquad / \quad [/] \quad / \qquad / \quad /}$$
Let us pause in life's pleasures   and count its many tears

This is crucial to the song's signature sound. It's reflected in a musical *syncopation* that gives a kind of lift to the unstressed syllable at the end of every line's first half, almost like a line break in a poem. A songwriter as skilled as Foster makes his words tag along with these musical operations in supple and unexpected ways. They don't come as naturally to poems because poetry never controls time with the precision that music depends on.

As in any poem or song that isn't primarily concerned with narrative, it's worth asking why these stanzas need to be in this order.

Temporal and Spatial Arts

Thinking about the order of the parts may be even more important in songs than in poems. Our relation to temporal arts – music, dance – differs from our relation to spatial ones – painting, sculpture. This isn't a sharp opposition: we walk around a statue to see it well and looking at a painting takes time. The painter has many ways of guiding our eye, which control the "story" of our seeing. On the other hand, as we listen to a piece of music we build up a kind of "picture" in our minds, a whole shape that carries the meaning of the piece.

On the spectrum from the most time-bound to the most spatial arts, printed poems lie slightly closer to the painting end than songs because – especially if the poem is short, occupying just a few square inches of the page in front of us – we move more readily toward comprehending it as a whole than we can do with a song that someone else is singing to us. To this degree the unfolding of a song in time – and therefore the order of its parts – is slightly more foregrounded than in poems. This subtle distinction, though, shouldn't be taken as undermining the essentially *sounded* event that a poem wants to be.

Foster's first line lays out the terms of the song's concerns: "pleasure" versus "tears." Throughout, "song" is suppressed to "sigh." In the second stanza the "voices" of the poor are "silent." The third stanza renders these victims more vividly concrete by embodying them in an individual "pale, drooping maiden." Her "voice would be merry" if it could – some performers alter this to "would be singing," making the contrast even simpler – but the voice is reduced to "sighing all the day." In the final stanza Foster does two things to this collective lamenting exhalation that feel climactic. First, he diversifies it into "sigh," "wail," and "dirge," all to be gathered again into the "song" of the final refrain. Second, in a move that reverses the individualizing gesture of the previous stanza, he disembodies the voice of the sigh/song and at the same time declares that it's audible even on the unpeopled "wave," "shore," and "grave." By the end of the song we know that we can hear the lament everywhere and anywhere if we listen as the song has urged us to.

The first and second stanzas both begin with "us" or "we" and then turn to others, "the poor." If we're tempted to think of ourselves as safely distinct from "the poor," however, the song instead insists on our solidarity with them. One of the most striking ways it effects this universalization is by *addressing* not any person or group but "Hard Times," which beleaguer all of us or can at any stroke of ill-fortune. It's not easy to say whether "Hard Times" feels like the plural it seems to be or becomes a singular, amorphous oppressor. In any case, the tone of "come again no more" is almost politely regretful, not an aggressive demand but a pained plea. There's no question of defeating or destroying "hard times": right up through the last refrain line of the last stanzaic refrain, "Hard Times" is a persecutor still there to be addressed.

Example: Whole-Song

As an example of whole-song form let's explore Bob Dylan's "You're Gonna Make Me Lonesome When You Go" from *Blood on the Tracks* (1974). This is not one of Dylan's massive songs that people sometimes call "epic": "Sad-Eyed Lady of the Lowlands" or "Desolation Row" from the 1960s, or "Ain't Talkin'" from *Modern Times* (2006). Dylan always uses stanzas to construct those grand-scale songs. This song instead shows the resources of whole-song form and how the writer can use it not only to lend variety to the song's surface but to articulate its deeper structure.

At the beginning of his career Dylan's songs were all stanzaic, either with refrains ("Blowin' in the Wind") or without ("Love Minus Zero/No Limit"). His first song in whole-song form was "Ballad of a Thin Man" on *Highway 61 Revisited* (1965). The bridge in that song (beginning "You have many contacts / Among the lumberjacks") is only subtly distinguished musically from the other stanzas. (For the musically minded: its bass line descends like that of the other stanzas, but diatonically rather than chromatically.) The rhymes are a little more dense and the melody tends to be a little higher in pitch than elsewhere in the song. But these differences don't emphasize the contrast between the A- and B-strains or give the bridge a very strong structural role in the song. Yet his next album, *Blonde on Blonde* (1966), is an almost explosive investigation of song forms and especially of the bridge as a structural element. (Earlier we examined the first lines of the two bridge sections of "Absolutely Sweet Marie." That song's overall form is AABABAA.) After *Blonde on Blonde*, though he writes in a wide variety of song forms, he returns with some frequency to the bridge as an element in a song's architecture. "You're Gonna Make Me Lonesome When You Go" has two bridge or B-strain sections, and we'll look at how he uses them.

When I teach courses on Music and Poetry or on Dylan in particular, I often begin with an exercise in which students are asked to listen to and transcribe (without consulting the Internet except to look up words and phrases) this song and "Imagine the Duchess's Feelings" by Noël Coward (1899–1973). Coward's song – British and from 1941 – gives current American students a lot of difficulty:

> Imagine the Duchess's feelings:
> You could have pierced her with swords
> When she discovered
> Her pet lamb, like Lenin,
> Had sold *The Daily Worker*
> Near the House of Lords.

Many of the references are unfamiliar: *The Daily Worker*, the American Communist Party newspaper, ceased publication in the late 1950s, and students are more likely to hear "Lennon" than "Lenin" (when they don't hear – perhaps by association with the "pet lamb"? – "lemon"). The point of having them try to write down the words for themselves is to help them realize how readily we skip over what we don't quite understand, substituting what we do know, even when we think we're listening carefully.

Despite its more familiar idiom, Dylan's "You're Gonna Make Me Lonesome" presents a few puzzles of the same kind. Some students don't recognize the name of Ashtabula, Ohio, or know that "Careless Love" (not "callous love") is the title of a song dating from before the twentieth century, or that Queen Anne's lace is the flower also called wild carrot. (It doesn't help that Dylan omits the possessive in the flower's name, so that students who hear "queen and lace" are listening faithfully to the phonetics, if not to the syntax.) The lines

> Relationships have all been bad
> Mine've been like Verlaine's and Rimbaud

give particular difficulty. To understand that Dylan means the French poet Arthur Rimbaud (1854–1891), not the American action hero Rambo, we need not only to notice the stress on the last syllable of the name rather than the first, but also to have some familiarity with literary history or enough acquaintance

229

with French pronunciation and spelling to be able to look up the name. Beyond these mondegreen moments, though, Dylan's song highlights some deeper problems with transcription – and by extension with listening to songs.

Here is my transcription of Dylan's song. It differs in some respects from the official one available on bobdylan.com, and we'll look at some of these differences in a moment:

> I've seen love go by my door
> It's never been this close before
> Never been so easy or so slow
> I been shootin' in the dark too long
> When somethin's not right it's wrong
> You're gonna make me lonesome when you go

> Dragon clouds so high above
> I've only known careless love
> It always has hit me from below
> But this time around it's more correct
> Right on target, so direct
> You're gonna make me lonesome when you go

> Purple clover, Queen Anne lace
> Crimson hair across your face
> You could make me cry if you don't know
> Can't remember what I was thinkin' of
> You might be spoilin' me too much love
> You're gonna make me lonesome when you go

> > Flowers on the hillside bloomin' crazy
> > Crickets talkin' back and forth in rhyme
> > Blue river runnin' slow and lazy
> > I could stay with you forever and never realize the time

> Situations have ended sad
> Relationships have all been bad
> Mine've been like Verlaine's and Rimbaud
> But there's no way I can compare

All them scenes to this affair
You're gonna make me lonesome when you go

    You're gonna make me wonder what I'm doin'
    Stayin' far behind without you
    You're gonna make me wonder what I'm sayin'
    You're gonna make me give myself a good talkin' to

I'll look for you in old Honolulu
San Francisco or Ashtabula
You're gonna have to leave me now, I know
But I'll see you in the sky above
In the tall grass, in the ones I love
You're gonna make me lonesome when you go

The listening difficulties here don't much involve the line and stanza format of the song. (Nor do the differences in my transcription, though I have chosen to indent the bridge sections to clarify the structure visually.) The main stanza or A-strain is unusual but clear: it's six lines long, rhymed aabccb. (It's worth noticing that because every main stanza ends with the refrain line, which is also the song's title, this rhyme scheme requires Dylan to find a third-line rhyme on "go" every time, five times all together. Dylan often sets himself rhyming tasks like this, partly because he so often favors one-line refrains.) The stanza is more odd metrically than in rhyme. The words in the first two lines fill all four musically available beats. This makes the first run directly into the second and the second into the third, and only rhyme marks these as separate lines. The next three lines similarly run together, so that on a higher rhythmic level the stanza sounds as though it has just two very long lines. The third and sixth lines, by contrast, fill five beats and therefore (by the powers-of-two logic of the music) leave a pause of three beats. This additional space in which they resonate goes along with the epigrammatic quality of some of these lines: "Never been so easy or so slow," "Mine've been like Verlaine's and Rimbaud."

The bridge or B-strain is quite distinct from the A-strain not only in melody and chord structure – always the strongest musical signal of a bridge – but also in the meter and rhyme of the lyrics. It's four lines long, not six, and rhymed abab (though in the second bridge it takes a lot of help from the equivalent

231

position of the lines for us to hear "doin'" and "sayin'" as a rhyme). More strikingly, the first three lines of the bridge are each five beats long just like the final (refrain) line of the A-strain stanza. This creates an unusual structural continuity from the end of the A-strain into the beginning of the B-strain. The fourth line of the bridge is much longer, in one case seven beats –

/   /   /   / / /   /

You're gonna make me give myself a good talkin' to

– and in the other, all eight:

/   /   / /   / /   /

I could stay with you forever and never realize the time

(Both of these lines, like many others in the song, are also bound together internally by rhyme, assonance, and consonance.) The length of this line makes the end of the bridge push on into the beginning of the next A-strain stanza. This gives the whole bridge – moving from lines with rests to a line with little or none – especially great forward momentum.

The overall form of "You're Gonna Make Me Lonesome When You Go," then, is AAABABA. This illustrates a more general point about this kind of form: because the bridge is sensed as a change in the song, it registers for us as an *event* more than the recurring A-strain stanzas. In the structure of a temporal work of art our sense of drama is heightened when events crowd together at the end, not when the pace relaxes. For this reason songwriters are unlikely to compose songs whose form runs ABABAAA (the reverse of Dylan's) or anything similar. The archetypal whole-song form, AABA, illustrates this dramatic tendency in the simplest possible way.

AABA as Fundamental

The appeal of this structure may be more fundamental still: it shows up everywhere. The pattern of doing thing A, doing it again, doing thing B, and returning to do thing A again turns up in many pleasing narratives on a range from tiny to enormous. A very compact instance is the refrain of a 1912 hymn by James Rowe and Howard E. Smith:

> Love lifted me! Love lifted me!
> When nothing else could help
> Love lifted me!

The limerick, too, acts out a kind of AABA, with its two-stress rhyming pair (B) following after the second of three three-stress lines (AA...A). Even in the pattern of line-groupings in George Herbert's "Matins" that we sketched in Chapter 3 we can glimpse a similar design: the first stanza divided asymmetrically; the second divided asymmetrically as well, though in the opposite direction; the next two stanzas divided symmetrically; and the last composing a symmetry of the opening asymmetries.

In my transcription I've used the "gonna" that also appears in the official version. This is not exactly for the sake of phonetic accuracy. We probably say (and Dylan would surely sing) "Yer" exactly the same as "You're," but I see no point to the official transcription's use of "Yer" in the refrain line – and in fact that nonstandard form doesn't appear in the official title. "Gonna" is different because "going to" has two different functions as an item of speech in English, though in prose we would spell both of them in the two-word form. When Dylan ends lines in "Mr. Tambourine Man" with "...there is no place I'm going to," no one would write it as "no place I'm gonna." The "going to" that denotes futurity is pronounced differently, and it seems reasonable to accept the (as it were) standard nonstandard spelling "gonna."

Perhaps it doesn't matter much how we transcribe "gonna," or whether we use spellings like "shootin'."

Final 'g' in Transcriptions

Keeping or dropping the 'g' at the ends of gerunds and present participles can be significant. It doesn't change the dictionary meaning of the word, but does alter its social meaning. It becomes a vehicle for "code switching," a term for how we shift our way of talking – in word choice, pronunciation, and even syntax – to different audiences. Several news commentators, particularly in 2008, noticed that President Barack Obama would switch nimbly from "living" to "livin'" and back in various public contexts. Sometimes the deciding factor seemed to be the racial or socioeconomic makeup of his audience, but the more general principle seemed to be the degree of formality that he felt the occasion called for.

But occasionally decisions that we make about punctuation in transcribing a song can be surprisingly telling and difficult. I've printed one of the lines in Dylan's third stanza as "You might be spoilin' me too much love," but that's evasive. The official transcription gives "You might be spoilin' me too much, love," but it's also possible to hear the line as "You might be spoilin' me, too much love." In the former case "love" is a vocative, a name he gives the "you" he's addressing, one that identifies the relation between them. Putting the comma after "spoilin' me," on the other hand, identifies "too much love" as the means by which she "spoils" him. Can a person be spoiled by receiving too much love? Certainly Dylan says so in a number of songs, including "Buckets of Rain," also on *Blood on the Tracks*: "You got all the love, honey baby, I can stand." If the notion seems at all paradoxical or counterintuitive, so does the alternative idea of "spoiling too much": doesn't "spoiling" by definition entail some kind of excess? On any ground, then – logical, psychological, rhetorical – it seems impossible to decide where to place the comma. Yet without a comma, as I've printed it, the line doesn't make sense. Writing the line down forces us to decide (or to evade the question as I've done). One point of transcription is that it makes us realize what we don't quite know about the song and think about what's at stake. Is the singer of this song someone who believes that a little spoiling (of him) is all right but too much is too much? Or is he someone who fears that getting too much of a good thing from someone else threatens his independent identity? I think Dylan's persona in many of his songs supports the latter idea more than the former, but other listeners may hear him otherwise. Who we think he (the singer) is, which is near the center of what we think his song means, can come down to questions that emerge when we simply try to place a comma.

Who this singer is, or how his song shows him perceiving and reacting to his situation, is intimately tied up with how the song progresses. If I'm right (as the official transcribers also think) that in the last stanza Dylan sings not "I see you in the sky above" (an announcement of his obsession with her) but the prediction that "I'll see you in the sky above / In the tall grass, in the ones I love" (presumably after she "goes"), how does he arrive at that relatively tranquil conclusion? Approaching this kind of large thematic question about the song's meaning turns out to be easiest when we examine the two bridges. They function differently, but both bear on the progress of the song as a whole, like tugboats steering this enterprise one way and then another.

The first bridge interrupts the personal story – which from the title onward has been directed toward an unhappy future – with a moment of delight in the present:

> Flowers on the hillside bloomin' crazy
> Crickets talkin' back and forth in rhyme
> Blue river runnin' slow and lazy
> I could stay with you forever and never realize the time

The first three lines are the culmination of a pattern in the song that began with earlier lines about "Dragon clouds" and "Purple clover." Here the vitality and harmony of the natural world are brought to the fore with the flowers "bloomin' crazy" and the rhyming crickets. The fourth line turns abruptly to the song's most ardent declaration: "I could stay with you forever and never realize the time." In several ways this song is about time: what makes it pass quickly or slowly, how the future (and the past) can weigh on the present. In this bridge the natural present suggests a conclusion about the future, but it's a wistful conclusion that the rest of the song says won't come true. The juxtaposition of the first three lines with the fourth is a little like what Lennon and McCartney do in the final stanza of "And I Love Her":

> Bright are the stars that shine
> Dark is the sky
> I know this love of mine
> Will never die

Claims of eternal devotion may be unconvincing on their own. Paired with astronomical commonplaces that have the advantage of being unarguable, the claim gains credibility by association. In Dylan's bridge a similar apparent digression may convey the same kind of authenticity – just as the world of crickets and

clouds is perennial, so my pleasure in your company would be if you let it –
though in the context of the song the claim it supports is doomed.

Dylan's second bridge works quite differently. It doesn't suspend the drive
toward the future but rather accelerates it by picking up the expression "You're
gonna make me" from the refrain and repeating it three times:

> You're gonna make me wonder what I'm doin'
> Stayin' far behind without you
> You're gonna make me wonder what I'm sayin'
> You're gonna make me give myself a good talkin' to

In the refrain line, the complement of "make me" is the adjective describing his
anticipated state, "lonesome." In this second bridge, the complements are verbs
instead: "wonder" twice and then "give myself a good talkin' to." These active
verbs emphasize the accelerating process he's undergoing, not the static condition he expects to end up in.

That expectation, summarized in the title and refrain, runs counter to his
mood of pleasure among the "clouds" and "hillside." Yet we understand how
these two tones – present joy and anticipated pain – intensify each other. We can
hear an analogous ambivalence play out in the jaunty music of Dylan's song. The
tempo is quick, the rhythm is carried by brisk guitar strumming, and the song
is in a major key. If the music directly supports the good humor of the first
bridge, it also deepens the predicted sense of loss. In this way it helps explain
how he arrives at the comparative serenity of the last stanza.

In "You're Gonna Make Me Lonesome When You Go" the complex story of his
feeling, developing and warring against itself, is told in several intertwined
ways. In the sequence of A-strain stanzas the anticipation of parting begins as
hardly more than a single line (though it's the inescapable refrain) and grows to
occupy the whole last stanza. The two bridges contrast with that sequence. The
first dwells more thoroughly inside the present relationship than any of the rest
of the song. The second bridge, on the other hand, gives the most abstract and
internal picture of his response to the relationship's disintegration. The emotional force of the song depends on these contrasts, which are bound up with
Dylan's particular realization of the whole-song form.

6

Advanced Topics

The method of scanning metrical verse introduced in Chapter 1 and used throughout this book represents what's sometimes called a "foot-substitution" theory of meter. Other names for it are "traditional" and "classical" – occasionally even "mainstream." Within the conversation about English poetry that has run from the sixteenth century through the twentieth, several different theoretical traditions have competed, crossed, and mingled. By around 1900, though, theories of "quantitative" meter (treating English as if it were Latin) and attempts to scan verse using musical notation (treating syllables as if they were notes) largely gave way to the approach used here.

This mere popularity or longevity has advantages of its own. First, it facilitates discussion among students and scholars who all speak the same critical language. Second, popularity may have some relevance to the nature of meter itself. If meter is an aspect of how a metrical poem means – as we've seen throughout this book – then it's part of a system of communication. The people at both ends of that system, poets and readers, have to hold *in common* a body of assumptions about what to listen for, about what to hear but set aside as peripheral, and ultimately about what does or doesn't sound like a metrical line. I might learn to read Classical Arabic, but if I don't know anything about the intricate rules of meter followed by poets in that language in the past thousand years their poems still won't fully "speak" to me. We need access to a poem's context of metrical tradition just as we need to know the idiom and dialect of its language. *What makes this a metrical poem?* is a question just as embedded in

Verse: An Introduction to Prosody, First Edition. Charles O. Hartman.

cultural assumptions as *What makes this a poem?* The traditional method of scanning a poem we have been using embodies a kind of common denominator – not necessary "lowest" – of ideas about how a metrical line works.

Besides this common-currency acceptability, the traditional approach to scansion also has the advantage of relative simplicity. It may not have seemed simple when you first encountered words like "spondee" and "caesura," but while poetic meter is a complicated phenomenon this way of marking and hearing it is relatively straightforward. At its base it relies only on our intuition (aided by the dictionary) about what syllables are stressed; a few rules of thumb about probable combinations of feet; and the concept that meter's influence on rhythm shows up in promoted stresses.

Scansion Rules of Thumb: Recap

It's worth repeating material from earlier chapters to list the "rules of thumb" for substituted feet. One common complaint against foot-substitution theories is that they might (meaninglessly) allow any line to count as metrical, since almost any combination of up to four syllables can be labeled with the name of some Classical foot. (The pattern /xx/ is a choriamb, x//x is an antispast, and so on.) But that would be a theory willfully blind to facts. In practice, and confining the question to iambic pentameter for the sake of brevity, we've found that most metrical lines in English – far more than 95% – can be accounted for with just a few constraints on substitutions for the iamb:

- spondees can go anywhere;
- so can double iambs replacing two iambs (xx//);
- a trochee can always go at the start of the line, sometimes after a caesura, never at its end, and hardly ever more than one in a row;
- bare stresses (defective feet) are distributed like trochees but are more damaging to stability;
- anapests can go anywhere but threaten to take over the line, perhaps ruinously shortening it by one foot;
- a line can end with an extra slack syllable (or more, if rhymed).

These guidelines work about equally well for a poet writing an iambic pentameter and for a reader scanning one to discover how it realizes the meter.

Yet explanations that people generally but vaguely accept aren't necessarily accurate. This is true not only in physics and statistics but also in matters concerning language. Language is something everybody does, but conscious knowledge of English grammar, for example, is not very widespread. It doesn't have to be: we can speak and understand English without ever thinking about prepositional phrases – though, as we've seen, being aware of a poem's grammar can add to our sense of its meaning. Perhaps what we know about English meter as accustomed readers and writers is as susceptible to finer analysis as what we know about other aspects of language.

In the past four decades, several alternatives to the method of scansion used here and the theoretical assumptions underlying it have come to a high degree of development. Each of them aims to give a more accurate and detailed explanation of the phenomena that competent readers experience when they read metrical verse.

By analogy, classical nineteenth-century physics works well until we start considering things smaller than atoms. Then we turn for greater accuracy to quantum mechanics, which is much more strange but is precise enough to lead to (for instance) the transistors at the basis of all modern electronic devices. One problem with this analogy is that traditional scansion, as presented in this book, doesn't represent a theory nearly as cogent as classical physics. The other problem is that while physicists have long agreed (more or less) about quantum mechanics, no approach to poetic meter, neither the traditional one I've tried to define, nor any of the alternatives, has gained universal acceptance. Modern metrical theories still (or again) compete as camps or schools. No consensus has emerged and it's doubtful that one will in the near future.

The main business of this chapter is to point to a couple of approaches to meter that differ from the traditional account I've given in the first five chapters of this book. These theories are much too substantial and complex to be explained or exemplified here in full detail. Still, it's helpful to look at the principles these alternative theories adopt and the insights they achieve. They make attractive claims to show how our experience of meter in poetry *really* arises and operates.

They also offer to illuminate in different ways the history of meter in English – a topic we have barely touched on. That history is usually thought of as running like this: After Old English with its accentual meters collides with French and evolves into Middle English, Chaucer introduces the iambic pentameter. Then the language changes again, so that a century later Wyatt and his contemporaries can't quite understand the sound of Chaucer's poems, and this leads them to a version of the meter that sounds very rough to us (with lines like "With his hardiness taketh displeasure"). The pentameter line is brought back into order during the sixteenth century, which takes us to Shakespeare's sonnets and plays. In the seventeenth century, while Donne loosens the meter a great deal, Milton imposes strict law on the ten-syllable line but varies the position of stresses dynamically. In the eighteenth century Pope and others enforce maximum smoothness again. In turn the Romantics loosen the meter once more and Victorians from Browning to Yeats explore even further variations. This historical picture is accurate as far as it goes, but it would be gratifying to have an explanation that could distinguish both historical moments and the practice of different poets in the same historical period. This could be one test of a metrical theory that might supplant the traditional account of varying fashions in metrical substitution.

Generative Metrics

One force behind the new growth of theories about meter has been the development of the modern science of linguistics. This makes sense not only because meter is obviously somehow connected with or embedded in language, but also because linguistics has undergone a transformation as radical as those which the early twentieth century brought to physics. We know a great deal more about language than we did fifty years ago (though the revolution began half a century before that in the writings of Ferdinand de Saussure, a Swiss linguist). Through the work of Noam Chomsky and others from the 1950s onward, linguistics has established a far more rigorous and detailed account of what we're doing when we create or comprehend sentences we've never heard before. Linguists seek to understand the systematic, implicit rules which describe or define our "competence" as users and consumers of language.

The implicit rather than explicit nature of our knowledge as linguists study it is important to emphasize. As an example take the distinction between **voiced** and **unvoiced** consonants. If you press your hand to your throat and repeat "sss" and "zzz" several times, you'll feel the vibration of your larynx – your voice box – on the "z" sound. Consonants in English come in pairs: like "z" and "s," "b" is voiced while "p" is unvoiced; "d" and "t" are another pair, and so on. You may never have thought about this, but if you didn't *know* it on some level no one would understand you and you wouldn't understand anyone else. The distinction between the members of these pairs, known as a "phonemic contrast," keeps your sentence about *drought* from being about *trout*. (Context helps – especially when you're whispering, when the voiced/unvoiced contrast disappears.) These are characteristics of a great many phenomena that linguists have uncovered: they turn out to be items of systematic knowledge held in the brains of language users, but knowledge acquired so easily in childhood that it takes a major research effort to make us aware of what we implicitly know. Whether meter resembles syntax and phonology in this regard is a question we'll return to.

Many of the leading developments in linguistics have occurred in the realm of syntax. Generative and transformational grammars have eclipsed the prescriptive grammar long taught in schools (which may be one reason that often *no* grammar is taught). Other progress has reached into territories more obviously related to metrics. Poems, as we've seen throughout this book, are as much webs of language *sounds* as they are sequences of sentences. The publication in 1968 of *The Sound Pattern of English* by Chomsky and Morris Halle marked a major advance in our understanding of **phonology**, the branch of linguistics that studies not just the sounds but the sound *system* of a language. Other linguists, including Kenneth Pike in the 1940s and Mark Liberman in the 1970s, have added important work on **intonation**, the pitch contours of speech, which a poem turns into a kind of speech melody that the poet uses expressively. Together these and other advances offer the tantalizing prospect of a complete theory of meter, one that would achieve what Chomsky calls "explanatory adequacy" as well as merely "observational" and "descriptive" adequacy. This theory would make meter a *component* of language, just as other research is promising to bring linguistics into the wider territory of cognitive science. It would explain how our brains do meter.

One central movement among linguists studying poetic meter is the field called "generative metrics." Metrical rules are sought which will "generate" metrical lines just as syntactical rules generate sentences and phonological rules generate the sounds of words we speak. ("Generate" here means "predict what native speakers will judge as correct.") A central figure in this field is Paul Kiparsky, whose long technical essay from 1977, "The Rhythmic Structure of English Verse," is as ambitious as its title implies. (This essay is far from the last word or even Kiparsky's last word. But it lays most of the groundwork for this approach to meter.)

241

Here is a small example of the kind of detail that Kiparsky's theory is capable of addressing. He notes that Shakespeare never uses the word "hierarchy" – which does seem odd since it's a term intimately related to all kinds of relationships that Shakespeare is very interested in. Kiparsky points out that the word has two adjacent stresses: *hier-ar*-chy.

The Syllables of "Hierarchy"

Kiparsky treats "hierarchy" as having three syllables. The first syllable differs among dialects: for many English speakers "fire" is one syllable, and for others it has two. Shortly we'll look at how Kiparsky's argument is affected if we hear "hier-" as two syllables.

He calls these "lexical stresses," defined as stressed syllables within a polysyllabic word. Shakespeare, he shows, does not allow lexical stresses to occupy the "weak" or W positions in a line. These are, roughly speaking, the odd-numbered syllables, while the even-numbered ones are "strong" (S):

W S W S W S W S

(Elision can sometimes make a position contain two syllables, but that's a complication we can leave aside for now.) This turns out to be the governing principle of Shakespeare's meter in Kiparsky's analysis: no lexical stress in a W position. There's an important exception for the first syllable of a line or of a major syntactical constituent – that is, the syllable right after a line break or a caesura. This follows from the idea Kiparsky develops that what happens in a W position is determined by its relation to the syllable just to its *left*. The line's first syllable has no left-hand neighbor to constrain it. But since "hierarchy" has two adjacent stresses, no matter which one falls on the "strong" or S position the other is bound to fall on a W position. Therefore this word would make any line unmetrical. Kiparsky doesn't claim to prove that this is *why* Shakespeare never uses "hierarchy" – he only points out the difficulty the word would cause in Shakespeare's metrical system – but the case is suggestive.

Furthermore, Kiparsky can point to four lines in John Milton's *Paradise Lost* that do contain "hierarchy" or its plural:

Each in his hierarchy, the orders bright ... (1.737)
Of hierarchies, of orders, and degrees ... (5.591)
Who speedily through all the hierarchies ... (5.692)
So sang the hierarchies: meanwhile the son ... (7.192)

(The parenthetical citations indicate the book and line number in the poem.) In all these cases the first stress in the word occurs in a "strong" or S position (the fourth, second, eighth, and fourth syllables, respectively). To force this into foot-substitution terms – which Kiparsky doesn't use – Milton sometimes allows a trochee to replace an iamb even if it's not preceded by any pause at all (it's in the middle of a word):

$$/ \quad x \mid x \quad / \mid / \quad x \mid x \quad / \mid x \quad /$$
Each in his hierarchy, the orders bright

This breaks one of our "rules of thumb," but that's all they are, and it indicates why the line sounds metrically strange. Shakespeare, however, by Kiparsky's account, does *not* break this rule. More precisely, Shakespeare's version of the rule outlaws trochees in these positions only when the two syllables of the trochee belong to the same *word*. He does use trochees not following a caesura in other circumstances:

There are more things in Heaven and earth, Horatio,
$$\mid \quad / \quad x \quad \mid$$
Than are dreamt of in your philosophy...

$$\mid \quad / x \mid$$
Grief fills the room up of my absent child

In these cases, however, the trochee is made up of two monosyllables.

The picture becomes slightly muddier when we notice some other lines in *Paradise Lost*. In one, a variant on the word "hierarchy" occurs with its first stressed syllable in a "weak" or W position, the third syllable in the line:

$$x \quad / \mid \quad / \quad / \mid x \quad / \mid x \; (/) \mid x \quad /$$
The great hierarchal standard was to move; ... (5.701)

Apparently Milton can place the word's first stress in a W position as well as in an S position. This suggests the possibility (which Kiparsky doesn't mention) that Shakespeare's own rules *could* have allowed him to use "hierarchy" at the beginning of a line, since a lexical stress is allowed in that special W position. The first stress in "hierarchy" would go in the specially licensed first position in the line and the second stress would fit normally in the second (S) position.

As Kiparsky describes them, Shakespeare's rules don't constrain what happens in S positions at all. An unstressed syllable can always occupy the position where the meter leads us to expect a stress. This coincides with the pattern we have been calling "promoted stress." In Kiparsky's system, in a line like Shakespeare's "Shall I compare thee to a summer's day?" the word "to," which is obviously unstressed, is permitted in an S position because anything is permitted in S positions, whether promoted or not.

In other lines Milton also uses a shorter noun related to "hierarchy":

> To whom the winged Hierarch replied. ...   (5.468)
> Under their Hierarchs in orders bright: ...   (5.587)
> War unproclaimed. The princely hierarch ...   (11.220)

"Hierarchy," as Kiparsky points out, is often pronounced with three syllables. However, it's clear when we scan these three lines that "hierarch" *also* has three syllables ("hi-er-arch"), but with a different stress pattern: /x/ versus //x, or in Kiparsky's terms, SWS versus SSW:

> x   / | x   / | x / |x   / | x   /
> To whom the winged Hierarch replied

Milton is very consistent about the number of syllables in a pentameter line, so there's no question about "winged" being disyllabic, for instance. The word "hierarch" wasn't available to Shakespeare – it really came into English only in Milton's time, somewhat after Shakespeare's death – but it raises a point about the related word "hierarchy," which Shakespeare *could* have used but didn't. If Milton could sometimes hear "hier-" as one syllable and sometimes as two, couldn't Shakespeare? This kind of optional syllabification is frequent in all periods of English verse. For most speakers "our" and "hour" and "flower" all rhyme, but many will perceive "our" as one syllable and "flower" as two (probably influenced by spelling). If "hierarchy" can therefore have four syllables which would be stressed /x/x, or SWSW – and this is how the word appears in many modern dictionaries – then

Shakespeare could have used it by placing its first syllable on some even-numbered position in the line. Though Shakespeare never used "hierarchy," we may not have a *metrical* explanation of the fact.

In other cases, Milton breaks our rules of thumb more sharply:

> Beyond all past example and future ...   (10.840)
> To the Garden of Bliss, thy seat prepar'd ...   (8.299)

The first of these lines seems to end with a trochee, and the other begins with two trochees. (*Any* metrical reading of this line must begin with a somewhat counter-intuitive stress on "To.") Both of these are highly unusual positions for trochaic substitution in a traditional scansion.

Trochees in Second Foot

Why is the trochee so rare in the second foot of the iambic pentameter? Some traditional metrists even include a rule against it, and it is indeed destabilizing. In our rules of thumb it's largely excluded by the fact that caesurae rarely occur so early in the line, just after the second syllable.

In both of Milton's lines the result is a real instability in the iambic meter. The lines want to topple over into triple rhythm –

> (?) x / | /   / | x / | x x   / x
>   Beyond all past example and future ...   (10.840)

> (?) x   x / | x x   / | x / | x /
>   To the Garden of Bliss, thy seat prepar'd ...   (8.299)

– at the usual cost, the disastrous loss of one foot in the pentameter.

Kiparsky can show that such lines, though they remain exceptional even in Milton, abide by a rule which requires these trochaic inversions to stay within *word* boundaries. In Kiparsky's terms, the "labeling mismatch" of a stressed syllable in a W position is not accompanied by a simultaneous "bracketing mismatch" between the boundaries of the foot and the word.

Labeling and Bracketing Mismatches

Kiparsky's full and exact explanations of "labeling mismatch" and "bracketing mismatch" require pages of diagramed examples. For our purposes, we can simply think of "bracketing mismatches" as moments when a word crosses a foot boundary. In a line by Shakespeare that Kiparsky uses as an example, "The lion dying thrusteth forth his paw," this happens three times, once in each two-syllable word. "Labeling," on the other hand, refers to the S and W labels on positions in the line: WSWSWSWSWS in iambic pentameter. A "labeling mismatch" happens when a "strong" syllable coincides with a W position in the line.

Milton, Kiparsky claims, wouldn't begin a line with "To regard an abyss" – even though it has the same stress pattern as "To the Garden of Bliss" – because the two syllables that reverse the iambic stress pattern ("-gard an") belong to different words.

More, Kiparsky can show that Milton's rule is almost always followed by Thomas Wyatt, an early and famously "rough" metrical poet, and by Gerard Manley Hopkins, also known for straining against the conventional rules of meter. On the other hand, John Donne (1572–1631) can write lines like "Shall behold God, and never taste death's woe." In foot-substitution terms, this isn't particularly hard to scan:

$$x \quad x \; / \quad / \; | \; x \;\; / \,| \, x \; / \quad | \; / \qquad /$$
Shall behold God, and never taste death's woe

Nothing in this scansion looks especially bizarre or excludes the possibility of Shakespeare or Milton having written it. (All three poets were near contemporaries.) Kiparsky's rules for Shakespeare's and Milton's meters, however, do exclude Donne's line in a principled way. For both Milton and Shakespeare, simultaneous labeling and bracketing mismatches make a line too hard to hear as metrical. Donne, in contrast, sometimes uses these radical variations to lend emphatic vigor to his rhythms, whatever the risk to metrical stability.

Kiparsky's theory results, then, not in a single generative formula for iambic pentameter, but in a method of analyzing and categorizing several variant rule systems. He systematically distinguishes the meter of Shakespeare from that of Milton; Wyatt's from both; and all three from that of Alexander Pope, whom he rightly calls "about as closefisted metrically as any English poet has ever been." Aside from his detailed rule sets for those four – which he shows to be related in symmetrical ways – he offers similarly precise descriptions of the practice of such strongly divergent poets as Hopkins, Donne, and Browning, all of whom differ, and in different ways, from Milton and Shakespeare, whose two metrical styles define something like the mainstream of English verse.

These are significant results. They represent an advance both in detail and in rigor over the common, casual understanding of English metrical history that I outlined earlier. People sometimes speak of a pendulum swinging throughout that history between strict or smooth (Pope) and loose or rough (Donne or Browning). But as Kiparsky remarks in the "Envoi" that ends his essay, this talk of two poles doesn't tell us much: "there is far more variety than a simple dichotomy would suggest." His claim, furthermore, is that this variety "involves not only overall metrical complexity" – which can be measured by simply counting the mismatches in a line – but also "clear-cut absolute differences in the specific types of mismatches allowed by the poets." This is a level of precision in historical discriminations that foot-substitution scansions can't reach.

What has happened along these lines since 1977? One development is that Kiparsky with Kristin Hanson published "A Parametric Theory of Poetic Meter" in 1996. Their title points to the notion, then newly current, of linguistic "parameters." We can imagine a set of switches in the brain, each of them set one of two (or three) ways, which together account for differences among languages. For example, one switch would determine whether declarative sentences are required to have an explicit subject (English: "It's raining," in which the meaningless "it" is present only to satisfy this rule) or not (Italian: "Piove," a complete sentence). Somewhat like the four-letter genetic code in our DNA, this system is highly economical, and so it might account for the baffling fact that our brains so effortlessly learn something as complex as language. All the child has to learn is the settings of a few dozen or a few hundred switches, not all the endless details of a language's syntactical structure.

In such theories the settings of the parameters in effect *define* a language's structure. Hanson and Kiparsky offer a very compact set of parameters for poetic meter which go beyond Kiparsky's "Rhythmic Structure" essay by aiming to define *all* possible stress-based meters in *any* language. This allows them to discover, for example, a startling affinity between modern meters in Finnish and the "sprung rhythm" developed by Gerard Manley Hopkins. There's unlikely to be any direct influence. Instead, because the number of parameters to be set is limited such coincidences are less improbable than they would seem otherwise.

Its economical compactness makes the parametric theory too dense to be explored here. But it seems important to consider Hanson and Kiparsky's crucial addendum to their list of parameters, which they call the Principle of Fit: "Languages select meters in which their entire vocabularies are usable in the greatest variety of ways." This may seem obvious – a meter that required all words to be six syllables long would lead to few poems in English – but it has subtle power. It can help us think, for example, about the complex question of why English settled on the iambic pentameter as its dominant line. Why not continue the Old English accentual (as William Langland did), or the octosyllabic line that Chaucer took from French and used in his earliest poems? What *are* the characteristics of English that meters like the iambic pentameter particularly fit? Hanson and Kiparsky give a detailed answer which is well worth considering. It's a question we will revisit in the next section of this chapter from a different perspective.

The Principle of Fit may or may not, as we saw, point to a gap in Shakespeare's metrical rules which Milton revised in such a way that he could use words like "hierarchy." Yet as a principle that underscores the connection between a language and the metrical system its poets use, it seems an important one for *any* theory of meter to take into account.

Theories of generative metrics, in the very form of the rules they discover, deeply entangle meter with other aspects of language which linguists study but which foot-substitution scansion more or less excludes. (That is, the meter-centered *scansion* excludes them, though the extended discussion of rhythm which scansion is meant to initiate will consider them all.) In Kiparsky's "Rhythmic Structure of English Verse" the rules that define each poet's practice entail concepts (and notations) from syntax, from morphology (the internal structures of words), and from corners of phonology concerning both stress (which Kiparsky, following Liberman, conceives in terms of binary-branching trees) and boundary (so that the differences among "lexical," "#-level," and "##-level" stresses – defined by various kinds of word and phrase boundaries – help to make the historical distinctions he achieves). This means, unfortunately, that those coming from outside a linguistic background have a steep slope to climb to enter into his system. While exploring a particular rule about fifth-syllable caesurae, he remarks that it is "the interplay of both these factors, stress and syntax, which we must look at to understand what is going on here." When he declares that, although Liberman's stress trees aren't the same as the trees used to investigate syntax, still "stress trees are congruent with the constituent structure," he is inextricably tying stress and the meter that depends on it to the syntactical system as analyzed by linguists. In contrast, in our scansions in earlier chapters syntax shows up only in one detail: syntactical boundaries define caesuras, and so set the normal conditions for some kinds of substitutions. Otherwise in a foot-substitution system syntax has no role in the *meter*, though it's often part of our exploration of the *rhythm* of the line.

Kiparsky's system, unlike some other alternatives to foot-substitution scansion, retains the notion of the metrical foot. In fact he puts more emphasis on it than I have in this book. Our scansions have used the mark between feet ('|') mostly as a step toward naming the feet so as to see what combination of them the line presents. But one of the most striking differences between Kiparsky's approach and the one used here is his focus not only on foot boundaries but on *word* boundaries. They define "lexical stress," for instance, which is crucial to his formulation of various poets' meters. He also speaks of many poems' "spontaneous expressions"

> of an intuition that no metrical theory so far to my knowledge has explicated: that the meter of a line is determined, even against the metrical context, by the predominant metrical structure of the *words* in it. (1977, p. 224, his emphasis)

He's referring to the "labeling mismatches" we saw before in a line like "The lion dying thrusteth forth his paw." He distinguishes among poets' rule sets by means of these different kinds of mismatches and whether they occur together. His distinctions therefore depend on both foot and word boundaries, while the scansions we have been using pay no attention to the boundary between words.

For generative metrics, this embedding of meter in the rest of language – conceiving of it really as a kind of sub- or super-language – is no disadvantage but a token of success. It's not a matter of new territory being flagged as conquered by the kingdom of linguistics. Rather it represents just the kind of unifying account of what are obviously related human activities – speaking and making poetry – that the discipline of linguistics always seeks. This unity is undeniably attractive. It has some further consequences, however, that distinguish Kiparsky's project from the ones of greatest relevance to most readers and writers of poetry.

First, as in other linguistics-based theories, Kiparsky's claims to success are ultimately embodied in tests for metricality in a line. As he says in his "Envoi,"

> We have focused on just one of the problems of metrics, but it is one that must be solved at least partly before much headway can be made on the others. It is the problem of formulating the principles that distinguish metrical from unmetrical verse for a given poet or period, and that govern the relative metrical complexity of lines. (p. 244)

Since the most prominent task which modern linguistics sets itself is the precise location of the intricate border between grammatical and ungrammatical sentences – sentences a native speaker would or would not normally produce – it seems natural to extend this task to the metrical realm. Yet it's not obvious that a test for metricality is needed "before much headway can be made" on the "problems" we face in scanning a line or learning to scan one. Quite crude tests for unmetricality – beginning with counting on our fingers! – can be of some use to the writer of metrical verse: they can act as a kind of filter that excludes unsuitable candidate lines or makes the poet fix them. As readers, however, most of us aren't often concerned with questioning *whether* a line is metrical. Since we're reading a metrical poem, we assume that the poet thought it was. Our goal is to come to terms with lines that are – whether deliberately or inadvertently or through historical change – difficult, that is, hard to scan, and to ask what bearing the line's quirks have on its meaning and effect.

Second, and for closely related reasons, Kiparsky treats meter as largely implicit knowledge like syntax. Earlier I quoted him speaking of poets' "spontaneous expressions" of certain metrical principles. He introduces one of his important distinctions among rule sets in these terms:

> In rebuilding the English iambic pentameter, Wyatt and his contemporaries had not yet hit on a principle that most later poets, *no doubt quite unconsciously*, were to stick to in one or another form. (p. 206, emphasis added)

As I suggested earlier, it's not obvious that the analogy between meter and syntax as implicit knowledge systems is such a close one. Poets and readers require a certain amount of learning which rarely goes on, like the learning of syntax, in infancy and early childhood. Often it goes on in classrooms, by definition places where conscious knowledge is acquired. A generative-linguistics approach to metrics, like the approach to syntax, tends to formulate its results in notation systems closer to mathematics than to critical prose. If the results are correspondingly counterintuitive, this is consistent with the fact that the rules defining our syntax are too complex for us to deploy them consciously. Poetic meter, on the other hand, is a territory in which our awareness of expressive effects is at least desirable. The mechanisms and techniques by which these effects are achieved often rise into the sphere of our consciousness and curiosity. As the linguist Thomas Cable summarizes, "A master poet should be able to tell the apprentice the basics of any meter in fifteen minutes. That is not true of *any* language."

Third, Kiparsky's theory is not what might be called a "reciprocal" one: it may work for readers but it doesn't help writers of metrical verse. His rules rely on lexical stress, and they restrict only the occurrence of stressed syllables in W positions, not constraining what goes in S positions at all. It follows that monosyllables are ungoverned, so that *any* monosyllabic line counts as metrical. T. S. Eliot's line in "The Love Song of J. Alfred Prufrock" about mermaids, "I do not think that they will sing to me," is a metrical iambic pentameter by all of Kiparsky's rule sets, but so is

/   x │ x   x   /   │   x   x   / │ x /

Nor could I have thought they would sing to me

and so is

x   /   │ x   x   / │ xx   /   │ x   /

The man in the hat is a friend of mine.

Foot-substitution scansion treats these lines as I've shown here: it finds them to be something other than iambic pentameters (in both cases, versions of anapestic tetrameter). It would advise the poet accordingly. Here's where a test for metricality does come in handy. In linguistic terms, Kiparsky's success is only partial: the goal of syntactic theory, for example, is to find rules which will generate all *and only* grammatical sentences. Each of Kiparsky's rule sets generates all of a poet's metrical lines and excludes specific kinds of unmetrical ones, but also generates lines we would warn a poet against presenting as metrical.

Perhaps the ultimate in non-reciprocal theories is the statistical approach to meter that is characteristic of various Russian scholars of language and meter. Marina Tarlinskaja's monumental 1976 study, *English Verse: Theory and History*, is a comprehensive compilation of metrical details minutely discriminated and arranged in tables. These allow us to watch the historical development of many aspects of metrical variation. This rich vein of data has been mined by various theorists – including Kiparsky and Derek Attridge, to whom we're about to turn – as a way to develop and check theories of meter. Invaluable as it is from this point of view, however, no one could imagine a poet reverse-engineering these tables into new poems.

Yet the preference for a reciprocal method is only a preference. Perhaps it owes too much to my own experience of teaching people both to read and to write poems. It has only this weak theoretical foundation: that since poets and readers must somehow share knowledge of meter it seems natural that its principles should be equally accessible to both. Just so, a single understanding of syntax enables us both when we speak sentences and when we hear them. On the other hand, I've suggested that metrical knowledge tends to be more explicit than syntactical knowledge. A reciprocal theory can accommodate both the shared nature of metrical knowledge *and* its explicit nature. These demands also favor the simplest adequate theory, since what we do at least half-consciously can never be as complex as what we do without thinking about it: speaking, climbing stairs, seeing things in three dimensions. Singing is complex, but not compared with the dynamic miracle of breathing.

The Native Sound of English

Derek Attridge is a literary scholar and critic known for far more than his work on metrics, but he is one of the most influential metrists of our time. Though not a linguist, he's well acquainted with modern linguistic theory and practice. Unlike some other literary metrists he is no devotee of what he calls the "classical" foot-substitution scansion. His most crucial book on meter is the 1982 volume, *The Rhythms of English Poetry*.

Attridge's Variants

I'll refer to *The Rhythms of English Poetry* as *REP*. In 1995 Attridge published a textbook, *Poetic Rhythm: An Introduction*, which presents a somewhat streamlined version of the theories worked out more fully in *REP*. Later we'll look at a couple of important developments in the later textbook. Later still, in 2003, with Thomas Carper he condensed much of his theory into a handbook called *Meter and*

Meaning: An Introduction to Rhythm in Poetry. These revisions usefully simplify Attridge's multi-symbol notation system. Since his theories are most fully worked out in *REP*, that's the source I'll concentrate on here.

Early in *REP* he acknowledges that "because of its importance in the writing of both poets and critics, the outlines of the classical approach, at least, have to be mastered by anyone with an interest in English poetry." Helping you master this approach has been the mission of this book. But Attridge's system is quite different, and he discusses what he calls "foot-substitution theory" mostly to explain "how it came into being, so that its sheer familiarity does not confer on it any unwarranted authority" (p. 5). The approach to meter we've used in this book is not precisely the version he is referring to, but it is a "foot-substitution theory."

Before *REP*, Attridge wrote another book that explored the sixteenth-century attempts by English poets and critics to import quantitative meters from Latin and Greek into our insistently different language. *Well-weighed Syllables: Elizabethan Verse in Classical Metres* (1974) points out that English schools at that time – roughly Shakespeare's time – taught Latin using a pronunciation system that badly obscured the sound of the language. (There were no Romans around to consult and no sound recordings of their speech. More modern reconstructions of the sound of Latin have depended on complex collaborations among scholars in many disciplines.) Consequently these poets and critics couldn't really *hear* the meter of the Latin poems they read so respectfully. At the same time, though, they studied the treatises of Latin authors writing *about* the metrical system. As a result, Attridge persuasively argues, they didn't expect a metrical theory to be very closely correlated with what the writer's or reader's poetic ear actually experienced. This was also the period when poets, critics, and readers were working out our modern understanding of English meter, and so they were prepared to theorize about it at a distance from what they actually heard in English. This is why poets eagerly tried to bring the high-status Latin meters – really no more audible to them in Latin than in English – into a language which, as we saw in Chapter 2, is not hospitable to those quantitative meters.

Attridge takes this standard rejection of Classical meters in English a step further. He would dispose of the whole Classical apparatus of metrical terminology and analysis. Above all, Attridge rejects the *foot* as a meaningful unit in English verse.

"Foot" in English

Part of Attridge's argument against feet in English is historical. He claims (p. 5) that the word "foot" was introduced very early in discussions of English poetry but was then left aside until the "new interest in Greece and Rome" in the nineteenth century. "The classical approach may also help us to understand certain features of verse written by poets who consciously adhered to such a view of metre, though their number is perhaps not very large." (p. 17). The evidence here isn't entirely clear. The *OED* cites Shakespeare's *As You Like It* (1616), "Some of them had in them more feete then the Verses would beare," and John Dryden's *Fables* (1700), "Some thousands of his Verses...are lame for want of half a Foot." The words "spondee," "trochee," and "anapest" all go back to the sixteenth century in English. Even if they were used primarily to discuss Latin verse, George Puttenham (1529–1590), in his influential book on *The Arte of English Poesie*, applies "anapest" and "trochee" to English. It's not clear why we should assume that poets, of all people, didn't read Puttenham.

What does he put in its place?

What the Elizabethan poets really heard, Attridge argues, both in their English predecessors and in popular verse and ballads, was a *beat*. Crude as beats might seem in comparison with the (inaudible) subtleties of Latin, beats, not quantities, are the native foundation of meters in English, as in other Germanic languages. As early as Chapter 2 I've occasionally used the word "beat" in talking about certain kinds of prominently pulsating, musically measured verse. Attridge, though, puts beats at the center of his system rather than stresses and slacks (though of course he acknowledges stress as a central fact of English). What's the difference between beats and stresses? As we noticed in Chapter 2, English is a stress-timed language, so that the interval between stresses *tends* to even itself out. But this tendency is a loose one, often violated. Beats in contrast are *defined* by **isochrony**, the equal time intervals between them (Attridge, 1982, p. 74). When the stress-timing of speech becomes most conspicuous and exact, stresses are becoming – or as Attridge rightly says, "are experienced as" – beats.

The notion of the beat is fully at home only in music, and music has a different relation to time from poetry and speech (and perhaps everything else). Perceptually speaking,

We cannot accurately judge time increments without a reference time unit. Regular reference time units are found in musical contexts and rarely in other types of human experiences. Even the human heartbeat is rarely consistent enough to act as a reliable reference. The underlying metric pulse of a piece of music does, however, allow for accurate duration perception. This accuracy cannot be achieved in any other context of the human experience. (William Moylan, *Understanding and Crafting the Mix: The Art of Recording.* Focal Press, New York and London, 2013, p. 19)

Words can never quite be notes, though we can sing them to notes. In Chapter 3 I quoted Ezra Pound saying that "poetry begins to atrophy when it gets too far from music." Though I agree with Pound that it's disastrous for poetry to lose that connection, a poem – even when performed aloud – is in a medium with some distinctly non-musical characteristics. Both in rhythm and in pitch, spoken language is much less strictly organized than music.

English speech displays *both* a tendency for stressed and unstressed syllables to alternate *and* a tendency for the interval between stresses to be isochronous.

The "Rhythm Rule"

One place where these tendencies are on display is in what linguists call the **Rhythm Rule**. It's also called the "thirteen men" rule: in sentences like "She just turned thirteen," the last syllable is stressed. But when another stress immediately follows – "thirteen men" – we shift the stress back to the first syllable to avoid "stress clash." We simultaneously equalize the time between stresses and re-establish alternation between stresses and slacks.

When both these tendencies are fully regularized we get lines whose meter we easily recognize, whether we begin from feet or from beats. Attridge relies on our experience of beats not only to discuss galloping anapestics and so on, but also in his analysis of "literary" verse forms like the iambic pentameter. Though he sometimes uses the term "iambic pentameter," he views this meter essentially as dictating a line of five beats. Stresses may be more or less aligned with the beats and there may be more or fewer stresses than beats, but it's the beat that defines the meter. The rest of his system is devoted to showing how stressed and unstressed syllables are organized into and around beats.

Attridge concentrates much of his attention in *REP* on the *four*-beat line. This makes sense: as we've noticed before, there seems to be something fundamental to our language (and our music) about fours, whether beats or stresses or lines in stanzas. Recognizing the fundamental role of the four-beat line in our music-poetic culture leads him to the notion of the "unrealized beat." This is the empty place, the "rest," that we hear at the ends of the second and fourth lines of the ballad stanza. In Chapter 2 we saw this stanza from Theodore Roethke's "My Papa's Waltz," and scanned it this way:

```
    x   / |/   x  | x /
You beat time on my head
  x  x  /  |  /   / | x  /
With a palm caked hard by dirt,
    x      /  | x / |x  /
Then waltzed me off to bed
  /  /  | x (/) | x    /
Still clinging to your shirt.
```

The context in which Attridge discusses this poem (p. 92) suggests that we might hear *all* of these lines as ending with unrealized beats. In our earlier examinations of the ballad stanza (Chapters 2 and 3), we saw the "rest" at the ends of the shorter lines as flowing from the musical background of which even highly literary ballads remain aware. Treating it also as the true structure of Roethke's iambic trimeter line is a more radical move – though Roethke's title does associate it with a "Waltz," and though his relatively end-stopped lines do encourage pauses.

Trimeter versus Waltz

People sometimes try to relate Roethke's choice of trimeter with the "Waltz." But the 3/4 time signature of a waltz indicates three quarter-note beats going by very much faster than the three feet (or beats) of the trimeter line. We might think of the whole line as three measures of waltz time – or Attridge would say four, the last being silent – but not as a single measure.

For Attridge the modern accentual-syllabic meters don't represent a radical break from the Old English metrical tradition but a transformation of it. He argues against driving "a wedge between metrical types which shade into one another, and, by denying English literary verse its intimate links with the popular tradition, [ignoring] one of its great sources of vitality" (p. 12). On the other hand, he doesn't argue as some critics have that the Anglo-Saxon line of four strong accents lives on underneath or within the iambic pentameter. Rather, he sees the five-beat line as "the only simple metrical form of manageable length which escapes the elementary four-beat rhythm, with its insistence, its hierarchical structures" (the tendency of four-beat lines to congregate in four-line stanzas) "and its close relationship with the world of ballad and song" (p. 124). On the other hand, that musical relationship does seem to motivate his focus on beats in the pentameter as well as in the lines of the shorter four-square meter.

At its strongest Attridge's argument is not just that "foot" is an unnecessary concept but that it's a misleading one. The best case is the kind of line that we also noticed in Chapter 2, as in this stanza by Auden:

> /   x /   x /   x   /
> Earth, receive an honoured guest;
> /   x   /   x   /   x /
> William Yeats is laid to rest:
> /   x / x   /   x /
> Let the Irish vessel lie
> /   x   (/) x   /x (/)
> Emptied of its poetry.

There we found such lines a puzzle: iambic or trochaic? Attridge's position is that the question is meaningless. The presence or absence of slack syllables at the beginning or end of the line is metrically a matter of relative indifference. Nor are lines like these as rare as they might seem, especially in popular verse. In any verse that we hear as relying strongly on beats, "feet" turn something deliberately rhythmically simple into what looks inappropriately complicated. How far does this argument run?

From beats Attridge derives his concept of the "offbeat." Offbeats are not quite the same as slack syllables, just as beats aren't the same as stresses – although in what we would call a regular iambic meter the offbeat that falls between beats lines up with a slack between stresses. More radically, though, Attridge gives rules allowing for zero, one, or two offbeats between beats under circumstances that vary with what he calls the "metrical set": an expectation generated in the mind of the reader by (among other forces) the poem. The zero option introduces complications we'll come back to in a moment. With the option of one and two offbeats the difference between duple and triple meters – iambics and anapestics for example – fades somewhat in importance. (Our treatment of anapestics, in contrast, had to introduce two new feet to account for the likely substitutions in triple meter.) The beat is primary and sufficient; regulating offbeats, Attridge says, is the province of "pairing conditions" that are characteristic of literary rather than popular uses of the meter. He suggests that only literary meters include syllable counting among their rules.

"Promotion" is a term that Attridge uses just as we have used it since Chapter 1. Here is his scansion of a line (from Shakespeare's Sonnet 18) that includes a promotion:

-s   +s -s -s -s +s   -s   +s-s   +s
And often is his gold complexion dimmed
o   B o B̄ o B   o   B o B

We would scan the line this way:

x / | x (/)| x   / | x   / | x   /
And often is his gold complexion dimmed

The two are exactly equivalent. Below the line, Attridge marks beats (B) and offbeats (o), with a line over the B of "is" to show that it's promoted. Above the line he adds – though he doesn't always include this annotation – marks that show whether the syllable is stressed (+s) or unstressed (-s). Our scansion, of course, doesn't make this distinction between beats and stresses.

Attridge also uses the complementary term "demotion." A syllable stressed in speech becomes "demoted" when it corresponds with an offbeat, as in this line from Shakespeare's Sonnet 55:

-s +s -s +s   -s +s   +s +s   -s +s
Nor Mars his sword, nor war's quick fire shall burn
o   B   o   B   o   B   ó   B   o   B

The mark under "quick" says that the syllable (marked as + s above the line) is metrically demoted to an offbeat. You'll recognize this as an iamb followed by a spondee. Again the difference between these analyses is not significant.

Attridge speaks of "double offbeat" not only as part of what defines a triple meter but also when two adjacent offbeats occur in a context where the norm is one. (We'd call such a context iambic or trochaic.) In our terms this may correspond to (i) an anapestic substitution (<u>xx</u>/), (ii) the beginning of a double iamb (<u>xx</u>//), or (iii) the end of a trochee followed by an iamb (/x|x/), three possibilities we'll come back to in a moment. Conversely, Attridge uses "implied offbeat" to refer to his zero option: two beats with no syllable between them. Here is a line from Shakespeare's Sonnet 140 that includes both a double offbeat ("when their") and an implied offbeat (between "sick" and "men"):

$$
\begin{array}{ccccccccc}
-s & +s & -s & +s & +s & -s & -s & +s & -s & +s \\
\end{array}
$$

As testy sick men when their deaths be near

$$
\begin{array}{ccccccccc}
o & B & o & B & \hat{o} & B & \breve{o} & B & o & B \\
\end{array}
$$

Here the "double offbeat" corresponds to the start of a double iamb, while the "implied offbeat" falls between "sick" and "men." He indicates it by placing a circumflex accent over the silent offbeat's 'o' mark.

The cases of paired stresses, where two consecutive beats occur with no audible offbeat between them, raise some of the most interesting points of difference between Attridge's approach and the one used in this book. Attridge unifies the three cases I just listed – anapest, double iamb, and trochee-iamb pair – since the distinctions among them depend on foot divisions and he rejects feet. He then works out explanations for why some cases of implied offbeat disturb the stability of a line and others don't – or equivalently why some placements of paired stresses within the line are less common than others. For example, the sequence ooBB (xx//) is, according to statistics Attridge cites from Marina Tarlinskaja, six times more common in the poems of Keats than BBoo (//xx) and the latter pattern *never* occurs in Pope. We'll return to this disparity shortly.

Attridge's analysis of the "pairing conditions" under which different combinations can occur is very thorough, and his seismologic sensitivity to rhythmic effects makes his analyses a pleasure to read. For purposes of comparison with the system of scansion used here, however, it's important to notice two kinds of strategies that he adopts in accounting for the detailed behavior of his beats and offbeats: "compensation" and a shift in the relation between meter and rhythm.

Throughout *REP* it's clear that Attridge sees variations from the norm of alternating stressed and unstressed syllables as generally entailing *compensation.*

Paired beats (with an "implied offbeat" between them) are very often matched with adjacent double offbeats, and these two displacements compensate for each other. To translate this into terms we're familiar with, the reason why the double iamb (for example) doesn't disrupt iambic pentameter is that the exceptional double stress is preceded by an exceptional double slack. This makes intuitive sense. Whether we speak of beats or of stresses, it feels reasonable to think of the pentameter as consisting of five prominences linked by spring-like connectors within a fixed frame: expansion at one point produces compression at another. As Attridge explains one such case:

> If one thinks of a regular duple rhythm as the matching of a beat-offbeat alterna-
> tion with a syllable-by-syllable progression, thereby satisfying both stress and
> syllabic principles, an implied or double offbeat constitutes a mismatch between
> the two types of rhythm. But this misalignment can receive some compensation
> if an implied offbeat is followed by a double offbeat, and vice versa. This process
> of compensation can also be seen in terms of the underlying rhythm: an implied
> offbeat momentarily speeds up the underlying rhythm … and the slight post-
> ponement of the following beat created by a double offbeat is perhaps sensed as a
> return to regularity (pp. 180–181).

He goes one step further: under some circumstances this compensation can be delayed. In a famously difficult line by Keats, "How many bards gild the lapses of time," the system we've been using is troubled by two consecutive trochees:

x   /| x / | / x | / x | x /
How many bards gild the lapses of time

This breaks one of our rules of thumb about substitutions in the iambic pen-
tameter, though it doesn't break any *defining* metrical rule. Attridge points out that a double offbeat ("lap<u>ses of</u> time") follows the disruption and perhaps makes up for it, even though it doesn't follow immediately. He calls this "postponed pairing." Even more strikingly, here is a line by John Donne (always a wonderful metrical troublemaker) that we would probably want to treat as headless so as to avoid a double trochee at the beginning:

/ | x | /   x | x / | x   / | x   /
Teach me how to repent, for that's as good.

Headless lines are moderately rare because they destabilize our reading of the line almost as much as adjacent trochees do. Attridge's scansion

> Teach me how to repent, for that's as good
> B   o B ŏ B   o B o B

suggests that the double offbeat ("how to repent") helps normalize the line. He uses a similar scansion to make metrical sense of the more famous but similarly difficult first line of Shakespeare's Sonnet 116: "Let me not to the marriage of true minds."

From this perspective variation ceases to be a strictly *local* alteration of one or two feet at a time. Meter becomes a property of the whole line. This dynamic vision of the workings of the metrical line is attractive. It allows Attridge to speak of the line or parts of the line "speeding up" and "slowing down" without sounding merely impressionistic. It has the side effect that *only* the whole line can be reliably scanned. This makes it somewhat more difficult for a person learning scansion to build up skill and knowledge a little at a time: it's not obvious where to begin.

Attridge is not satisfied with the strict dichotomy between abstract meter and concrete rhythm that underpins the system we've used since Chapter 1. It leaves out "the important role of elementary rhythmic forms in determining what patterns are possible" (156n). The systematic rhythmic behavior of a poem depends for him not on two layers – meter and rhythm – but on "underlying rhythm[ic structure]," "metrical pattern," "realization rules," and sometimes "conditions," as well as the "metrical set" referred to earlier. Within his system the boundaries among these layers are porous. In this book's approach, in contrast, the strict opposition between abstract meter and concrete rhythm creates the little arena in which they interact.

From one angle, the question of where and how sharply to draw the line between meter and rhythm is a question about how much to include in *scansion*. For example, Attridge calls our attention to these two lines, both from Wordsworth's *The Prelude*:

> And growing still in stature, the grim shape ...
> Remembering not, retains an obscure sense ...

The stress patterns at the ends of these lines are the same (xx//) and our method of scansion doesn't distinguish between them. Yet Tarlinskaja's statistics say that the second line, in which the middle syllables of the final double iamb belong to the same *word* ("obscure"), is a much rarer type of line than the first. Attridge doesn't claim that this difference depending on word boundary belongs to meter as such, but he does say that it plays "a part in the realising, or thwarting, of metrical structures." At various points he introduces, besides word boundary, both syntax and phrase structure into discussions of how lines realize meter. There's no doubt that all of these factors (and others besides) are important to the rhythms of lines, and since a scansion diagrams the relation between a line's rhythm and its meter there is no theoretical limit to how much *might* be included in a scansion. The question may be how much *needs* to be included for scansion to do its job. Of course this depends on how we define its job. I've defined it as minimal – scansion roughly diagrams the interaction between speech stresses and metrical pattern – or rather as preparatory: the purpose of scansion is to encourage and inform discussion of broader rhythmic effects, which we haven't tried to diagram.

Attridge's abundant analyses enrich our sense of how the complexities of linguistic rhythm interact with the simple principles of meter, but sometimes they seem to threaten that simplicity. His two-line scansions especially – one for beats and one for stresses – while they convey useful information, deliberately blur the opposition between rhythm and meter. Though many writers have yearned toward a scansion that will describe *everything* relevant to the rhythm of a line, no such system exists. If it did it would be unwieldy, to say the least. It would record not only syntax and phrase structure but the duration of syllables, intonation contours, phonetic structures, and so on. Aside from being difficult to read and to learn, it would soon raise doubts about whether the scansion was describing the line or an individual performance of the line. The question for someone practicing metrical criticism is how much we need to include in the scansion and how much we can leave to the ensuing discussion of rhythm that scansion should initiate.

The greatest success of Attridge's beat-based metric is that it greatly simplifies our account of some fundamental, especially song-related meters in English. Aside from the "Earth, receive an honoured guest" variety, beats provide the most efficient description of the limerick: two three-beat rhyming lines, two two-beat rhyming lines, and a three-beat line that rhymes with the first two. Here, talk of "feet" seems tediously complicated.

On the other hand, the version of "classical" scansion used in this book arguably simplifies the account of literary meters like iambic pentameter. The pentameter may grow out of beat-based lines – surely it does – but as Attridge notes in illuminating detail, it has grown a long way out. The elaborations required in order to keep accounting for it in terms of beats complicate the analysis of meter's basic operation in the verse.

Here is a line from Keats that I admired in Chapter 1:

```
 /   x |  /  /  |x   x   /   / |x   /
Cool'd a long age in the deep-delved earth
```

We saw this trochee-spondee opening also in several other lines from the "Ode to a Nightingale" and in one by Pope, and Attridge supplies further examples from Spenser, Dryden, Pope, and Tennyson. To make these into five-beat lines, he says, "one has to reduce the stress on the third word" (p. 170). At first he treats it as "an exception to the rule," since it doesn't fit the conditions for what he calls "demotion." Later he explains it as "metrical subordination" (pp. 230–239). There he gives still more examples, including Keats's own "Hold like rich garners the full-ripened grain" (from "To Autumn"). In all these cases Attridge treats the third word in the line as "subordinated" to the fourth because of the recurring *syntactical* situation: in English speech, an adjective in a noun phrase is subordinated in stress to the noun that follows it. Because this is a phonological effect of syntax, and because (unlike Kiparsky and other generative metrists) Attridge doesn't want to make his metrical system actually dependent on syntax, he argues "that it would be best not to handle it within the metrical rules" (p. 231). Therefore "subordinated stresses need not be distinguished in rules or scansion" (p. 230) – that is, in the primary, beat-based scansion he places below the line. Instead, he indicates what's happening in his supplemental "stress pattern" scansion above the line.

It's true that English phonology makes us subordinate adjectives to the nouns that follow them: in "the blue house," "house" gets more stress than "blue."

Phrases and Compounds Revisited

Don't be confused by "the White House": as a name, it's a compound noun, not a noun phrase. As we noticed in Chapter 1, compounds are stressed at the beginning.

Phonologically, then, in the speech rhythm of Keats's line "rich" is subordinate to "garners." Yet a metrical context inevitably alters the operation or at least the dominance of various phonological rules. If we read with a constant underlying awareness of the abstract metrical pattern – if our "metrical set" depends on foot-based scansions – we may hear an emphasis on "rich" that resists its phonological subordination to the noun. (Does the extra stress on "rich" comport with its meaning? At the least it encourages us to linger, a luxury that poetry enjoys and encourages, as does the word itself.) This possibility leads to our spondee in the second foot –

$$/ \quad x \mid / \quad / \mid x \quad x \mid / \quad / \mid x \quad /$$
Hold like rich garners the full-ripened grain

– while Attridge relies on phonology to reduce what would otherwise be (for him) an unmetrical sixth beat in the line. All the assumptions we bring to the reading of metrical verse affect many details of that reading.

The simplicity of our scansion system may, of course, come at the cost of exactness. How exact do we want or need to be? Lines that create interesting problems for Attridge's highly refined system can often be scanned easily with the simpler tools we've developed. About Browning's line, "The deep groves and white temples and wet caves," Attridge declares that "a momentary expansion of the metre to accept six beats is the only linguistically acceptable solution" (p. 238). But we can treat it as

$$x \quad / \mid / \quad x \mid / \quad / \mid x \quad x \quad / \quad /$$
The deep groves and white temples and wet caves

The trochee in the second foot – an uncomfortable place for it as we've noticed before – combines with the spondee and the double iamb to make this a very unusual line, but we don't need to doubt that it's metrical. The same is true of this other line by Browning that Attridge also treats as a six-beat outlier:

$$/ \quad x \mid / \quad / \mid x \quad / \mid x \quad x \quad / \quad /$$
Hands and feet, scrambling somehow, and so dropped

(Browning is full of vigorous, metrically rebellious lines like this.) He quotes this line by Yeats: "And that must sleep, shriek, struggle to escape." "Read as prose," says Attridge, the three stresses would certainly all function as rhythmic peaks; in the context of duple verse, it may be possible to suppress the beat on the middle syllable in some way. However, as with extreme cases of metrical subordination, it may be more accurate to say that we sometimes accept six-beat lines in pentameter verse, though only under certain very special conditions which we have learned to recognise (p. 252).

But we can scan this at least as easily as Browning's thorny lines, with a spondee in the middle and promoted stresses in the first and next-to-last iambs:

$$x \quad (/) | \quad x \quad / \quad | \quad / \quad / | x \quad (/) | x \quad /$$
And that must sleep, shriek, struggle to escape

Finally, Attridge is as dissatisfied as we were on finding that Kiparsky's method fails to exclude as unmetrical any line that is all monosyllabic: "John is dead drunk and weeps tears from red eyes" is his example (p. 42). But it's not clear that this is unmetrical. With a taste for spondees we could admire

$$/ \quad x \quad | / \quad / \quad | \quad x \quad / \quad | \quad / \quad x \quad | / \quad /$$
John is dead drunk and weeps tears from red eyes

– though the trochee in the fourth foot, not preceded by a caesura, does make the scansion more complicated than most.

Unlike Kiparsky, Attridge is not eager to make a formal test for metricality the centerpiece or goal of his analyses. Instead he seeks ways to talk about meter that will force or at least draw attention to the nuances of rhythm, and at this he succeeds.

Attridge's later textbook *Poetic Rhythm: An Introduction* (1995) makes a number of changes to his system and one major addition. The most immediately striking change is his simplification of the marks for scansion. This may seem a minor point, but the transition into the modern desktop-computer age clearly made him recognize the advantages of a set of marks that could easily be typed. His newer scansions have a clean look:

$$/ \quad \angle \quad x \angle \ x \qquad \angle \ [x] \angle \quad x \quad x \quad \angle$$
Far round illumined Hell. Highly they raged

He uses the same marks for stressed and unstressed syllables that we have been using. Beats are now indicated by underlining the syllable's stress mark (or slack in the case of promotion). His system requires about a dozen scansion marks all together. Of course there are still no feet, which his system replaces.

He also adds half a dozen notations for the "Phrasal movement" that is the other topic this later book brings into metrics. Attridge is not alone among metrists in feeling that the account of a poem in rhythmic terms is incomplete if we pay no attention to how syntactical phrases interact with more immediately metrical phenomena like stresses or beats. Perhaps the most highly systematized example is offered by Richard Cureton, whose *Rhythmic Phrasing in English Verse* appeared in 1992. Cureton develops elaborate analyses of at least three major levels of organization in the poem, which he calls meter, grouping, and prolongation. Applied fully to a poem such as William Carlos Williams's "Without invention nothing is well spaced," his method results in forty pages of diagrams and closely packed argument. His system comes closer than any other theory so far to comprehending every aspect of the poem's language as events in time.

One of the most intriguing aspects of Cureton's approach is how extensively he exploits the insights in Fred Lerdahl's and Ray Jackendoff's *A Generative Theory of Tonal Music* (1983). This is an ambitious and widely admired project in which the discoveries of generative linguistics are applied to music, particularly to its rhythmic structures and to the principles that govern musical phrasing. Cureton's terms "grouping" and "prolongation" come directly from Lerdahl and Jackendoff, for whom they are the major categories of analysis. By perceiving how this linguistics-based way of treating music might be brought back to the study of language, particularly in poetry, Cureton in one obvious sense closes an essential circle. In another sense he may help us see how poetry, and metrical verse in particular, differs from other uses of language. He reminds us – by transcending them – of certain old, doomed attempts to scan verse using musical notation. (Sidney Lanier championed this approach early in the twentieth century.) Those musical scansions always ended up notating only performance, not underlying structure. Cureton demonstrates – if not simply – how metrical and musical underlying structures resemble each other on a much more fundamental level, even though the syntax of language and the syntax of music are different.

Scansion by Computer

In the Introduction to his 1995 *Poetic Rhythm* Attridge says, "This book does not ... offer a metrical *theory* in the strong sense of the word." Such a theory would "formulate rules that would enable a reader (or a computer) to decide if a given line is an acceptable example of a given meter. No successful metrical theory in this sense has yet been produced..." (p. xviii). This raises a question that probably interests Attridge less than it does generative metrists: is it possible to write a computer program that will scan metrical verse? The answer is a conditional yes. In this final section we'll look at a program called the Scandroid which embodies that provisional answer. Watching how it does the job of scansion and what the conditions or limitations are on the job it does reveals some aspects of meter and our comprehension of it in a new light. The program is available on charlesohartman.com/verse.

My interest in this question began in the same place as most other computer investigations I've pursued as an amateur programmer. I was curious about how I knew how to do something: harmonize a chorale melody, make an English sentence, scan an iambic pentameter. One way to approach this kind of question is to tease out and write down *all* the stages of doing the thing. An algorithm is an explicit specification of the steps in some procedure down to the level of primitive operations.

"Primitive" Operations

What makes an operation "primitive" depends on context. In computer hardware terms it might be something like adding two numbers or displaying an alphanumeric character on a screen.

In Chapter 1 we developed an outline of the process of scanning a line of iambic pentameter. At the time I called it an "algorithm," but it was not nearly detailed enough to serve as instructions for a computer.

When we try to fill in the gaps in such an outline down to the necessary primitive level, we often find some holes that on closer inspection gape so wide that we don't know how to fill them in. A procedure containing cracks this wide may turn out to be incomputable, or it may be one that will eventually yield to greater computing power or – more interestingly – to more precise knowledge of our own procedure. How well can we fill in the gaps in the procedural sketch laid out in Chapter 1?

The first step in our scansions, you'll recall, is to look for polysyllabic words, count the syllables, and decide which one gets a primary stress.

Step Zero and Computers

Actually the first step is to read the line aloud. The computer could do this, but it would be useless since it can't intelligently hear its own voice – at least in metrical terms – at least so far. This casts a sidelight on how we do scansion and why computers are far from being able to do it our way.

Can we "teach" the computer to parse the line's syllables like this? Yes, to a great extent. There are well-known principles for dividing an English word into syllables. (This lexical-level aspect of the Scandroid is applicable only to English, of course, though other parts of the program would be relevant in some other languages as well.) There are complications: "staked" versus "naked," for instance. Locating the main stress in an English polysyllable is also a rule-driven activity – which is presumably how *we* do it, since we certainly don't memorize all words individually. Again there are quirks. The British and American pronunciations of "controversy" (stressed on the second syllable or the first) demonstrate one kind of example, and the many verb-noun or verb-adjective pairs like "rebel" and "addict" present another, as we saw in Chapter 1.

Input to the Scandroid

Where does the Scandroid get lines to scan? The user can type in a line or read in a whole text file of lines (a poem, for instance). This text is displayed in the middle of the program's screen. Then the user can double-click a line to watch it being scanned. There are both Scan and Step buttons, which run the scansion operation all at once or bit by bit. In either case the program displays a brief explanation of what it is doing at each step.

If the user gives the Scandroid a whole poem in a text file, the program first decides whether the basic foot (the "metron") is the iamb or the anapest. To do this, it takes the first ten lines as a sample and runs them through a streamlined version of its scansion procedures, both the iambic and the anapestic versions, and determines which works better. Then it tries to calculate the number of feet per line. If all the lines are close to the average in length, the program just divides this average by two (for iambs) or three (for anapests). If the lines vary too much in length – or if the program is dealing with a single line – it does without the pre-calculated assumption of line length. That makes some operations a little harder or a little less reliable, but doesn't much diminish the program's performance. This suggests something about the stability and persistence of metrical lines in general.

Just as we can consult our dictionaries to settle tricky cases or remind our ears about the structure of a polysyllabic word, it seems not *too* bad a cheat to provide the Scandroid with its own dictionary. Depending on how other parts of the program are going to deal with a suffix like "-ed," we might leave "staked" and "raked" out of the dictionary but include "naked," indicating the syllables and stress as "NA#ked." A word like "convict" we might notate as "con#vict" to show that *either* syllable might be the stressed one. If the program can do the rest of its work properly, then the context of a metrical line will help it distinguish these invented cases:

<pre>
x   /|x   / | x   / | x   / | x (/)
</pre>
They never did convict the murderer,
<pre>
x   / | x   / | x x   /   / | x   / x
</pre>
But now they think an escaped convict did it.

(Alternatively, we could omit the word "convict" from the dictionary entirely and leave the Scandroid on its own. Which tactic works best is a question to settle by experiment.) As we try the Scandroid on more and more lines we collect odd words or odd situations for words. In this first line from Shelley's "Ozymandias," we need to hear "antique" as *front*-stressed:

<pre>
x /| x /|x x (/) | x /|x   /
</pre>
I met a traveler from an antique land

(This may be due to the Rhythm Rule we saw earlier in this chapter, though there's also a component of historical change.) If we put "an#tique" in its dictionary with no indication of which syllable is stressed, the program can both scan Shelley's line correctly *and* deal properly with a line like this invented one:

<pre>
x / | x   / |x / | x /| x   /
</pre>
Antiques and trinkets line the village streets.

269

Whether there are problems that still escape – polysyllables whose syllables or stress we can't compute but for which a dictionary entry would create ambiguities that undermine the scansion of other perfectly good lines – is a question for further research. Also, some special effects of verse can never be captured by this kind of word-by-word lexical information. A good example is the "wrenched accent" which we saw earlier in some ballads:

> I am a prisoner far from home,
> But if you'll only steal the key,
> I'll take you where the grass grows green,
> And make of you a great lady.

The Scandroid is fundamentally unable to deal with the last line of this stanza.

As a last resort the Scandroid lets the user double-click on a word that the program has treated incorrectly. This brings up a dialog box in which the user can type the correct syllable and stress pattern. The user is temporarily editing the dictionary, mostly to take care of a special case like "AN#tique" that may have been omitted from the dictionary.

Next the Scandroid, like us, must decide which monosyllables demand stress. The best way to do this would be the way we do it (when our hearing feels uncertain), by considering whether the word belongs to one of the open-class parts of speech: nouns, verbs, adjectives, adverbs. That would be an attractive option for a programmer these days because "POS taggers" – plug-in program modules that identify each word in a text by its Part Of Speech – are publicly available off the shelf. This was not true when I first formulated the main procedures that now make up the Scandroid. Instead I relied on brute force – that is, the dictionary. Because closed-class words are by definition limited in number, it's not a large task to insert them into the dictionary all marked as unstressed monosyllables: "to," "the," etc. Then the Scandroid can assume that any monosyllable *not* in its dictionary is an open-class, stressed word. This turns out to be fairly reliable, though there are still exceptions: "like" is sometimes an unstressed preposition (though one that is often subject to promotion), sometimes a verb. The Scandroid must rely on context, and occasionally this might yield either a spondee that ought to be an iamb (if the word isn't in the dictionary and is therefore treated as stressed) or a promoted stress that ought to be a full one instead (if the word is in the dictionary as unstressed but would be stressed in speech because of contrast, for instance). Only a fully parsing POS tagger could get around this problem, but in practice the problem comes up very rarely. Even with all the "grammar" words, a dictionary of under a thousand entries is enough to handle a very large proportion of lines of verse.

Once the line's syllables and main stresses have been located, the next task is to divide the line into feet. Within the system used in this book, this is the step where humans seem to run into the most confusion while learning to scan lines. I was curious to see how difficult it would be to program. The short answer – since the computer has no problem with memorizing names and thrives on sorting out logical possibilities – is that it was not very difficult, though there are a large number of subsidiary tasks to accomplish along the way. These include identifying headless lines (ones that begin with /x/, if the line's remaining marks would otherwise come up one foot short); locating anapests (again relying partly on the count of syllables in the line, and looking for sequences like /xx/ at likely positions); and distinguishing the kinds of patterns that Attridge declines to distinguish: xx/|/x versus xx// versus |xx/|/x.

What may be more interesting is that in the process of automating all this bookkeeping about the line I discovered *two different* algorithmic approaches to dividing it into feet. The one I programmed first I later came to think of as Corralling the Weird. It begins by looking at the start and end of the line for things like final extrametrical slack syllables, initial trochees and bare stresses (headless lines), and so on. These are not always easy to identify, but the right set of interlocking tests in the right order performs well. All that remains then is to look for a way to divide the remainder of the line – typically the middle of it – into the appropriate number of feet. This is usually not complicated, and often it's simply a matter of dividing the remaining syllables into pairs.

The other algorithm occurred to me because I had been reading the essay by Paul Kiparsky that we examined earlier in this chapter, though the connection is not entirely straightforward. This method I named Maximizing the Normal. It uses a combination of special operators called "regular expressions" to find the longest string of syllables within the line that is all iambic (such as x/x/x/) or that *could* be after we allow for promoted stresses (such as x/xxx/). The program assumes that these stretches are indeed iambic. Whatever may be left over at the beginning or end – which will be nothing if the line is all regular or is varied only by promoted stresses – is usually easy to recognize.

Both algorithms do well with a large majority of lines. Each fails occasionally. Usually a line that one can't handle the other can. The Scandroid tries both

271

algorithms in a quick run-through. If both work the program chooses at random. It announces which it has chosen and also allows the user to force the choice. This is not very useful, of course, except for research purposes. It's a way to learn something about what goes wrong with one algorithm or the other when applied to specific lines.

Promotions in the Scandroid

One of the last tasks the Scandroid performs is to mark promoted stresses. Since it can't hear and knows nothing about speech rhythms except what it calculates or finds in its dictionary, it does this in a simple-minded way: when the foot-division process is finished, if the line seems to be one stress too short a pattern like xxx/ or xxxx/ is likely to contain a promotion. Two or more promotions in a line rarely add much more trouble. In its scansions the program marks these promotions not with "(/)" as we have done, but with the abbreviated "%" instead. Lining up scansion marks over syllables – a trivial task for people – requires a large amount of tedious calculation which becomes still harder if any of the marks are more than one character long.

On the whole the Scandroid performs well. Yeats's poem "The Second Coming" contains many lines that a student might find difficult to scan and about which two scholars might (and do) disagree. The program's scansion of these lines largely agrees with mine. Since I can't predict the outcome in detail, this is more surprising than it might seem.

The fact that the Scandroid is largely successful at what it attempts has a great deal to do with the method of scansion it uses. During the process of dividing the line into feet the program knows nothing at all about syntax. It doesn't even know word boundaries: it works exclusively with a preliminary line of stress and slack marks:

x x x / x / / / x x /

As we've seen, the Scandroid isn't even capable of deciding about a monosyllable's stress by knowing its grammatical part of speech. One way to put this is that during this central stage of scansion – dealing with feet – the program's knowledge is purely *metrical*, with no *rhythmic* input except the preliminary stress marks on polysyllables and monosyllables. These marks, produced word-by-word from the simplest principles of lexical knowledge, are apparently enough to produce the diagram of relations between meter and rhythm which is all that this system asks a scansion to be. Both in what it requires, then, and in what it produces, the Scandroid, by reducing foot-substitution scansion to a mechanical process, emphasizes how very far it is from Attridge's ambition to bring all of the line's rhythmic complexity into a comprehensive system.

Beyond the Scandroid

If someone were to create a program – far more complicated than the Scandroid – that could perform Attridge's or Kiparsky's kinds of scansion, it would be interesting to run them against each other like competing chess programs, operating on a large corpus of metrical lines. This might or might not reveal more about what's going on when we read metrical lines or specify distinctions among metrical poets, or at least add to Marina Tarlinskaja's statistical tables of metrical variation.

It's important to emphasize that the success of the Scandroid in the absence of syntactical and other rhythmic information does *not* demonstrate that Attridge and Kiparsky and Cureton in their different ways are wrong to tie syntax, phrase structure, and word boundary closely to the meter. They all differently require scansion to include a great deal more information about the line's rhythm. All that the program proves is that the system of scansion we've been studying in this book – a system largely agnostic about the larger structures that words participate in and that are crucial to their making sense, since the system attends *only* to metrical questions of stress – is particularly ready to be computerized. Whether this endorses it as an approach for humans to use is a complicated question that you can explore and answer for yourself.

Glossary

AABA — A whole-song form, popular since early in the twentieth century, comprising four **strains**, the third contrasting with the first, second, and fourth. The contrasting B-strain is often called the **bridge**. Typically the music for each of the four strains is eight measures (or bars) long, so the form is also known as "32-bar form." Examples: the Gershwins' "I Got Rhythm"; the Beatles' "I Saw Her Standing There"; Bob Dylan's "Just Like a Woman." See pp. 216–217, 232.

accent — see **stress**

accentual meter — A **meter** in which the **line** contains a set number of **stresses** or accents. No count of syllables is maintained. The most typical length is four stresses; the four-stress line can be traced back to Old English (Anglo-Saxon) poetry. See pp. 82–83, 85–86, 182.

accentual-syllabic meter — A **meter** in which the **line** is measured according to two different elements: a count of syllables and a count and positioning of **stresses**. An example is the **iambic pentameter**: typically ten syllables, the even-numbered ones stressed. The two interlocking elements make it possible to analyze the line as being made of **feet**: set combinations of stressed and unstressed syllables. See pp. 82, 257.

acephalous line (also **headless line**) — An **iambic** line whose first **slack** syllable is missing. An iambic line that begins with a **stress** *may* not be acephalous; it may instead begin with a **trochee substituted** for the first **iamb**. See p. 21.

Verse: An Introduction to Prosody, First Edition. Charles O. Hartman.
© 2015 John Wiley & Sons, Ltd. Published 2015 by John Wiley & Sons, Ltd.

Alcaic — A Greek and Roman **stanza** of four **lines**. There are variations, but a typical pattern (with the Classical long and short syllables translated into **stresses** and **slacks**) is this:

```
/ / x / / / x x / x /
/ / x / / / x x / x /
/ / x / / / x / /
/ x x / x x / x / /
```

See p. 116.

alliteration — The repetition of consonant sounds at the beginnings of successive or nearby **stressed** syllables. A more specific term than **consonance**. All vowels are treated as alliterating with each other. "Delight in living alone" is an alliterative phrase; so are "envy of affluence" and "rhyme or reason." See p. 83.

amphibrach — A **foot** consisting of a **stress** between two **slacks**: x/x. In some foot-based theories of **iambic** meter a **line** may end with an amphibrach, but the amphibrach will appear nowhere else in the iambic line. That is an alternative to the approach used in this book, which instead accepts extrametrical slack syllables at the ends of iambic lines. (Compare **paeon** and **palimbacchius**.) See p. 22.

amphimacer (also **cretic**) — A **foot** consisting of a **slack** between two **stresses**: /x/. Rarely encountered in **iambic** meters, but common in **anapestic** ones.

anacrusis — A musical term for which "upbeat" is a synonym: rhythmic material preceding a "downbeat." See p. 226.

anapest (adjective **anapestic**) — A **foot** consisting of two **slacks** followed by a **stress**: xx/. The anapest is the basis for anapestic verse, the second most common group of **meters** in English after the **iambic**. The anapest is also used as a **substitution** in iambic meters, more frequently in some historical periods, and in the practice of some poets, than in others. See pp. 19, 23–24, 65.

anaphora — As a rhetorical term: the repetition of a word or phrase at the beginnings of a series of **lines** or clauses. In linguistics the term denotes a word that replaces another word to avoid repetition, like "one" in "I'm an oddball, and you're one too." It can also be used more broadly to include syntactical devices of continuity such as pronouns: "I like Dave, and you'll like him [that is, Dave] too." See p. 222.

appositive — Two words or **phrases** are "in apposition" if they have parallel grammatical structures (two noun-phrases, for instance) and share the same reference. In "my father the King" or "the street, the place I used to play as a child," the second part of the phrase is an appositive which gives additional information about the first part. See p. 145.

assonance — The repetition of vowel sounds in successive or nearby syllables. In the phrase "out and about" the first and last syllables are linked by assonance (which is one factor that makes phrases of this kind persist). Since vowels are more continuous with each other than consonants, subtle patterns of *similar* vowel sounds can register as assonance also. In Shakespeare's line (the opening of Sonnet 30) "When to the sessions of sweet silent thought," we may hear not only the 'e' in "when" and "sessions" but also the stressed vowels in "sweet" and "silent" as joining into assonantal pattern. See p. 104.

assonantal rhyme — A kind of **near rhyme** in which the similarity of the rhyming syllables depends on their vowels. "Boast" and "close" are an assonantal rhyme. See p. 104.

bacchius — A **foot** consisting of a **slack** followed by two **stresses**: x//. Very rare in iambic verse but common as a **substitution** in **anapestic** verse. See pp. 20, 67–68.

ballade — A French form, in English usually written in **iambic tetrameters** or **pentameters**. The poem is typically three eight-line **stanzas** plus a four-line envoi. All the stanzas use the same two **rhymes**, which makes the form difficult in English. The stanzas and the envoi all end with the same **refrain** line. The stanzas rhyme ababbcbC (the capital C being the refrain) and the envoi rhymes bcbC. Variations such as the double ballade, ballade supreme, and ballade royal also exist. See p. 127.

ballad stanza — A four-line **stanza** (**quatrain**) in which the first and third lines are four beats long and the second and fourth lines are three beats long. "Beats" suggests the song origin of this form. In written poetry the lines are usually at least approximately **iambic tetrameters** and **trimeters**. (If the iambic **meter** is regular the stanza becomes **common measure** or **hymnal stanza**.) The second line always **rhymes** with the fourth; the first line sometimes rhymes with the third. See pp. 56–57, 108–109, 215, 256.

bare stress (also **defective foot**) — A **foot** consisting of a single stressed syllable: /. In **iambic** verse it occurs most frequently at the beginning of a **line**, producing an **acephalous** or **headless** line; less frequently it follows a **caesura**. Elsewhere it is rare. See pp. 19–20, 67.

blank verse — **Iambic pentameter** without **rhyme** (not to be confused with **free verse**). Some estimates say that blank verse accounts for three-quarters of all English verse; if so it's because this is the measure of epics from Milton's *Paradise Lost* (1667) through Wordsworth's *The Prelude* (1799–1850) and beyond. The absence of rhyme and **stanzas** means that blank verse is usually organized, above the level of the **line**, as **verse paragraphs**. See p. 103.

blues — A song form as well as a musical style. The most typical blues **stanza** is three **lines**, each of about five beats. The second line usually repeats the first. All three lines rhyme. (Therefore any **heroic couplet** *can* be sung as a blues, appropriately or not.) See pp. 215–216.

breve — A symbol, ˘, used in **scansions** of Classical **verse** based on **quantitative meters** to indicate a short syllable. Greek and Latin had rules determining whether a syllable was long or short; English does not. In **stress**-based **accentual-syllabic meters** like most of those in English we use 'x' rather than the breve to mark **slack** syllables. See pp. 12, 93.

bridge — In **whole-song forms** comprising more than one kind of **strain**, such as **AABA**, the B-strain is most often called the bridge. "Channel" and "middle eight" are equivalent terms sometimes used by musicians. See pp. 199, 216–217, 228–229.

caesura (plural **caesurae**) — A pause within a **line** associated with a **syntactical** juncture such as the boundary between sentences or clauses. The boundary between phrases might yield a weaker caesura. A majority of lines as long as the **iambic pentameter** have a caesura; it is unusual for a line to have more than one. Caesurae have some influence on **metrical substitutions**. In this book, the symbol ″ is used when it is desirable to include a caesura in a **scansion**. See pp. 29–30.

catalectic — Missing a final **slack** syllable. This applies to **trochaic lines** ending with a **bare stress**, and is the inverse of an **acephalous** or **headless iambic** line, one that begins with a bare stress. See p. 62.

chain rhyme — In some poems built in **stanzas**, **rhyme** is not confined within the stanza but connects (chains together) consecutive stanzas. A basic example is **terza rima**, whose three-line stanzas are rhymed aba, bcb, and so on.

chant royal — An elaborate French form, in English most often written in **iambic pentameters**. The poem is in five eleven-line **stanzas** plus a five- or seven-line **envoi**. All the stanzas use the same five **rhymes**, which makes the form difficult in English. The stanzas and the envoi all end with the same

refrain line. The stanzas rhyme ababccddedE (the capital E being the refrain). The envoi rhymes either ccddedE or ddedE. See pp. 127–128.

choriamb (or **choriambus**) — A **foot** in which two **slacks** surround two stresses: x//x. It is rare in English; there is little point in **scanning** an **iamb** (x/) and a **trochee** (/x) as a single foot. In Greek and Latin the **quantitative** foot of two long syllables preceded and followed by a short syllable is more frequent. See p. 116.

clitic — A word or partial word that never stands by itself in a normal sentence. Examples are the possessive "'s" in "dog's" and the article "a" in phrases like "a dog." The term belongs to **phonology**. Clitics are phonologically joined to the word they depend on (whether it follows or precedes the clitc): we don't typically pause when speaking the pair, and the clitic typically receives no stress. See p. 174.

closed class — A closed class of words is a word-type to which new examples are rarely added. Prepositions are an example: English has one or two hundred ("on," "to," "among," etc.), though many of them are rarely used ("abaft," "modulo," "betwixt," etc.). Compare with an **open class** such as nouns, of which English has at least tens of thousands, with new ones frequently added. See p. 15.

common measure — A four-line **stanza** (**quatrain**) consisting of an **iambic tetrameter**, an **iambic trimeter**, another tetrameter, and another trimeter, rhymed abab. This is the same as **hymnal stanza**. It can be seen as a stricter poetic version of the **ballad stanza** common to poems and songs. See pp. 56, 109.

compound — A word made of two or more other words, such as "starfish," "simple-minded," or "interest rate." Some compounds are spelled as single words, some are hyphenated, and some are spelled as separate words. Over time there is a tendency for the space between words to become a hyphen and for the hyphen to disappear, as the compound becomes more familiar and therefore feels more like a single unit. In English **stress** falls at the beginning of a compound, while in a **phrase** stress falls at the end: thus "*black*board" as opposed to "a black *board*." See p. 13.

consonance — The repetition of consonant sounds in nearby or successive syllables. **Alliteration** is a specialized form of consonance. There is consonance between "jabber" and "bottle" (the 'b' sound), but strictly speaking no alliteration because the repeated sound does not begin the **stressed** syllable in both cases. Like **assonance**, consonance can help unify a passage of verse, as in

Tennyson's famous line, "The murmuring of innumerable bees." While consonants tend to be less continuous with each other than vowels, in Tennyson's line the fact that 'm' and 'b' are related (the nasal and **stop** versions of the same articulation) probably contributes to the effect of consonance. See p. 104.

continuant — A phoneme (a language sound) through which the breath continues, as opposed to a **stop**. The letters 'm,' 'l,' 'f,' and 's' all represent continuant phonemes in English. By some definitions, continuants also include the vowels. See p. 204.

contrastive stress — **Stress** on a word or syllable that is created by the speaker's awareness of an opposition to some actual or potential alternative. A speaker who says "I gave him *three* apples" is probably emphasizing her or his generosity: not just one or two. As listeners we are aware of this stress, so contrast is a way to communicate distinctions and emphases. See pp. 13, 159.

couplet — A **stanza** of two **lines** that **rhyme**. (An unrhymed pair of lines joined by theme or syntax or isolated by surrounding blank spaces is more exactly called a **distich**.) Series of couplets are usually printed without stanza breaks. See **heroic couplet**. See p. 31.

cretic (also **amphimacer**) — A **foot** consisting of a **slack** between two **stresses**: /x/. Rarely encountered in **iambic** meters, but common in **anapestic** ones. See pp. 20, 67–68.

crown of sonnets — A **sonnet** sequence in which the last line of each sonnet is repeated as the first line of the next. Usually the first line of the sequence is repeated as its last line, closing the circle. See p. 130.

dactyl (adjective **dactylic**) — A **foot** consisting of a **stress** followed by two **slacks**: /xx. It is rare as a **substitution** for the **iamb**, and never used in **anapestic** meters. A small number of poems in English are in **meters** based on the dactyl. The **quantitative** version of the foot, however (a long syllable followed by two shorts), was the basis of the dominant meters in Greek and Latin. See pp. 20, 64.

defective foot (also **bare stress**) — A **foot** consisting of a single stressed syllable: /. In **iambic** verse it occurs most frequently at the beginning of a **line**, producing an **acephalous** or **headless** line; less frequently it follows a **caesura**. Elsewhere it is rare. See pp. 19–20, 67.

dimeter — A line of two **feet**. Rare, except as part of a **stanza** pattern among longer lines (as in the **limerick**). See pp. 51–52.

distich — A pair of **lines** not necessarily **rhymed**. (Compare **couplet**.) Unrhymed lines may be perceived as paired because they are preceded and followed by stanza breaks, or because they are linked thematically or syntactically. See p. 211.

double iamb (also **rising ionic**) — A **foot** consisting of two **slacks** followed by two **stresses**: xx//. In **iambic** meters it is a frequent **substitution**, always replacing *two* consecutive iambs. See pp. 19–20.

dramatic monologue — A poem understood to be spoken by someone other than the poet. It differs from most drama — even from "closet drama" not meant to be staged — in having only a single speaker. See p. 139.

duple — A **rhythm** or a **meter** is duple if it is based on pairs, in poetry particularly pairs of syllables. Among poetic **feet**, the **iamb** and **trochee** are both duple. Duple is opposed to **triple** in the sense that basic rhythms of *more* than three units are somewhat unusual and can be built up out of twos and threes. See pp. 24, 64.

elegiac couplet — A Greek and Roman **quantitative** form in which **hexameters** and **pentameters** alternate. If we translate Classical long and short syllables into the **stresses** and **slacks** more natural to English, the basic pattern is this:

$$/ \, x \, x \, / \, x \, x \, / \, x \, x \, / \, x \, x \, / \, x \, x \, / \, /$$
$$/ \, x \, x \, / \, x \, x \, / \, '' \, / \, x \, x \, / \, x \, x \, /$$

(The ″ indicates an obligatory **caesura**.) In the longer line, any **dactyl** (/xx) except the last can be replaced by a **spondee** (//). In the shorter line a spondee can be **substituted** for either of the first two dactyls. See p. 116.

elision — To elide something is to leave it out. In the context of **meter** the term means erasing the boundary between two syllables. In this way two syllables — always **slack** syllables — can be counted as one. This turns what would locally be a **triple** rhythm into a **duple** rhythm that fits more regularly into a duple meter such as **iambics**. This is helpful when **anapests** are out of fashion or threaten to destabilize the meter. The traditional rule is that two syllables can be elided if the first ends with a vowel or a liquid ('l,' 'r,' 'm,' 'n') *and* if the second begins with a vowel or liquid. Thus "the amazing air" and "the returning king" and "then a burning bush" could all be read as iambic **dimeters**. See pp. 23–24.

end-stopped — A **line** of **verse** is end-stopped if it does not continue **syntactically** into the next line. Because language provides many levels of possible continuity, a line's end can manifest many degrees of closure. Therefore "end-stopped" refers not to an absolute condition (at least until the end of a poem) but to a spectrum of stronger and weaker suspensions of the poem's forward motion. Conversely, **enjambments** can be stronger or weaker: the more enjambed a line the less end-stopped, and vice versa. See pp. 145, 146–148, 152.

English sonnet (also **Shakespearean sonnet**) — A poem typically of fourteen **iambic pentameter** lines rhymed

a b a b   c d c d   e f e f   g g

See p. 135.

enjamb (verb), **enjambment** (noun) — A **line** of **verse** is enjambed if its **syntax** continues into the next line. (We also speak of the *pair* of lines as enjambed.) The "strength" of an enjambment, as it is often called, depends on how closely bound together by syntax are the segments separated by the line break. A line broken at the end of a clause is less strongly enjambed than one broken at the end of a **phrase**, and an enjambment in the midst of a phrase is stronger still. The strongest possible enjambment divides a word between lines; the absolute zero of enjambment occurs at the end of a poem. The more weakly a line is enjambed the more **end-stopped** it is. See p. 145.

envoi — A **stanza** at the end of some French and Italian **whole-poem forms**, shorter than the other stanzas, which addresses or "sends" the poem (like an envoy) to the poet's mistress or patron. The **sestina, ballade,** and **chant royal** are some forms whose formula includes an envoi. Usually pronounced as in French. See p. 128.

epistrophe — A rhetorical term for the repetition of a word or **phrase** at the ends of a series of **lines** or clauses. See p. 222.

falling — A **rhythm** or **meter** is described as falling if its beginning is more strongly emphasized than its end. Among poetic **feet**, the **trochee** and the **dactyl** are both falling. See p. 64.

feminine rhyme — Another name for **two-syllable rhyme**. For two words to rhyme this way, their last stressed vowel must be the same, as must any following consonant and the whole following unstressed syllable. For example: "river / sliver." See p. 102.

foot (plural **feet**) — A group of syllables seen as a **metrical** unit. In English feet are one to four syllables long, one or more of them **stressed**, in a particular order. Greek and Latin feet are patterns of long and short syllables instead. In any **meter** based on two different elements, such as syllable count and stress, it is convenient to think of **lines** as composed of repeated units — the feet — which are replaceable under various rules for **metrical substitution**. See p. 17.

fourteener — A **line** of fourteen syllables, almost always an **iambic heptameter**. These lines usually appear in rhymed couplets which therefore sound very much like **ballad stanzas** printed as two lines rather than four. This is particularly true when a **caesura** falls regularly after the fourth foot in each line. See pp. 56, 110.

free verse — Nonmetrical **verse**. Not to be confused with **blank verse**. More subtly, not to be too much confused with the French *vers libre*, since the linguistic and historical conditions of the "freeing" are distinct and the metrical rules from which the French **line** is "free" are more rigid than those used in English verse. See pp. 37, 63, 151–192.

full rhyme — Or more simply, **rhyme**: a pair of words identical in sound from the final **stressed** vowel to the end of the word. The term is used in various equivalent ways: "tame" and "flame" both match an "-ame" rhyme, "tame" is a rhyme for "flame," and "tame" rhymes with "flame." See also **feminine rhyme** or **two-syllable rhyme**. Compare **near rhyme** (though there are other terms like **slant rhyme**, **half rhyme**, and **off rhyme**). See pp. 23, 100–105.

ghazal — A form from the Middle East and India made up of separate (and relatively disparate) two-line **stanzas** or **distichs**. The rules followed by most poets in English (not identical to those in Persian and Urdu) are: (i) the lines are equal in length, usually measured syllabically; (ii) the second line of each distich ends with a single-word **refrain**, which also ends the first line of the poem; (iii) the last **stressed** syllable before the refrain-word at the end of each distich **rhymes** with the syllable in the same position in all stanzas; and (iv) the final stanza includes the poet's name, perhaps in indirect or punning form. See p. 115.

haiku — A form, originally Japanese, which in English is a **tercet** whose lines are five, seven, and five syllables in length. See p. 129.

half rhyme — Used in this book as one of several synonyms for **near rhyme**, though some authors systematically distinguish various divergences from **full rhyme**. See p. 104.

headless line (also **acephalous line**) — An **iambic** line whose first **slack** syllable is missing. An iambic line that begins with a **stress** *may* not be acephalous; it may instead begin with a **trochee** substituted for the first **iamb**. See p. 21.

hemistich — A half-line. The term is most often used for each of the two-stress parts of an Anglo-Saxon **accentual** line. It is sometimes generalized to refer, for instance, to the parts of an **iambic pentameter** before and after a **caesura**. See p. 211.

hendecasyllabic — Named "eleven syllables" in Greek, this **line** has been a very common **metrical** pattern in a number of European poetries, especially Greek, Latin, and Italian. When the Classical **quantitative** long and short syllables are translated into English **stresses** and **slacks**, the line runs more or less like this, though there are variations:

$$/\ /\ |\ /\ \text{x}\ \text{x}\ |\ /\ \text{x}\ |\ /\ \text{x}\ |\ /\ /$$

Either of the first two syllables may be unstressed (though not both); so may the final syllable. The rules for the Italian hendecasyllable are somewhat different; and it has been suggested that this line helped give rise to the English **iambic pentameter**. See pp. 93–94.

heptameter — A **line** of seven **feet**. Uncommon in English except for the **iambic** heptameter also known as the **fourteener**. See p. 56.

heroic couplet — A **rhymed** pair of **iambic pentameters**. Consecutive heroic couplets in **verse paragraphs** were the dominant form in English in the eighteenth century, and important before and after that period as well. See pp. 109–110.

hexameter — A **line** of six **feet**. In English the **iambic** hexameter is probably less common than the **trimeter**, certainly less than the **tetrameter** or **pentameter**, as a continuous **meter**. Isolated hexameters show up in some versions of **blank verse** and at set positions within forms such as the **Spenserian stanza**. The dactylic hexameter, which in the **quantitative** meters of Greek and Latin poetry is the most dominant line, has occasionally been tried in English in a **stress**-based version. See pp. 18, 55–56.

hymnal stanza — A four-line **stanza** (**quatrain**) consisting of an **iambic tetrameter**, an **iambic trimeter**, another tetrameter, and another trimeter, rhymed abab. This is the same as **common measure**. It can be seen as a stricter poetic version of the **ballad stanza** common to poems and songs. See pp. 56, 109.

iamb (adjective **iambic**) — A **foot** consisting of a **slack** followed by a **stress**: x/. The iamb is by far the most common basis for **metrical lines** in English. Iambs also occur frequently as **substitutions** in **anapestic** verse. See pp. 8, 17–18.

iambic pentameter — The dominant metrical **line** in English almost since Chaucer used it in *The Canterbury Tales*. It is a line of five **iambs**, with **substitutions**. See p. 18.

inflected language — A language in which the grammatical function of a word is associated with changes in its sound and spelling. In Latin, for example, nouns and verbs have endings that indicate gender, number, tense, and case. English has lost most of its inflections, though Old English (Anglo-Saxon) was an inflected language like German. Modern English retains the "-s" to form most noun plurals and the third-person singular indicative of most verbs, and vowel changes in other verbs ("write," "wrote," and so on), but few other inflections. See p. 133.

internal rhyme — **Rhyming** between syllables within a **line** as opposed to (or in addition to) rhyme at the ends of lines. See pp. 103, 201.

intonation — Changes in the pitch of the voice in speech. These shifts are less definite and more continuous than those of musical melody. English uses intonational *contours* to convey certain kinds of meaning. The standard example is the rise in the voice at the ends of questions ("Would you like a cookie?") — though alternatives like "Who ate my cookie?" (the voice first rises and falls at the end) and "Would you like a cookie?" (when the speaker would really rather *not* offer the cookie) suggest the complexity of the actual speech system of intonation. This aspect of language is a concern of **phonology**. See pp. 206, 241.

isochrony (adjective **isochronous**) — Greek for "same time." A series of events such as **stresses** in speech are isochronous if the time-intervals between them are constant. See p. 254.

Italian sonnet (also **Petrarchan sonnet**) — A **whole-poem form** typically of fourteen lines, in English usually **iambic pentameters**. (In Italian the **line** was a **hendecasyllabic**.) The poem is divided by a **volta** (turn) between the first eight lines (the **octave**) and the last six (the **sestet**). The octave is almost always rhymed abbaabba. The sestet may be rhymed cdcdcd, cdecde, or other variations. See pp. 130–135.

limerick — A **whole-poem form** in five lines. The first, second, and fifth are three beats long, roughly **iambic** or **anapestic trimeter**, and all rhyme together. The third and fourth lines are two beats long, or **dimeters**, and rhyme with each other. See pp. 127, 233, 262.

line — The basic unit of printed **verse**. In verse as opposed to **prose**, the breaks between lines are arranged by the poet, not happenstance results of the printing process. In other words, the line is a compositional unit. This means that a verse line can be too long to be printed as a single physical line. (In this case, parts of the line after the first physical line are customarily indented.) A further complication is that readers can be well aware of these compositional units even when the poem is not in print, or in song (see Chapter 5). The line is a visual unit, but it is more than a visual unit. See p. 8.

long hymnal stanza, long measure — Variants on **common measure** or **hymnal stanza** in which all four lines of the **stanza**, not just the first and third, are in **iambic tetrameter**. Always rhymed abab. See p. 109.

macron — A symbol, ‾, used in **scansions** of Classical **verse** based on **quantitative meters** to indicate a long syllable. Greek and Latin had rules determining whether a syllable was long or short; English does not. In **stress**-based **accentual-syllabic meters** like most of those in English we use '/' rather than the macron to mark stressed syllables. See pp. 12, 93.

melisma — A term in music indicating that a single sung syllable is extended over more than one note. The first syllable of "The Star-Spangled Banner" is sung to two notes. See p. 203.

meter (adjective **metrical**) — A **prosody** based on counting. A **syllabic** meter is a simple example: every **line** is a set number of syllables in length. The **accentual-syllabic meters** common in English are a more complex example. The poetry of every language favors one or a few meters; which element or elements are counted varies according to the properties of the language. **Nonmetrical** poetry is often called **free verse**. See pp. 8, 10–12.

metrical substitution — A foot-based **meter** such as the English **iambic pentameter** or the Classical **dactylic hexameter** is defined by a base foot repeated a set number of times. However, it is rare for all **lines** using such a meter to repeat the base foot with no variation at all. If one of the iambs in a pentameter is replaced by a **trochee**, for example, we call it a trochaic substitution. Some possible substitutions disturb the meter too much for poet and reader to keep track of it. Which substitutions are "allowed" in this sense is governed, if not strictly, by historical trends and by the internal dynamics of the metrical line. Rules of thumb for usual substitutions in English **iambic** verse are given on pages 20–21 and 238, and for **anapestic** verse on pages 66–68.

molossus — A **foot** consisting of three **stresses** (or, in Classical **quantitative** verse, long syllables): ///. Though it is a theoretically possible **substitution** in English **anapestics**, examples are not easy to construct. See p. 67.

monometer — A **line** of one **foot**. Extremely rare as a continuous form, though occasionally used as part of a recurring **stanza** pattern. See p. 50.

monosyllable — A word of one syllable. Compare **polysyllable**. See p. 9.

near rhyme — Used in this book as one of several synonyms, though some authors systematically distinguish various divergences from **full rhyme**. Since rhyme depends on several conditions — identity of vowels and of consonants and of stress positions — there are several ways that a rhyme can be "near" (or "off" or "slant" or "half"). See p. 104.

nonmetrical verse — **Verse** whose **prosody** is not based on a numerical rule. The most common name for nonmetrical verse is **free verse**. See p. 8.

octameter — A line of eight **feet**, which is uncommon. See pp. 18, 81.

octave — The first, eight-line part of a **sonnet**, especially an **Italian** or **Petrarchan sonnet**. See pp. 46, 131–135.

off rhyme — Used in this book as one of several synonyms for **near rhyme**, though some authors systematically distinguish various divergences from **full rhyme**. See p. 104.

open class — An open class of words is a word-type to which new examples are frequently and easily added. Verbs are an example: English has at least tens of thousands, and new verbs (often adapted from other parts of speech) are constantly added. A few decades ago "impact" was only a noun, and a few decades earlier the same was true of "contact." Writers often coin new verbs, as in Tennyson's "Diamond me no diamonds." Compare with a **closed class** such as pronouns, of which English has only a few dozen. See p. 15.

ottava rima — A **stanza**, originally Italian ("eight rhyme"), which in English is usually written in **iambic pentameter**. The **rhyming** pattern is abababcc. See pp. 112–113.

paeon — A **foot** consisting of four syllables one of which is **stressed** (or long, in **quantitative meters**). The four possible feet are called "first paeon" (/xxx) and so on. In English meters the second paeon (x/xx) occurs at the ends of lines participating in three-syllable **rhyme** ("a scrivener / has given her"). The third paeon (xx/x) occurs at the ends of lines when an **anapest** has been **substituted** for an **iamb** and the line also ends with an extrametrical slack syllable. Theoretically in **anapestic** meters the third paeon would result if an extra-metrical slack were added to the last foot of a line, but in practice this is rare. If we maintain the principle that extrametrical syllables never count as part of a foot, we have no need of the paeon; compare **amphibrach** and **palimbac-chius**. See pp. 23, 67, 191.

palimbacchius — A **foot** consisting of two **stresses** followed by a **slack**: //x. It never occurs as a **substitution** in **anapestic** meters because it too confusingly reverses the movement of the anapest (xx/). In **iambic** verse it occurs almost exclusively at the ends of lines, when a **spondee** has been substituted for the last iamb and the line also ends with an extrametrical slack syllable. If we maintain the principle that extrametrical syllables never count as part of a foot, we have no need of the palimbacchius; compare **amphibrach** and **paeon**. See p. 23.

pantoum (or pantun) — A **whole-poem form**, adapted from Malay, in **quat-rains** (four-line **stanzas**). The poem is organized by repeated lines rather than by **rhyme**. The second and fourth lines of the first stanza are repeated as the first and third lines of the second stanza, and so on. Usually the last stanza's second and fourth lines are also the first and third of the first stanza, closing the circle. See p. 115.

pentameter — A **line** of five **feet**. In English it is the most common length in **iambic** meters, though unusual in **anapestic** ones. See **iambic pentameter**. See p. 8.

Petrarchan sonnet — (also **Italian sonnet**) — A **whole-poem form** typically of fourteen lines, in English usually **iambic pentameters**. (In Italian the **line** was a **hendecasyllabic**.) The poem is divided by a **volta** (turn) between the first eight lines (the **octave**) and the last six (the **sestet**). The octave is almost always rhymed abbaabba. The sestet may be rhymed cdcdcd, cdecde, or other variations. See pp. 130–135.

phonology — The branch of linguistics that studies the sound systems of languages. Phonetics — the study of phonemes, the sounds of a language that its speakers perceive as distinct — is a central concern, but phonologists also study aspects of sound patterning beyond the level of the word (including **intonation** and **prosody** as linguists use that term) which are also relevant to the study of **meter** and **rhythm** in poetry. See p. 241.

phrasal verb — Roughly, a verb spelled as two words. English abounds in phrasal verbs: "turn down," "buy out," and so on. A complete definition is beyond the scope of this book, let alone this Glossary, and exact diagnostics by which to distinguish phrasal verbs from prepositional verbs and other forms are difficult to specify briefly. However, native speakers recognize that "I'll pass on dessert" does not imply that dessert will be in my will or my genes, as in "I'll pass on my farm [or my green eyes] to my son." Some characteristics of phrasal verbs: (i) the first word is always a common verb such as "go," "catch," etc., to which is added a particle that looks like a preposition or adverb; (ii) the verb and particle are sometimes separated by other words; (iii) the meaning of the phrasal verb is impossible to deduce from the parts, so that looking up "look" and "after" in the dictionary does not reveal the meaning of "He looks after his sister"; (iv) the particle, unlike a preposition, is always **stressed**. See pp. 41–42.

phrase — A group of words, not a complete clause, that stands for a conceptual unit and is also a **syntactical** constituent: for example, a prepositional phrase ("of the teacher"), a noun phrase ("the brother of the teacher"), or a verb phrase ("visited the class"). The term is used also in music. The intuitively close relation between the language and music meanings is borne out by the fact that a phrase of words when sung is usually matched exactly with a musical phrase. See pp. 13, 204.

polysyllable — A word containing more than one syllable. Compare **monosyllable**. See p. 9.

poulter's measure — A **couplet** in which the first line is an **iambic hexameter** and the second is an **iambic heptameter**. See p. 111.

promoted stress — A syllable that is **stressed** because of its position in a **line** of metrical **verse** — it occupies a place where **meter** creates an expectation of stress, and it is surrounded by silence or unstressed syllables — rather than because it is the main stress of a **polysyllable** or a **monosyllable** of an **open class**. See pp. 19, 27–30.

prose — Printed language broken into **lines** merely because the page is not wide enough to hold (for example) a complete paragraph. The opposite of **verse**. See p. 7.

prosody — In poetry: a system of **rhythmic** organization understood in common by poet and reader; therefore, a means by which the poet can control and enrich the reader's experience of rhythm and through it the whole temporal experience of the poem. There are many prosodies in many languages and even within English, including but not limited to **metrical** ones. In linguistics the term has a broader meaning; **phonologists** study not only the **rhythm** and **stress** on which (for example) English **accentual-syllabic meters** depend, but also phenomena such as **intonation**. See pp. 2, 87, 152.

pyrrhic — A **foot** consisting of two **slacks**: xx. In the system adopted by this book, the pyrrhic is not an "allowed" **substitution** for the **iamb**. Situations where it might seem to appear are referred instead to the **double iamb** or to the concept of **promoted stress**. See p. 19.

quantity, quantitative meter — Quantity is a term for the duration of syllables. In Greek and Latin, quantity was determinable by rule, and was binary: a syllable was either long or short. The same is not true in English; though obviously a syllable like "put" takes less time to say than a syllable like "spoils," one like "pine" probably falls in between. Consequently quantity is not very useful as the basis for a **meter** in English, though it was the primary basis of meters in the Classical languages. See pp. 88, 93.

quatrain — A **stanza** of four lines, generally bound together by **rhyme**. (There is no separate name for unrhymed four-line stanzas.) Many specialized forms of the quatrain are common, such as **ballad stanza**. The quatrain is the most common length for stanzas. See p. 43.

refrain — A repeated word, **phrase**, or whole **stanza**. Refrains (of all sizes) are very common in songs and not uncommon in poems. Some poetic forms depend on refrains: the **villanelle** and **triolet** both have two alternating refrain lines, the **pantoum** is in a sense *all* refrain, and the **ghazal** uses a refrain word. See pp. 115, 128, 213–215.

rhyme — A link between two words (or the words themselves) that depends on the sounds at the ends of the words. "Rhyme" by itself is a synonym for **full rhyme**, in which the final **stressed** vowel and everything after it is identical in the two words. In various kinds of **near rhyme** the identity is loosened to similarity. See pp. 23, 100–105.

rhyme royal (or **rime royal**) — A **stanza** of seven **iambic pentameter** lines rhymed ababbcc. See pp. 111–112.

rhythm — The distribution of similar or commensurable events in time. In the context of **verse** this means particularly the distribution (regular or irregular) of the events of language sound, including all aspects of **stress**, pacing, and **intonation**, as well as phonetic recurrences such as **assonance** and **consonance**. In the particular context of **metrical** verse, rhythm is in a sense opposed to meter: it is the wide, widely varying, and multi-dimensional field of speech sound from which meter abstracts one or a few elements and regularizes them according to some kind of numerical rule. See pp. 2, 9.

Rhythm Rule — **Stressed** syllables in English speech tend to alternate with one or more unstressed syllables. (Stresses also tend toward **isochrony**. These are characteristics of a **stress-timed language**.) When two stresses happen to fall next to each other, we often adjust our pronunciation of one of the words to avoid this "stress clash." The word "Japanese" is pronounced with stress on its last syllable, but in the phrase "Japanese cars" we shift stress to the first syllable. See p. 255.

rising — A **rhythm** or **meter** is described as rising if its end is more strongly emphasized than its beginning. Among poetic feet, the **iamb** and the **anapest** are both rising. See p. 64.

rising ionic (also **double iamb**) — A **foot** consisting of two **slacks** followed by two **stresses**: xx//. In **iambic** meters it is a frequent **substitution**, always replacing *two* consecutive iambs. See pp. 19–20.

rondeau — A **whole-poem form**, or rather a family of forms, originally French. There are many variants: rondeau tercet, rondeau redoublé, rondeau cinquain, and others. All versions include just two rhyme sounds, which makes the form difficult in English. All versions begin with a **refrain** (as short as a phrase or as long as a whole **stanza**) that is repeated after other stanzas of set length. "Rondel" is sometimes used as a synonym. See p. 127.

Sapphic stanza — A four-line **stanza**, used by Sappho and later by Catullus and others, comprising three **lines** of equal length and a shorter fourth line. In Greek and Latin its **meter** was **quantitative**. When the Classical long and short syllables are translated into English **stresses** and **slacks**, the longer line's pattern is roughly this:

$$/ x \mid / / \mid / x x \mid / x \mid / /$$

— though the **spondees** in the second and last feet can be replaced by **trochees**. The fourth line is

$$/ x x \mid / /$$

Again a trochee may be **substituted** for the final spondee. See pp. 95–97.

scansion (noun), **scan** (verb) — To scan a **line** of **metrical verse** — to produce a scansion of the line — is to mark the line indicating the **feet** it comprises. It follows that only lines in foot-based meters can properly be scanned: the **accentual-syllabic** lines common in English, or the **quantitative** lines of Greek and Latin poetry. In these contexts a scansion diagrams certain aspects of the relation between meter and **rhythm**. Chapter 6 touches on the question of how much information must or can be included in a scansion. See pp. 3, 10.

sestet — The second, six-line part of a **sonnet**, especially an **Italian** or **Petrarchan sonnet**. See pp. 46, 131–135.

sestina — A **whole-poem form** of thirty-nine lines in six **stanzas** plus a three-line **envoi**. The form is originally Provençal (or Occitan: a language of southern France). In English the lines are most often **iambic pentameters**. Instead of **rhyming**, the stanzas permute their six end words. If we number the last word of each line in the first stanza 1 through 6, then the following stanzas' lines end with the same words in this order:

(123456) 615243 364125 532614 451362 246531

The envoi uses all six words; usually its lines contain 1, 3, and 5, and end with 2, 4, and 6. See pp. 129–130.

Shakespearean sonnet (also **English sonnet**) — A poem typically of fourteen **iambic pentameter** lines rhymed

abab cdcd efef gg

See p. 135.

short hymnal stanza, short measure — Variants on **common measure** or **hymnal stanza** in which the first line of the stanza, as well as the third, is shortened to an **iambic trimeter**. (Compare **long hymnal stanza, long measure**.) Always rhymed abab. See p. 109.

slack — An unstressed syllable (marked 'x'), in the context of **accentual-syllabic meter**. Here **stress** and slack are treated as a binary pair even though in speech stress occurs in varying degrees. A slack syllable is therefore unstressed not absolutely but in relation to the syllables around it and the simultaneously perceived context of meter governing the **line**. See pp. 11–12.

slant rhyme — Used in this book as one of several synonyms for **near rhyme**, though some authors systematically distinguish various divergences from **full rhyme**. See p. 104.

sonnet — Though the early French or Italian name meant just "a small song" (originally "a sound"), the term is now firmly associated with an extremely popular fourteen-line **whole-poem form**. Its rhyme scheme has two major varieties, the **Italian** or **Petrarchan sonnet** and the **English** or **Shakespearean sonnet**, and others such as the **Spenserian sonnet**. See pp. 40, 130–137.

Spenserian sonnet — A poem of fourteen **iambic pentameter** lines rhymed

a b a b b c b c c d c d e e

See p. 135.

Spenserian stanza — A **stanza** of nine lines rhymed

a b a b b c b c c

all **iambic pentameter** except that the last line is an iambic **hexameter**. See pp. 25, 55, 113–114.

spondee (adjective **spondaic**) — A **foot** consisting of two **stresses**: //. A common **substitution** in **iambic** meters, also not uncommon in **anapestics**. See pp. 19–20.

stanza — A regular grouping of **lines** of **verse** bound by **rhyme**. But this definition should be hedged: a grouping of lines, usually recurring, usually regular in length, often though not always bound by rhyme. It is conventional to print stanzas with a blank line between them (a stanza break), at least if they are longer than a **couplet**. The regularity of stanzas distinguishes them from **verse paragraphs**. See pp. 23, 52, 99–100.

stanzaic-syllabic meter — A **prosody** in which the length of **lines** is determined by a count of their syllables, but regularity is maintained at the level of the recurring **stanza** rather than the **line**. Thus the first line of every stanza may be three syllables long, the second line twelve, and so on. See p. 91.

stichic — A song or poem can be described as stichic if it is made of **lines** that do not combine into larger **stanzaic** structures. See p. 211.

stichomythia — A dramatic passage in which two speakers trade single lines of dialogue. See p. 211.

stop — A phoneme (a language sound) that interrupts the breath, as opposed to a **continuant**. The letters 'p,' 't,' and 'k' all stand for stop consonants in English. See p. 204.

strain — A section of a musical piece such as a song. A strain may comprise several **phrases**. The term is generally used only when the piece includes more than one distinct strain, as in **AABA** song form. See p. 216.

stress — (In this book, though not universally, "accent" is a synonym for "stress.") A **stressed syllable** (marked '/'), in the context of **accentual-syllabic meter**. Here stress and **slack** are treated as a binary pair, even though in speech stress occurs in varying degrees. A stressed syllable is therefore stressed not absolutely but in relation to the syllables around it and the simultaneously perceived context of meter governing the **line**. See p. 11.

stress-timed language — A language such as English that tends to regularize the time interval between **stresses**, with more or fewer unstressed syllables intervening. See p. 65.

substitution — see **metrical substitution**

syllabic meter (also **syllabics**) — A **meter** based on a numerical rule that determines the lengths of lines by a count of syllables. See pp. 88–92.

syllable-timed language — A language such as French that tends to regularize the time interval between syllables, usually with a weakening of **stress**. See p. 65.

syntax (adjective **syntactical**) — In ordinary usage the term refers first of all to the order of words in a sentence, but more importantly to the set of grammatical principles by which native speakers construct and interpret sentences. Syntax is also a name for the branch of linguistics that investigates and formalizes these principles, a branch distinct from **phonology**, semantics, and pragmatics. *Passim.*

tanka — A form, originally Japanese, which in English is five lines whose lengths in syllables are five, seven, five, seven, and seven. Sometimes two or more poets trade a "tanka chain," the first writing the first three lines, the other the next two and the first three of the following stanza, and so on. See p. 129.

tercet — A **stanza** (or whole poem) of three lines. See p. 114.

terza rima — A **verse** form in any number of **tercets** linked by **chain rhyme**:

aba bcb cdc...

The most common way to close the poem (or section of a poem) is with a **quatrain** rhymed yzyz to pick up the last rhyme. In English, terza rima is most often written in **iambic pentameter**. See pp. 114–115.

tetrameter — A **line** of four **feet**. In English it is the most common length in **anapestic meters** and the second most common in **iambic** meters. See pp. 17, 58–63.

trimeter — A **line** of three **feet**. In English it is a moderately common length in both **anapestic** and **iambic meters**. See pp. 17, 53–56.

triolet — A **whole-poem form** in eight lines using just two **rhyme** sounds and including two **refrain** lines, arranged as follows (with the refrains indicated by capital letters):

A B a A a b A B

See p. 128.

triple — A **rhythm** or a **meter** is triple if it is based on threes, in poetry particularly trios of syllables. Among poetic **feet**, the **anapest** and **dactyl** are both triple. Triple is opposed to **duple** in the sense that basic rhythms of *more* than three units are somewhat unusual and can be built up out of twos and threes. See pp. 24, 64.

trochee (adjective **trochaic**) — A **foot** consisting of a **stress** followed by a **slack**: /x. In **iambic** verse the trochee is a very frequent **substitution** for the iamb, especially at the beginning of the line. Trochaic verse, using a **meter** based on repeated trochees, is not very common in English. See pp. 18–21.

two-syllable rhyme — Also called **feminine rhyme**. For two words to rhyme this way, their last stressed vowel must be the same, as must any following consonant and the whole following unstressed syllable. For example: "river / sliver." See p. 102.

unvoiced — A consonant is unvoiced if the vocal cords do not resonate during its production. Examples are 'p', 't', and 's' as opposed to 'b', 'd', and 'z'. See pp. 240–241.

verse — Language that is (or can meaningfully be) printed in **lines** which, as opposed to the incidental physical lines of **prose**, are determined purposefully by the writer. See pp. 1, 7.

verse paragraph — When **blank verse** or **heroic couplets** are used as continuous forms, structures larger than the line or pair of lines are often indicated, like paragraphs in **prose**, by an indented first line. Also as in prose, such structures are usually logical or narrative ones, irregular in length, as distinct from the regular, formal groupings of **stanzas**. See p. 109.

villanelle — A **whole-poem form** of nineteen lines using just two **rhyme** sounds and including two **refrain** lines, arranged in five **tercets** and a **quatrain**. Designating the rhymes as a and b and the refrain lines (which rhyme with each other) as A1 and A2, we can diagram the whole poem this way:

$$A^1 \, b \, A^2 \quad a \, b \, A^1 \quad a \, b \, A^2 \quad a \, b \, A^1 \quad a \, b \, A^2 \quad a \, b \, A^1 \, A^2$$

The history of the form is somewhat murky, but it has been popular in English for over a century. It is usually in **iambic pentameter**. See p. 129.

virelai — A **whole-poem form**, or rather a family of forms, perhaps originally French. A **refrain stanza** begins the poem and follows each succeeding stanza. Typically the stanzas interspersed among refrains are three in number, each in three parts, the first two rhyming with each other and the third with the refrain. See p. 127.

voiced — A speech sound is voiced if the vocal cords resonate during its production. Examples are 'b', 'd', and 'z' as opposed to 'p', 't', and 's'. All vowels are voiced sounds. See pp. 240–241.

volta — Italian for "turn": the turning or balance point in a poem, particularly between the **octave** and the **sestet** in an **Italian sonnet**. See p. 134.

whole-poem form — A poetic form that must be specified completely if it is to be specified at all. To describe a **stanzaic** form, in contrast, all that is necessary is to describe the base stanza and perhaps the number of repetitions. The **sonnet** is the most common whole-poem form. See p. 127.

whole-song form — A song form built of two or more different kinds of parts in some specified order. The most common and basic example is **AABA** form. (The B-**strain** is also called the **bridge**.) The parts are usually distinct both musically and lyrically; for example, the B-strain may have a different rhyme scheme from the A strains. See p. 216.

wrenched accent (or **wrenched rhyme**) — Especially in old **ballads**, some lines are clearly meant to **rhyme** although their final words are **stressed** differently and would not be heard as rhyming in ordinary speech. Thus in "Sir Lionel": "And as he rode by one hawthorne, / Even there did hang his hunting horne." (But this is not a simple case: as a compound, "hawthorn" retains some stress on its last syllable, and in earlier centuries the stress may have been stronger.) The point is not so much the distortion of a word for the sake of rhyme — which might merely be a sign of incompetence — but the readiness of language in song to yield to the **rhythmic** dominance of music. See p. 198.

Index of Poets and Poems

Note: Lines quoted in isolation are attributed to their source and indexed in italics.

Verse: An Introduction to Prosody, First Edition. Charles O. Hartman.
© 2015 John Wiley & Sons, Ltd. Published 2015 by John Wiley & Sons, Ltd.